JX
1974.7
K735
992

D1431766

A volume in the series

Anthropology of Contemporary Issues

EDITED BY ROGER SANJEK

SOCIAL & BEHAVIORAL SCIENCES Anthropology

30-2150   JX1974   91-55538 CIP

Krasniewicz, Louise. **Nuclear summer: the clash of communities at the Seneca women's peace encampment.** Cornell, 1992. 259p bibl index afp ISBN 0-8014-2635-9, $34.50; ISBN 0-8014-9938-0 pbk, $13.95

In the summer of 1983, a group of women purchased land near the Seneca Army Depot in upstate New York and planned a summer encampment to protest nuclear arms deployment and the patriarchal society that they perceived as supporting and fostering militarism and oppression. Krasniewicz has undertaken an anthropological study of the interactions and conflicts within the camp and between the encampment women and the people of the nearby communities. She employs several theoretical tools, including Geertz's concept of "thick culture," Turner's "liminal period," deconstruction of texts and symbols, and a variety of narrative techniques, including a "textual collage." Both the events described and Krasniewicz's approach are interesting, but she is ultimately unable to offer much in the way of fresh interpretation or provocative analysis. Some of her material deserves much fuller discussion, e.g., how the lives of women attending the camp were changed. This is a fine case study that offers useful material for scholars of radical feminism and of social change and conflict in late 20th-century America. Excellent photographs, good bibliography. General; undergraduate; graduate; faculty.—*M. L. Meldrum, SUNY at Stony Brook*

Nuclear Summer

*The Clash of Communities
at the Seneca
Women's Peace Encampment*

Louise Krasniewicz

Cornell University Press

Ithaca and London

First published 1992 by Cornell University Press.

International Standard Book Number 0-8014-2635-9 (cloth)
International Standard Book Number 0-8014-9938-0 (paper)
Library of Congress Catalog Card Number 91-55538

Printed in the United States of America

*Librarians: Library of Congress cataloging information appears on the
last page of the book.*

⊚ The paper in this book meets the minimum requirements of the
American National Standard for Information Sciences—Permanence of
Paper for Printed Library Materials, ANSI Z39.48-1984.

To my mother

Contents

Preface

In the summer of 1983, a large number of women established the Seneca Women's Encampment for a Future of Peace and Justice near a military nuclear weapons storage depot in Seneca County, New York. There, women gathered to protest nuclear weapons and to critique the "patriarchal society" that created and used those weapons. During that summer the protests led to verbal and physical clashes between the encampment and the people residing in surrounding communities. The encampment became a major regional news event of the summer and was noted regularly in the national media.

This book looks at the conflicts between the women at the encampment and their neighbors, at the strategies these people used to deal with their differences, and at some particularly intense confrontations during which their conflicting views and positions came into play. Both groups found the differences between them very disturbing, but perhaps even more upsetting were the differences within each group. As the events of the summer revealed these differences and forced public acknowledgment of them, deeply held assumptions about what constituted membership in each community were challenged. In emphasizing conflicts and disagreements, however, I do not mean to suggest that only disharmony existed in Seneca County or the women's encampment. Rather, I hope these confrontations can provide a window on our social mechanisms, for these kinds of differences between and within communities are not unique to this set of events; they should be seen as an expected part of social life.

In negotiating their differences, both internal and external, each group attempted to build a coherent identity, to define who they were and to state their place in a confusing and threatening world. To this end, they constructed representations of themselves and the "other," which they used to defend their identities and communities. Here, to analyze the processes involved in building and using these self-representations, I ex-

amine a wide range of narratives and actions that made up social, psychological, and political dramas.

In the tradition of Arthur Vidich and Joseph Bensman's *Small Town in
Mass Society* (a study conducted in the 1950s in a community near Seneca
County), this book is concerned with the often uneasy relationship between local communities and the larger society in which they exist. But
unlike the earlier study, which took place before the globalization of mass
communication and the massive presence of multimedia forms in the
home, this book does not assume that mass culture is an "external agent,"
somehow separable from the local community into which it "transmits"
policies and information (1958:82). Instead, all the aspects of mass societies intricately intertwine, generating much confusion and tension in
their members, who then try to separate these interwoven aspects of their
lives into identifiable communities and influences. Their attempts are
what interest me here. I want to understand how people defined and
juggled what *came to be seen as* separate personal, community-based,
and mass-culture narratives as they were trying to make sense of the world
around them.

The question that arises for an anthropologist studying these events is
not who was right and who was wrong but how the participating communities defined all that was happening around them that summer. This book
analyzes constructed texts, identities, and narrative representations in
order to show their rhetorical composition and the discursive constraints
that affected their production and utilization. I conclude that constructing
representations is a powerful political act that controls not only the
crucial definition of self and other but also the differential access to power,
resources, influence, and status.

The results of my work are presented here in the form of an experimental ethnography that employs, at the same time that it is exploring, a
variety of textual forms and voices. Such textual experiments are becoming more common in anthropological texts. Myra Bluebond-Langner
(1978), for example, uses the same technique of organizing narrative
information into the form of a dramatic play that I have employed in
Chapter 13. The fictionalized narrative in Chapter 12, though not common in standard ethnography, is being seen more often as anthropologists
turn their field experiences into novels (Barbara Tedlock, Billy Jean Isbell,
Dan Rose, and others are actively exploring this genre). Even the inclusion
of substantial transcripts of conversations and written textual productions of the community under study is still relatively uncommon in ethnography. Peter Davis's portrait of an American community, which com-

bines "social research with techniques of storytelling" (Davis 1982:10), covering events from a wedding to a murder in a small town, perhaps comes closest to the project attempted here. These experiments in textuality, wedged into more traditional analysis, are designed to demonstrate the complexity of textual production not just in ethnographies but also in the everyday lives of the people anthropologists study.

The events described and analyzed here took place in 1983, at a time when there was much concern and discussion about the nuclear threat to the world. When events in Europe in 1989 and 1990 signaled the "end" of the cold war, concerns about nuclear weapons and policies came to seem almost unnecessary. Suddenly it seemed as if we could put behind us the powerful cold-war narratives of self and other that had been sustaining and driving us. The attempts to replace these old stories with new narratives of a neutral, unthreatening world were short-lived, and the war in the Persian Gulf brought back in full force the types of narratives described here. I hope this analysis helps the reader to make sense not only of the events of 1983 but of the similar processes of narrative construction and textual self-defense that continue to rule our understanding of the world situation.

My research was conducted in two communities in conflict with each other; yet both encouraged and supported my project. I thank all the women of the Seneca Women's Encampment for a Future of Peace and Justice who were willing to share their experiences, ideas, and written accounts. Some I only know by first name and others are identified this way for anonymity. I particularly thank Jody, Shad, Andrea Doremus, and Pam Flanigan for their comments and interest, and Nancy Zucchino, my video partner. Other women whose support and critical comments were especially helpful were Helen, Didi, Hershey, Skysong, Estelle, Kim, Anet, Woodi, Robin, Judy, and Joan. Jean Aceto provided invaluable newspaper files on the encampment. Sharon Chapman and Lucinda Talbot graciously granted me access to the accounts of their encampment experiences. Michelle Crone deserves special thanks for her years of encouragement, friendship, and caring and for her wisdom in guiding me through alternative women's worlds. The Schlesinger Library at Radcliffe College provided materials from their encampment archives. The Boston Women's Video Collective provided me with copies of their extensive videotape documentation of the encampment, which proved to be extremely valuable.

Residents in and around Seneca County also were willing to share their experiences and perceptions, and I especially acknowledge Emerson and Carolyn Moran, Wisner and Barbara Kinne, Jerry McKenna, Joe Bromka, Judy Hart, Terry Mansell, Brian Dombrowski, Howard and Jean Burtless, Nikki Greer, Gwen McLeod-Webber, Ed Polk Douglas, Ferdinand Nicandri, Father Michael Conboy, Father Albert Shamon, Doyle Marquardt, and Robert Zemanek for the time and information they provided. The Seneca County Cooperative Extension and Ray Zajac and Sharon Secor of the Seneca County Board of Supervisors helped with crucial information. Seneca County sheriff Tom Cleere generously gave me access to the records of the events of 1983 and the facilities to study them. Dale Arcangeli, also of the sheriff's department, provided a fascinating orientation to life in Seneca County and was an excellent source of information and reflections.

The men and women of the Waterloo VFW Post made me feel welcome in their community, and my special appreciation goes to Ron and Nancy Bush, and to my friend Barney Olschewske, for all the help they provided. In Waterloo, Melley and Tom Kleman also extended warm hospitality, and Melley was particularly instrumental in integrating me into community life. In this regard I also thank all the women of the weekly Trivial Pursuit games!

In Seneca Falls, Mary Curry was a wonderful source of historical information on women's activities in the area, and Gwen Henderson (pseudonym) provided a moving and significant account of life in her town. Howard Van Kirk, Jr., shared his perceptive observations in an ever-delightful manner, and Pam Quiggle provided excellent photographic documentation of the encampment as well as her friendship and an introduction to a softball team in need of another player. My thanks to the women of that team for the chance to participate in another aspect of Seneca County life.

My apologies to any at the encampment and in Seneca County I may have forgotten, and my thanks to some very helpful people who have chosen to remain anonymous.

Members of the Seneca County news media—particularly Dave Shaw of the Syracuse *Post-Standard/Herald-Journal*, Carol Ritter of the *Democrat and Chronicle*, Marty Toombs of the *Finger Lakes Times*, and Bob Appel and Greg Cotteril of radio station WSFW—gave me their time and access to their records. The Auburn *Citizen* also made its records available.

I thank Roger Sanjek, the editor of this Cornell University Press series, the Anthropology of Contemporary Issues, for excellent guidance in improving this book and making it accessible to a wider audience. He and an anonymous reader offered perceptive and valuable suggestions.

I thank members of the Department of Anthropology, University at Albany, State University of New York, for general support and also for particular contributions: Gary Gossen for the inspiration to come back into anthropology; Jorge Klor de Alva for introducing me to models of critical thinking; Gail Landsman for suggesting the women's encampment as a topic; Walter Zenner for reminding me of the more general anthropological contexts for my work; and Iris Berger (Department of History) for her careful and perceptive readings and comments. I have been significantly influenced by Helen Elam of the Department of English, University at Albany, who has been instrumental in moving my thinking in exciting and productive directions over the past several years. For this I am particularly grateful.

Many fellow students, friends, and colleagues at the University at Albany, too numerous to mention, provided a valued forum for the discussion of my research. Special thanks do go to Susan Stebbins, Rhonda LaFleur, Laurie Donaldson, and Julie Goodson-Lawes for their discussions and for their visit in the field. Kathy O'Connor made expert transcriptions of my taped interviews as well as humorous, insightful comments throughout the project. Many thanks to Michael Blitz for inspirational conversations and for always knowing what I was saying and doing even when I couldn't figure it out. He continues to be my most important collaborator.

My thanks finally to my family, especially my sister, Joanne Stetson, and my mother, Mary Torok, for always being there and for not asking too often when I would be finished. And special thanks to Richard M. Leventhal, whose generous support and encouragement throughout made my work possible.

This research was funded in part by SUNY Benevolent Association Research Grants from the SUNYA Foundation, and by a grant from the Sigma Xi Grants-in-Aid of Research Program. All photographs not attributed to others are my own.

LOUISE KRASNIEWICZ

Santa Monica, California

Nuclear Summer

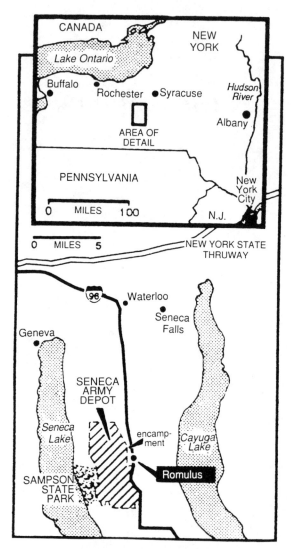

I

The Lost Summer

I neglected everything, . . . cost me personally a lot of financial grief too. Christ, I wasn't even there to take in the festivities my kids had in school. . . . Just like it was a lost summer, that's what it was, a lost summer, absolutely lost summer.

—Ray Zajac, Romulus Town Supervisor

In the summer of 1983 war raged in Chad, Chileans protested against Augusto Pinochet, Guatemalans overthrew Efrain Rios Montt in their second coup in seventeen months, and President Ronald Reagan said he was optimistic about peace in Central America even while he planned extensive U.S. war games in that region. Later in the year, the Soviet Union shot down a Korean airliner, killing all 269 persons aboard, and 241 U.S. military personnel died in the destruction of U.S. Marine headquarters in Beirut.

Also that summer, the spacecraft *Pioneer 10*, carrying a message to our extraterrestrial neighbors, crossed outside the boundaries of our planetary system. Earlier in the year, the space shuttle *Challenger* completed its maiden voyage, and in June, Sally Ride became the first U.S. woman astronaut to fly beyond the earth. Back on the ground, news reporter Christine Craft sued a Kansas City television station for demoting her because she was "unattractive, too old, and not deferential to men." Ginny Foat, former president of the California chapter of the National Organization for Women, was charged with murder, and Ling-Ling, a panda at the National Zoo, lost her first baby.

In the summer of 1983, the House of Representatives censured and reprimanded two male members for having had sex with teenage male

House pages. Witnesses at a congressional hearing testified that there was inadequate federal action on the AIDS problem because most of its victims were homosexual. Earlier that year, the Supreme Court reiterated that the right to an abortion was constitutionally protected.

At the movies, *War Games,* a film about a computer accident that starts a nuclear war, was popular. So were the James Bond film *Octopussy* and the third film in the Star Wars series, *The Return of the Jedi,* in which the Evil Empire is defeated. The French provided *The Return of Martin Guerre,* a movie about questionable identities and the power of storytelling in a small sixteenth-century French village. The April edition of the Marvel comic book *The Thing* featured a story titled "The Arena of No Return," which had the Fantastic Four superheroes crash-landing at the Seneca Army Depot. On television in November, the movie *The Day After* caused a controversy because it depicted the horrible devastation that would follow the detonation of a nuclear bomb in the United States.

In the small upstate communities in and around Seneca County, New York, the most memorable events of that summer took place much closer to home. In this county tucked between two of the scenic Finger Lakes, summer is usually filled with outdoor, family-oriented activities—parades, fishing contests, fairs, festivals, and softball games—that let residents savor the company of their neighbors and the natural pleasures of the region.

But the summer of 1983 was different. From the Fourth of July until Labor Day, thousands of women came to Seneca County to participate in the Seneca Women's Encampment for a Future of Peace and Justice, a protest against nuclear weapons and America's nuclear policies. The women came individually, in small groups, and in large contingents to camp on a fifty-two-acre parcel of land near the rural towns of Varick and Romulus and adjacent to the eleven-thousand-acre Seneca Army Depot (SEAD), a suspected repository of nuclear weapons. The express purpose of the encampment in that first summer of its existence was to stop the scheduled deployment of Cruise and Pershing II missiles before their (suspected) shipment from the Seneca Army Depot to Europe that fall.

The Seneca encampment was patterned on a similar peace camp at Greenham Common in England, where women had been protesting since 1981 against the planned deployment of these same nuclear weapons at the U.S. military base there. In addition to protesting nuclear weapons, the Seneca encampment, like Greenham, also served as a critique of the "patriarchal system" that was considered responsible for producing nuclear weapons and threatening to use them.

Protester at SEAD fence. Photo by Pam Quiggle

The women who came to the encampment were not drawn from any one group or movement. Rather, the encampment united women who might not otherwise ever have found a reason to work, protest, and talk together. Women with a history of activity in liberal and radical politics, feminism, countercultures, civil rights, or the antinuclear movement joined for a summer of protests and dialogue with women who were concerned about the seemingly more personal or perhaps "conservative" issues of family, religion, governmental accountability, and individual responsibility. As the summer's activities were to show, it was just this ability of the encampment to focus simultaneously on the political and the personal aspects of antinuclear issues that made this diverse collection of women so stimulating and ultimately so threatening.

The women who attended the 1983 encampment expressed their antinuclear or antipatriarchal sentiments by staging protests at the army depot and in the surrounding communities. These protests, which were designed to educate the country on the dangers of nuclear weapons as well as to provide a forum for feminist and peace issues, soon developed into occasions for heated and sometimes violent clashes between the encampment women and the local residents. The questions of risk and danger in a nuclear world, which the encampment women hoped to address by their

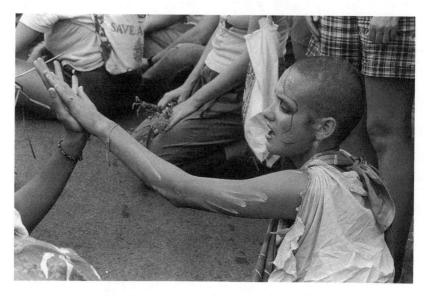

Ritualized protest. Photo by Pam Quiggle

protests, were soon overshadowed by questions of morality, lifestyle, politics, patriotism, women's roles, and sexuality.

The local residents expressed shock and anger at the actions of these female "outsiders," who were seen as disturbing their peaceful rural communities. One group of people formed the USA (United for a Strong America) Committee to counter what they saw as threats to the freedom, morals, and religious values of the country. These and other residents accused encampment women of being unpatriotic because they refused to fly the American flag on the Fourth of July; of being witches because their protests and performances were often odd and ritualistic; of being sexually perverse because they condoned lesbianism and created the encampment as a women-only space. They feared that the women would close down the depot, thus worsening an already high unemployment rate, and that taxes would have to be raised to cover the cost of policing the protests. They considered the women noisy, vocal, and unpredictable, and they accused the protesters of abandoning commonly respected notions of womanhood, the family, and authority. The residents could not see how all the personal and political issues the encampment women raised were related to nuclear weapons, and they refused to accept the logic of such protests in a democratic society or their relationship to peaceful Seneca

Encampment women walking through Waterloo. Photo by Pam Quiggle

County. As one resident explained, "These are well-intentioned dedicated women who feel they have a duty to perform. But I wish they'd gone someplace else" (*Ithaca Journal*, June 30, 1983).

As the women developed their antinuclear and antipatriarchal protests, the people in and around Seneca County began responding with counter-demonstrations, heckling, jeering, flag-waving and physical harassment during the protests and also at the encampment land. The USA Committee exhorted its neighbors in a flyer it circulated to oppose the communist-humanist-feminists who were threatening "pro-family biblical values." Tensions built toward August 1, when the largest mass demonstration of the summer was planned, and thousands of protesters were expected at one time. Just before the big protest, these tensions exploded in a series of particularly violent and frightening confrontations between the people of Seneca County and the women of the encampment.

On Saturday, July 30, about seventy-five encampment women walking from Seneca Falls (celebrated as the birthplace of women's rights) to the gate of the Seneca Army Depot fourteen miles away were stopped by an angry crowd as they tried to cross a bridge in the town of Waterloo (the birthplace of Memorial Day). Three hundred to four hundred townspeople threatened and harassed the women, who sat down on the bridge in a circle in order to diffuse the tensions and protect themselves. Fifty-three of the women were arrested, along with two local men, one of whom was carrying a rifle, and a Waterloo woman who sat down with the protesters in support of their right to march through her town. The encampment women were held for five days in a makeshift jail in a local elementary school (while the violent confrontations continued) before the charges of disorderly conduct against them were dismissed in a raucous trial. There were counterdemonstrations at the August 1 protest but no more overt violence. The encampment continued its first summer of activities until Labor Day and joined in a large antinuclear demonstration at the depot organized by other groups in October of that year. The encampment remained open on a smaller scale and with varying political and social agendas, although discussions about closing it gained momentum in the summer of 1990. At the time of this writing it is still open.

The clashes that took place between the encampment participants and groups of local "counterdemonstrators" seriously affected the encampment's agenda. Although the women had expected local opposition to their antinuclear protests, they had not anticipated such intense hostility to their lifestyle and antipatriarchal politics. The severe reactions, as well as some internal dissension, forced the participants to refocus their activities and energies in order to deal with these threats and challenges to their project and to the encampment's view of itself as a viable alternative to the patriarchal form of social organization. At the same time, these confrontations also forced the local people to reevaluate their stances, strategies, and categories when, by attacking the women, they themselves began violating the same "American" rights, privileges, and way of life that they claimed to be defending against these "invaders."

These differences of opinion, beliefs, and values between and within communities proved very disturbing because they challenged the deeply held assumption that such concepts as women and men, Americans, the family, religion, patriotism, and authority were stable, easy to understand, and shared by all members of a community. A person's stance in relation to categories based on these notions became crucial for confirming that person's identity as a local or an outsider, as a proper male/female or a pervert, and as a good American or a communist dupe.

Since categorizing, or putting things and ideas into their proper place, is one of the main ways of defining the differences between communities, challenges to each other's categories were particularly disturbing to all the participants in these events. These battles between communities that had different ways of categorizing and interpreting the world were serious social, political, and psychological dramas that had as their agenda the confident definition of self and other in a plural, conflict-ridden world. The disagreements are useful for illustrating how all communities define and maintain themselves, especially in moments of crisis, when those identities are most threatened.

The events of the summer of 1983 came to signify different things to different people. For some it was an occasion to reconfirm their belief in tradition, family, and authority; for others it was a celebration of alternative social, religious, and political relations. For some it was a chance to make new interconnections between feminist and antinuclear issues; others saw the events of the summer as a political joke, a media-hyped farce. Some people saw a chance to reconfirm the local history of Seneca County as either the birthplace of women's rights or as the source of the kind of all-American patriotism that had given birth to Memorial Day. Others (or sometimes the same people) would always remember Seneca County as the site of significant historical and contemporary fights between locals and outsiders, citizens and the government, good and evil. Many different people for many different reasons saw Seneca County as a Garden of Eden, a place deserving protection and veneration; yet many others saw the same place as the site of evil, either because of the presence of nuclear weapons (if one were antinuclear) or because of the unwelcome protesters (if one were opposed to the encampment). Many people wanted to rewrite both the history of the past and the course of the future, and many wanted to impose their reading and writing of history on others.

In the summer of 1983 Seneca County, New York, was an arena for the expression, evaluation, and reconsideration of the most treasured and respected beliefs and values of several different communities. For each group and each individual, what was at stake that summer was nothing less than the definition of who they were and what was their rightful place in the social world. In conflicts, dialogues, confrontations, accusations, and threats, the people around Seneca County and the women of the peace encampment struggled to define themselves in relation to each other and fought to defend these identities against erosion and misinterpretation.

These differences of opinion and belief were offered up for public consumption and consideration through a variety of expressive forms, including songs, signs, costumes, slogans, rituals, letters to the editor, newspaper and television interviews, photographs, gossip, rumors, conversation, and personal narratives. The participants used these expressive forms to argue, manipulate, and redefine the meanings and significance of the summer's activities.

Many of these expressive forms took the shape of narratives, stories that appear to be constructed in a "logical" and familiar order. As one of the "fundamental modes of explication" (Martin 1986:189), narrative is a common way to share meanings and understandings. One such narrative was offered to me as an orientation to Seneca County when I began my research. Dale Arcangeli, then chief deputy of the sheriff's department, had been assigned to coordinate the police coverage of the encampment's activities in 1983. When I met him in the summer of 1986, he agreed to take me on an orientation tour of the county and show me all the important places associated with that summer.

As we drove along, Deputy Arcangeli identified each place he pointed out by associating it with a story. Some of the stories were about the encampment, but most were from his own past or from the history of the county. My view of the county became informed by where he had lived at different ages, where he had worked as a teenager, where the local kids go parking, where businesses and families had come and gone. When we passed the Seneca Army Depot, Arcangeli told me about the herd of white deer that live there, thought by the local residents to be genetic mutations caused by the radioactivity on the base. We searched for the deer but could not find them.

By the time we entered the lower part of the county, a heavy thunderstorm had moved in with blinding rain, lightning, and heavy fog. It got so bad that I could not see the things he was pointing out and I repeatedly had to ask where we were. Later I found it impossible to retrace our path. I had thought that we were driving into this part of the county to see the school where the women arrested at the bridge in Waterloo were held for five days, but before we got there, Deputy Arcangeli had one more detour.

"Well, it doesn't have much to do with protests," he said, "but as long as you're here I just figured . . ." He hesitated and then asked, "Remember *Twilight Zone?*"

"Oh, of course!" I answered.

"Rod Serling?"

"Yeah."

"I'm probably one of the few people," he said proudly, "that had the fortunate childhood to grow up with his children."

"You're kidding!"

"In the summertime. Right down here, right here, there is a private drive." He pointed as we passed elegant summer houses on the lake side. "And if you go down, Rod Serling used to live down there!"

Deputy Arcangeli was selling garden seeds or something as a fund-raising activity for the Boy Scouts when he met Serling and his family. He thought the Serlings were just regular people, even if they did have a lot of money.

We continued to drive on and as the rain let up Arcangeli pointed out one of the new local wineries and a place where his deputies had had to disarm a man with a steak knife who was threatening his family. "I've got to show you something. It wouldn't make my day if I didn't show you," he said suddenly. We drove up to a cemetery just as the rain stopped. "Of course we could dig up some graves! Isn't that more archaeology than anthropology, though?" It was only his status as one of the chief order-keepers in the county that persuaded me to follow him into the graveyard.

He swung the beam of his huge flashlight over the gravestones as we walked. "No that's not it. That's not it. I thought it was around here someplace. There it is. There you go. And he *is* there! Because I was here when they put him in the ground."

My comment as I looked at the small, simple gravestone that was illuminated by his torch was that it was just a tiny, little thing. "Yeah, that's all," he agreed, "you'd think he'd have a great big stone. His wife told me, they got a big stone out in California, but he always wanted to be buried here so they put him here and put this here so there wouldn't be much publicity. All that is, is a veteran's stone." Buried here, in a tiny cemetery in Seneca County, New York, with plastic flowers decorating his veteran's headstone, was Rod Serling, creator of the *Twilight Zone*, who died June 28, 1975.

My purpose in relating this experience is not to suggest that Seneca County is reminiscent of the *Twilight Zone*. Rather, it is to demonstrate vividly how we all couch our explanations and communications in terms of familiar and conventional stories that we already know and cherish. To Deputy Arcangeli, Rod Serling was not only the ominous purveyor of alternative macabre realities but the summer neighbor whose children were enjoyable playmates and whose story was just one of many that defined his landscape. Yet Serling's national reputation as the host of disturbing and unconventional narratives can never be far from our assimilation of his literal emplotment in the grounds of Seneca County. These multiple narrative realities, based simultaneously in the local community and the larger society, work both with and against each other as we try to make sense of stories, ideas, and events. Like Serling himself, the master of narrative manipulations, Deputy Arcangeli was able to demonstrate this complexity and this usefulness of narratives.

Deputy Arcangeli's disorientation tour directly challenged my assumptions about the proper kinds of data to seek in studying American community life. It reoriented me, as the *Twilight Zone* program claimed it also did, to "that middle ground between light and shadow, between science and superstition, and between the pits of man's fears and the summit of his knowledge," to that "wondrous land whose boundaries are that of imagination" (Zicree 1982:31).

2

The Anthropology of Fallout

The culture of any society at any moment is more like the debris, or "fall-out," of past ideological systems, than it is itself a system, a coherent whole.
—Victor Turner

"I always thought that anthropologists studied the skulls they dug out of the ground instead of the skulls that were still walking around," one resident of Seneca County teased me while we were discussing my project to study the events that had taken place in his community. Many of his neighbors agreed that an anthropologist didn't seem the appropriate person to study their community. "Some of us were talking," one law enforcement officer explained, "and we were trying to figure out what anthropology is." He explained that they could understand that some anthropologists dug up old bones (he had worked with some physical anthropologists on murder cases) and that some dug up old civilizations, but didn't all the other kinds of anthropologists work in places like Africa?

It is not surprising that Seneca County residents were confused by the idea of an anthropologist studying a contemporary U.S. community. Like many who call anthropology their profession, this general public associates anthropology with archaeological excavations, with the physical anthropologist's search for the remains of evolutionary precursors, or with the study of non-Western, nonindustrialized societies. Anthropology retains for the initiated as well as the uninitiated an association with the study of the exotic, the esoteric, and the other.

Yet thinking of anthropology this way—as a discipline concerned only with people and things distant in time, place, and habit—belies anthropology's history, its present-day circumstances, and its applicability to the events in Seneca County in 1983. Actually, anthropology never exclusively focused on the untouched, unstudied "primitive" society idealized as the object of anthropological inquiry. Such researchers as Margaret Mead, Cora Du Bois, Marvin Harris, Hortense Powdermaker, Jules Henry, Evon Vogt, John Bennett, Constance Perin, Herve Varenne, and David Schneider are prominent in a rich tradition of American studies. Anthropology has always studied culture contact, contemporary societies, the West and the rest, and the nonindustrialized as well as the overindustrialized.

Today, for a variety of practical, ethical, political, and theoretical reasons, American anthropology no longer wants or needs to be seen as primarily studying the "primitive" other. Practically speaking, the extensive influence of global industrial, cultural, technological, and informational practices means that the so-called pristine, isolated societies that anthropology thought it needed to seek for analysis now exist only in anthropological nostalgia. In addition, the extensive post–World War II development of new nation-states has not only blurred the lines between groups that had previously been considered culturally and politically distinct but has also created economic and military conditions that make fieldwork in many parts of the world impractical. Access to subject societies is thus often not financially feasible or safe for anthropologists.

Ethical and political considerations have been influenced by the ability of former anthropological subjects to gain access to the same universities that have trained generations of anthropologists. Former subjects are discovering the need and desire to study themselves from their own perspectives and not to rely on Western interpretations of their lives, which have been criticized for their colonialist or neocolonialist bent. Many anthropologists came to share the concern of formerly colonized and studied peoples that anthropology was implicated in colonialism. They began to rethink the anthropological project, particularly after the temporary radicalization of academia in the 1960s and the revelation that anthropologists had collaborated in counterinsurgency against indigenous peoples in Indochina and Latin America by gathering anthropological data to be used against them (Marcus and Fischer 1986:35). The questions of whom we should study, why we should study them, and what we do with the information we collect have helped redirect anthropological projects.

In American anthropology, for many reasons, theoretical shifts have been quite complex in recent years. Interest has increased in interdisciplinary study; the use of textual analogies; the analysis of class, race, and gender; and emphasis on conflict and change instead of rules and consistencies. In consequence, anthropology has been opened to new subjects, new methodologies, and new theoretical possibilities. For some anthropologists, the changes have meant closer alliances with the biological and physical sciences and with statistical, quantitative, and computer analyses. Others have found their new allies in the humanities and the interpretive sciences. My work is aligned with theirs. Like them, I am interested in how literary criticism, the new historiography, revisions in psychoanalytic theory and the many facets of feminist studies can expand the horizons of anthropology. With these anthropologists, I am involved in crossing or redrawing disciplinary boundaries, exploring how to revamp our way of thinking altogether.

The changes due to the increased emphasis on interdisciplinary connections have resulted in what Clifford Geertz has called a blurring of genres or disciplines. Something is happening "to the way we think about the way we think" says Geertz (1983:20), and one grounding for this transdisciplinary, humanities-oriented work is the shift from the use of mechanistic or organic analogies to textual ones. Literary criticism has now become a major influence on anthropological inquiry. As George Marcus and Michael Fischer tell us (1986:5), "Theoretical developments in the field of literary criticism and interpretation ha[ve] replaced linguistics as an influential source of new ideas about theory and methodology in anthropology." Certain subfields of anthropology—notably symbolic, interpretive, feminist, and psychological anthropology—have been most open to these influences.

What is this textual analogy and what does it offer anthropology? Anthropology readily admits that access to such cultural features as identity, community, belief, motivation, or interpretive strategies cannot be direct. We cannot see a motivation or a plan; we can see only their effects—how people act, what they say and don't say about what they do, what they produce and consume. As anthropologists have long been aware, aspects of culture, indeed "culture" itself, are mediated, and anthropology's job has been to make sense of culture from the traces it leaves behind. Some anthropologists have approached the problem of mediated, indirect access to "culture" by defining culture as if it were a kind of text. According to this textual approach, "social actions can be 'read' for their meanings by the observer just as written and spoken materials more conventionally are" (Marcus and Fischer 1986:26). What is studied in this approach is not so much "life itself" as texts and performances about life.

Still, if this "culture-as-text" approach has been stimulating for anthropologists, it has also created some dangerous traps that are just beginning to be recognized. Text building is a major social activity, not confined to any one type of person but produced by everyone. As Shirley Nelson Garner, Claire Kahane, and Madelon Sprengnether remark, "The stories we tell ourselves about who we are or hope to be play a primary role in creating and sustaining our identities as we move through an uncertain world" (1985:9). Gayatri Spivak (1987:95) suggests that seeing life as a text is not simply an abstract invention of social scientists but parallels the way people actually conduct their lives. Texts are read and interpreted in a variety of ways and the particular method one chooses for reading depends on a methodological orientation or interpretive strategy. Texts can be seen, for example, as stable entities that contain their own meaning or, alternatively, as contested forms with negotiated meanings. Between these two poles are a whole range of strategies that radically alter the textual project. The danger for anthropology is in choosing a conservative strategy that tries to limit the possible range of meanings for a text rather than one that encourages a wide play of meanings and interpretations. Some anthropologists (inappropriately, I believe) have used the textual analogy to suggest that a text/culture need only be properly read in order for the correct and accurate interpretation of the text/culture to become clear (that is, for the meaning of the text/culture to be evident).

Like the now-unfashionable New Critics, who perceived the literary text as a stable source of meaning, anthropologists who see the text as representation of reality approach it as directly reflecting or embodying the culture that made it. Taking a "functional" attitude, they see the text as essentially coherent and integrated, its stable and definitive meaning available after a close, careful reading that tends to concentrate on the symbols and tropes (figures of speech such as metaphors) of the independent and self-sufficient text. The New Critics took the text as a coherent object that could be read apart from its cranky author or the peculiarities of a particular reader. The anthropological equivalent of the New Critics may have been the structural-functionalists, who were concerned with formal, idealized qualities and how they were integrated in a culture.

In the structural approach to textual analysis (both literary criticism and anthropology are indebted to Claude Lévi-Strauss here), texts were seen not as independent forms but as examples of recurring narrative and social patterns and themes. Structural analysis, as originally developed, "sought to reconstitute a common language for all narratives," according to Josué Harari (1979:23). This concentration on the form rather than just the content of the text was the hallmark of structuralism; the content could be changed but the structure could remain the same as long as the "relations between units is preserved," wrote Terry Eagleton (1983:95). Structuralism also introduced the notion of conflict into the text when it tried to delineate the binary oppositions (hot/cold, nature/culture, male/female) underpinning the narrative. It showed how these binary oppositions (which it tended to see as universal structures of the mind) determined the stable and identifiable meaning of the text.

Poststructuralists have challenged this model in recent years. If structuralists "are convinced that systematic knowledge is possible," as Jonathan Culler notes, then "post-structuralists claim to know only the impossibility of this knowledge" (1982:22). Criticism of structuralism, particularly for its notion of universal narrative structures as inherent elements of the human mind, does not entirely negate its potential contribution to textual methodology for anthropology. Structuralism did suggest the importance of seeing texts as constructed rather than as a reflection of external reality. What poststructuralism attempts to do is push this constructedness to the forefront without attributing it either to universals of the human psyche or to individual creative action.

The poststructuralist approach sees meaning not as residing in the text but as a function of the complexity of language and a product of the interaction of textual form, content, production and reception. Deconstruction is one such poststructural strategy, whose goal is to undermine the seeming stability of the text by showing that in order to posit one meaning, a text necessarily has to repress others. Deconstruction shows how the text itself contains the information to undermine the meaning that it is at the same time trying to promote. A text can be neither mined for its symbolic, hidden meaning nor categorized by its structure, form, content, or theme. Instead, deconstruction points out the contradictions in a text's logic and content. It is interested in the binary oppositions of structuralism, but it "tries to show how such oppositions, in order to hold themselves in place, are sometimes betrayed into inverting or collapsing themselves" (Eagleton 1983:133).

Feminist criticisms (of which there are many forms) can be seen as another strategy that attacks one of the most pervasive and oppressive structuralist binary oppositions—that between male and female. Feminist critics question not just the male and female roles seen in a text but also the general notion of dividing people into such rigid categories and power relations. They are concerned with the constraints on textual production that arise because of gender relations, and they believe it is crucial to place a text in the larger context of such relations, which profoundly affect its reading and writing. In this view, texts do not reflect an inherent biological gender nature; they have been constructed to support a particular politically motivated image of male and female.

Traditional psychoanalysis enacted an odd analyst-patient relationship with texts, attempting to identify the "unconscious" themes ruling a textual construction. More recent revisions in psychoanalytic theory (particularly those drawing on the work of Jacques Lacan and Jacques Derrida) look at how texts attempt (and fail) to control their own readings. In its concern for the style of repression a text uses to reveal and conceal what it does, current psychoanalytic thinking shows the inherent ambiguity and unresolvable conflicts residing in all texts. Lacanian analysis looks at how language and texts constitute us as subjects, and it refuses to let either our own reading of the text or the reading of ourselves remain stable. Since psychoanalysis studies the "internalisation of the social in the formation of the individual," as Victor Burgin puts it (1986:40), it can be useful for textual anthropology in relating text, society, and the individual.

What revisionary textual strategists (poststructuralists, feminists, deconstructionists, and Lacanian psychoanalysts) are pointing out is that it is necessary to avoid stabilizing the meaning of texts, behaviors, and events and always to consider the politics surrounding textual production and reception. It is the play of meanings resulting from the interaction of text, textual production, and textual reception that makes textual analogy useful for the field of anthropology.

The notion that texts are continually negotiated and always wrapped up in the intrigues of representation is useful for anthropology because it reminds us that texts are not only structures of meaning but also structures of power. "No reading is innocent," Susan Rubin Suleiman tells us, because "every reading is an interpretation, and every interpretation is an appropriation of the text for its own purpose" (1986:122). Every society tries to organize and control the ways that events, people, and objects are perceived, interpreted, reacted to, and acted upon. This system of control and relations is called discourse. Discourse is concerned with setting limits on how people talk and interpret by the establishment of a set of shared expectations about what things mean.

A discourse, writes Mark Philp, is "a system of possibility for knowledge . . . what rules permit certain statements to be made; what rules order these statements; what rules permit us to identify some statements as true and some as false; what rules allow the construction of a map, model, or classificatory system; what rules allow us to identify certain individuals as authors; and what rules are revealed when an object of discourse is modified or transformed. . . . When sets of rules of these kinds can be identified, we are dealing with a discursive formation or discourse" (Philp 1986:68–69). As a system of possibilities, discourse is used by individuals in their social relations, but it may or may not be used consciously: in most cases it operates "behind the backs" of the social actors (ibid.). Michel Foucault suggests that an analysis of discourse should consider not only how actors are constrained by discourse and in turn challenge it but also the modes of "circulation, valorization, attribution, and appropriation of discourses" (Foucault 1979:158). As we look for these discursive rules in a particular setting, we can see the relation among various social actors, between individuals and groups, and between community members and the larger system that contains and articulates their discursive fields.

Discourse, according to Edward Said, "is not mere formalization of knowledge; its aim is the control and manipulation of knowledge, the body politic, and ultimately the State" (1978b:678). Whoever can control, convince, or seduce others into accepting a particular discourse is exercising power by controlling interpretations and the social behavior influenced by them. The strategies of power acts are revealed in a discourse analysis, for discourse lays out the possibilities and the boundaries of choice and action in particular power relations.

Some discourses are dominant or more authoritative and have a greater chance of exercising this power. The authoritative discourse is the "already uttered" prior discourse that is backed by legal, political, and moral authority. It enjoys a privileged position because it dominates official public performance, expresses the established position, and "sees itself as giving the correct interpretation" (Bruner and Gorfain 1984:59). Challenges to the dominant discourse always appear to be coming from the margins of society, as if they were voices that were "other." Edward Bruner and Phyllis Gorfain explain that "authoritative voices attempt to fix meanings and stabilize order, whereas challenging voices question established meanings and tend to be deconstructive" (ibid.:56).

A text must make its own discursive features seem natural and normal and those of the challenging discourse seem perverted and absurd. Discourse analysis assumes that a text produced within a specific discourse tries to hide its workings and its mechanisms in order to maintain this facade of normalcy and naturalism. It seeks to uncover these workings, to show how the discourse works to manipulate knowledge, to persuade its adherents, to define itself as natural and true, and to stimulate people to social action. But discourse analysis, especially when used in anthropology, requires us to consider not only how these texts are constructed but how they are actually used and what effects they have when they are brought into the public arena. How a text is experienced affects its interpretations and reception; in fact, the text has no meaning until it is put into circulation, and it is these circulating, flexible, and ever-changing readings of texts that should concern the anthropologist.

Since anthropology sees "people as active agents in the historical process who construct their own world" (Bruner 1986a:12), rather than implementers of a predetermined textual strategy, we need to see how people do things with texts, not just how they articulate and read them. As active agents in the production, reading, resistance to, and reinterpretation of texts, people are neither dupes of discourse nor free-wheeling agents of action and power. Rather, they are conflict-ridden actors, simultaneously confident and uncertain, bold and reticent in their production of meaning. This aspect of agency is what is generally missing from many nonanthropological textual analyses and also from many of the anthropological ones.

The emphasis on textuality coincides with another change in anthropological inquiry. Anthropology (as well as other disciplines) has shifted emphasis from harmony models to conflict models. Anthropologist Victor Turner has called this adjustment the "postmodern turn" (1979:66). It leaves behind the traditional emphasis on the delineation of sociocultural rules in favor of exploring a society's practices and performances, seeking "in the very flaws, hesitations, personal factors, incomplete, elliptical, context-dependent, situational components of performance, clues to the very nature of human process itself" (ibid.:66–67). It is a change from trying to predict behavior, prove cause and effect, and determine origins toward trying to understand, explicate, and interpret without closing off other readings of textual materials.

Earlier anthropologists were not unaware of the conflicts and contradictions that existed in social life; as Sally Moore notes, they "chose . . . to ignore them in order to concentrate on the element of order" (1975:216). Moore explains that in the development of what is often called the practice approach, "there has been a shift of emphasis from the study of normative models to the study of specific situations and specific sequences of events . . . full of inconsistencies, oppositions, contradictions, and tensions" (ibid.).

Many factors contributed to the disillusionment with the social harmony theories and their static models of analysis. Among them were Freudian theories of motivational ambivalence and the inevitability of psychic conflict in human development. More recently, linguistics, always a source of inspirations and theoretical trends for anthropology, shifted its interests from the *langue*, or grammar, aspect of Ferdinand de Saussure's model of language to the *parole*, or speech/performance aspect. Lévi-Strauss's structuralist application of this linguistic model, with its emphasis on uncovering the underlying *langue*, or structures, of sociocultural data, has given way to a sociolinguistic emphasis on *parole*, or speech, which is studied not only in relation to the rules of the language but also in relation to its social context and performative features.

Inherent social conflict, especially as expressed in symbolic behavior, is a central theme of the influential work of Victor Turner. According to Turner, ritual is the place where conflict is acknowledged, the place where a society delineates the things that did not work and the steps necessary for a tentative and somewhat temporary social reconsolidation (Turner 1967). It is in ritual that a society has the most to say about itself, and what it is talking about is conflict. Conflict is thus not necessarily a destructive force but rather the means by which some form of continuity can be achieved. In fact, Turner points out, this continuity is difficult without the conflict that allows people to reemphasize and recreate the social categories that define and give meaning to their lives. Texts are produced in this atmosphere of conflict, out of a desire to understand and resolve the contradictions of social life. They are not the storage place for stable and shared meanings but the sites at which we can see meanings in conflict.

The postmodern turn in anthropology also promotes a shift in subject matter, or as Hal Foster tells us, "The mandate of postmodernism is also: 'change the object itself' " (1983:x). This mandate, combined with one that instructs anthropologists to be self-reflexive, has led to a change in the cultures studied. Now when anthropology studies the other, it is often in relation to the self, "while seeing itself as other" (Clifford 1986:23). Some anthropologists have turned to analysis of the "American" or United States culture that has nurtured and educated them and necessarily provides the context for all their work. This anthropology at home has created a whole range of new subjects, including the ones considered in this book.

Many of the early American studies focused on either of two entities—the local community or the national culture. There was less interest in explicating the relationship between the two. A postmodern analysis can help here because it will reify neither the local identities nor the national ones. Whether we like it or not, says Paul Rabinow, we all share "a specificity of historical experiences and place, however complex and contestable they may be, and a world-wide macro interdependency encompassing any particularity" (1986:258). We live in a state of "cosmopolitanism" no matter where we reside—in the biggest city or the smallest rural hamlet. We live "in-between," in what Turner would call a liminal state. It is this in-between state, this negotiation between the local and the national/global that is the subject of the postmodern study of American "culture."

We can approach the study of this liminal state by looking at moments of exchange and negotiation between local discourses and events and the more widely available national discursive and symbolic formations. Local discourses are readable in all the familiar places: in behavior, events, ritual, language, local texts, and local history. National discourses, because they are mass discourses, are available to us through aspects of the mass culture of late twentieth-century patriarchal, capitalist-consumer society: in national symbols, advertising images, high culture, and the mass-media texts of television, motion pictures, and the popular arts.

The line between what George Marcus calls the "local world of subjects and the global world of system" (1986:171) blurs as we apply a critique of representation and textuality to it because the local situation is framed by a simultaneous resistance to and accommodation of larger discourses. Microdiscourses, the local organization of knowledge which highlights certain meanings and deemphasizes others in order to achieve coherence, are reciprocally related to macrodiscourses. The local selects and promotes aspects of the general, while the general supplies ideological representations that can be used to legitimate and organize the local constructions and the resulting distribution of power and status (Chilton 1985:xvi).

The problem, suggest George Marcus and Michael Fischer, is "how to represent the embedding of richly described local cultural worlds in larger, impersonal systems of political economy" if "outside" forces are part of the construction of the local "inside" world (1986:77). How a local world simultaneously processes its own "culture" and that which is thrown at it from outside and above is one of the major concerns of this book. I do not look for large metanarratives to explain the events under consideration, but I use the postmodern strategy of discursive and textual analysis to evoke a sense of life during a series of inter- and intracommunity conflicts. But beyond just evoking these events, I hope to provide a strategy for analyzing how these events are constructed and interpreted locally and globally and for delineating the effects of these practices on people's lives and on the representations they create about those lives.

3

Coming Home

You can have no idea, said Peter irrelevantly, how refreshing it is to talk to
somebody who has a grasp of method. . . . You've got to show how the thing
was done, and then, if you like, bring in motive to back up your proof. If a
thing could only have been done one way, and if only one person could have
done it that way, then you've got your criminal, motive or no motive.
                                                          —Dorothy Sayers

An anthropologist studying her own culture has more to worry about
than just whether the people she is working with understand what anthropology is. In some ways working in your own society is easier—you are
familiar with the language, the "national identity" of your subjects, and
the general political, economic, and cultural milieu in which they exist.
You are less likely to make major mistakes in etiquette, and you already
know how to locate food, mail, entertainment, transportation, and restroom facilities. You probably can identify different types of kin relations,
have a general sense of what people in different occupations do, and have
a basic history of race, class, and gender relations.

Yet any anthropologist who has "come home" to work knows the
difficulties. Carol Greenhouse describes the situation well: "Americans at
work in the U.S. must become anthropologists all over again" (1985:261).
An important part of this reeducation is learning to see the everyday and
the mundane as data that help tell the ethnographic story. Road signs,
graffiti, newspaper ads, the movie playing at the local theater, the mer-
chandise in the local market or mall, clothing and hairstyles, the appearance of yards and houses, the food in restaurants—all things that an
anthropologist working in another culture would never think of ignor-
ing—need to be considered as data here too.

The traditional participant-observer role that an anthropologist can play in a foreign land also gets subverted at home. In this role anthropologists actively participate in the community they are studying while also trying to maintain a "scientific" or "objective" distance. Objectivity is difficult to maintain, however, for communities have every reason to assume that you, as another American and an incipient community member, ought to fit into preexisting roles or categories and should not be maintaining this illogical distance from your neighbors, asking them all sorts of questions.

During my work in Seneca County and at the peace camp, the roles assigned to me by different groups provided a record of how people classify themselves and outsiders. It also indicates that each group attempted to appropriate me, as they would try to recruit any potential new community member, to their own camp. Accepting the anthropologist as a community member is in some ways designed to neutralize her research or at least to confuse her loyalties. For example, one of my interviewees introduced me to a group of middle- and upper-middle-class women who met weekly to play Trivial Pursuit. They accepted me as a player, but I was never able to direct their attention away from the game and toward addressing my own pursuit of peace camp gossip. A group of working women accepted me as a member of their softball team, but only one postgame session in everyone's favorite softball bar led to a fruitful, if uneasy, discussion of the peace camp.

Many of the local veterans and members of the Veterans of Foreign Wars post considered me a friendly ear, willing to listen to their side of the story and enabling them to relive and relieve the tensions of the summer of 1983. More than one person commented that talking to me was like a session with a psychiatrist! Despite a sign in the VFW bar which said, "What you see here, What you hear here, When you leave, Leave it here," I was encouraged to take the stories they told away with me. And many of the community women that I talked to on a more formal, less involved basis used the opportunity to air their concerns not only about the peace camp but also about local conditions for women.

At the encampment I was required to play different roles at different times. In 1983 I was quite simply another participant, albeit one carrying a video camera. Upon my arrival in Seneca Falls with my female video partner to visit the historical sites before we went to the camp, an encampment women came up to us and said, "I would recognize two dykes anywhere!" We didn't want to counter her incorrect assumption, and we laughed to ourselves that we were so readily identified as members of the

Louise Krasniewicz at the encampment, 1983. Photographer unknown

encampment constituency. I was to learn through my research in the next several years that appearing to be a lesbian because of clothes, manner, or interest in women's issues was a key factor for acceptance in the post-1983 encampment community. The "discovery" that I was not a lesbian (usually because someone would directly question me) while I was doing this later research often led to hostility and suspicion at the post-1983 encampment. By contrast, this information usually comforted Seneca County residents, who then more easily assimilated me into their conversations and groups.

Those at the encampment assumed that any woman coming to the peace camp would actively and fully participate in routine and ritual. Although it was easy in 1983 to spend more time observing than participating, my observation habits were noticed and commented on in the smaller encampment community of later years. During a particularly emotional regional meeting in 1985, some women noted that I did not become involved in the antagonistic or emotional discussions that took place "from the heart," and they objected to my aloofness. My refusal to walk on hot coals in a ritual fire walk was not problematic, however, because I had participated in other aspects of the ritual and many other women also did not actually do the walk. Some of the encampment organizers believed that my study of their community legitimated their efforts, and they were willing to accept any level of participation or observation. Other women were unwilling to accept anything less than complete immersion in a separatist ideology and goddess-based spiritualism, and some became suspicious that I was spying for the army.

An anthropologist working in the United States thus has not only the traditional problem of juggling participation and observation but also the problem of switching sympathies among the many communities and factions that try to claim her as a logical member of their group. In a foreign place, an anthropologist is a clear and definite outsider, but in her own country, she discovers little comfort in trying to fall back on her professional status as an excuse for distancing herself from the communities she studies.

In the summer of 1986 I returned to Seneca County for four months of field research. I had attended the peace encampment in 1983 not quite as an anthropologist but also not exactly as a participating protestor. I was acquainted with some of the early organizers, who, as plans were being developed for the encampment, encouraged women with access to media equipment to document the activities. I joined in the effort to record the planning, building, and operation of this all-women's peace camp, attending twice in the summer of 1983 for a total of six days.

I have to admit that at first I had doubts about the ability of a group of feminist activists to carry out such an impressive enterprise. I had already seen the political and philosophical differences among women collapse concrete action into a pile of rhetoric many times. I was convinced that the organizers had miscalculated the amount of food, money, portable toilets and neighborly goodwill needed for the encampment's development. I was later to learn that many of the encampment organizers had had extensive experience organizing successful and safe music festivals that attracted thousands of women from throughout the country.

Although I was not "officially" an anthropologist at the time, my documentation work provided me with a chance both to participate and to distance myself from a project in which I did not have much confidence The use of a video camera provides the documenter with the same kind of participant-observer status that the anthropologist employs. It provides a license to observe from both inside and outside at the same time and to participate only as desired, with the "need" to record sometimes providing a good excuse not to be actively involved.

My decision to conduct more extensive research on the events surrounding the encampment arose at least partly from the nature of the experience. Many, or perhaps even most, women (myself included) were greatly moved by their participation. My initial misgivings were wiped away by a politically and socially stimulating community that offered a view of an alternative world. In 1984 I began attending regional encampment meetings as well as visiting the encampment, talking to some of the early organizers, and consulting the extensive encampment files. My analysis of 1983 was planned to include both accounts recorded at that time (from videotapes, audiotapes, photographs, journals, records, newspapers, etc.) and retrospective narrative accounts obtained from local residents and encampment women.

Not all anthropologists agree that the changes and trends described in the previous chapter are significant or positive for the discipline called anthropology. My own confrontation with this other current voice of anthropology came in the middle of my summer of fieldwork in Seneca County. I was in the offices of Seneca County's weekly newspaper, the *Reveille*, one day when Howard Van Kirk, the publisher, mentioned that another anthropologist had just walked in to use the copying machine. I was relieved to find out he was a folklorist collecting traditional folk stories until he told me that he had done his own brief study of the events related to the nuclear protests. The problems of that summer were easy to understand, he assured me, and they did not merit a summer of fieldwork or lengthy study. Echoing the exact words used by so many residents, newspaper reporters, and local officials, he told me that the problem in 1983 was that "the women came into a rural, conservative community that was not used to these kinds of activities." The most significant thing to understand, he insisted, was that people's main concern was economic—the local people were economically dependent on the army depot and were afraid of what would happen to people's jobs if it closed. It was plain and simple, he explained; people were motivated by economic factors and all the other so-called issues—witchcraft, lesbianism, nudity, and the American flag—were peripheral and basically insignificant. He didn't see what I could possibly have left to study: he felt he had answered the most important question of why Seneca County reacted so negatively toward the encampment women. From his point of view, my only options were to do an intensive analysis of the local economy or give up the project and go home.

My approach to the situation, I tried to explain to him, was quite different. I was not so much interested in proving *why* the events of 1983 took place as in describing *how* they took place and how people organized their understanding of these events. Asking *why* certainly leads to a reassuring closure (Why did the local people dislike the encampment women? Because they were afraid of losing their jobs and having higher taxes), but it is a closure that suppresses the richness of human social action. Such a mechanistic explanation is also too removed from the far-reaching effects of these events on the everyday lives of the individuals and the communities involved.

I was sure that my interest in effects rather than causes required me to analyze social action as Clifford Geertz has suggested, using a multi-disciplinary approach that considers culture semiotically, as a "web of significance" requiring interpretation (1973:5). Geertz's interest in "connecting action to its sense rather than behavior to its determinants" (1983:34) works with a culture-as-text analogy and with the search for *how* a text means. This shift to behavior and action as textual discourse seemed to provide the right approach for my study. When applied to the events of 1983 in Seneca County, New York, this approach led to an analysis of the texts produced about the discursive conflicts that took place that summer.

It was to become a major goal of my project to investigate the not-so-innocent purposes for which the people involved in this conflict produced, interpreted, manipulated, and experienced narratives or stories about the summer of 1983. In uncovering these narratives, I wanted to see how individuals and groups were both in control of and controlled by their stories; I wanted to see how they used narratives to make sense of those activities they supposedly were not used to seeing or experiencing. This search for the *how* of human behavior through the analysis of textual strategies was more complex than a search for the definitive *why*, but I thought it would provide a richer story of these events.

I wanted to approach social actions as textual products used in the context of a discourse. These textual actions asked not for definitive explanation but for careful readings; the delineation of their discursive context would show how people made the decisions they did and what constraints affected both collective and individual decisions and actions. I was interested in how people textualize their lives, how they both read and write themselves in and into the world.

The conflicts of that summer produced texts in many forms and about many subjects. By considering a range of these texts (for example, newspaper accounts, conversations, videotapes, letters, symbols, rituals, brochures, signs, clothing and appearance, songs) and analyzing their underlying assumptions, rules of organization, exclusions, and applications, we can see how these texts are constructed. The desired result of these productions, which all factions attempted to achieve, was a control of the interpretation and effects of the summer's events.

How did people know, as the other anthropologist claimed they did, how to interpret and categorize the women properly and correctly if, as everyone insisted, the local communities had never been confronted with this type of behavior or these kinds of women before? To me it seemed clear that the answer was in discourse because all social activities necessarily take place within discursive constraints, and the meaningfulness of any action is limited by what the discourse allows as a proper interpretation. I wanted to study Seneca County as an "interpretive community" (Fish 1980) that shared an outlook on actions and events. I did not feel that an economic explanation could cover everything that had occurred in 1983.

I explained all this (not in so many words) to the other anthropologist over coffee and later over lunch with him and his father in a Seneca Falls restaurant called Red's Place, which sported a sign that read, "Men's Hall of Fame," mocking the Women's Hall of Fame across the street. We parted ways after lunch, never to communicate again, and I went on to construct a study that had as its purpose the delineation of discursive, interpretive, and textual strategies in Seneca County in 1983.

The suggestion that the most important discourse informing the events of 1983 was economic did not sit well with me when I first heard it. It seemed too simplistically determinist and tended to denigrate non-material analyses as unimportant and less real. Initially, I completely rejected all economic explanations and kept my investigation focused on the symbolic. But economic factors are not inconsistent with the interpretive approach. Our symbolic constraints are heavily affected by material considerations, just as material conditions and explanations are certainly focused and guided by our interpretations. In addition, economic explanations embrace more than just material conditions; they, too, constitute a type of discourse involving the processes of representation and interpretation. This other anthropologist was not wrong to suggest a look at the material conditions of Seneca County; but it is important not to restrict the concept of economics to the traditional concern with the material aspects of life. Clearly some of the motivation for hostility to the encampment can be found in the economic background of Seneca County.

The encampment generated much opposition and had significant effects throughout the entire region. Nevertheless, the county is a useful bureaucratic, economic, and self-identification unit in New York state. It is used to organize such services as sheriff's departments, health departments, and welfare agencies. State funding for special programs in the arts, education, and farming are often determined on a countywide basis. In addition, local residents often organize their own groups such as church parishes or clubs within rather than across county lines. I use "Seneca County," therefore, as a shorthand designation for all the regional people who found themselves drawn into these conflicts, keeping in mind that not all of them resided in Seneca County proper and that not all the county residents were opposed to the encampment.

Like most rural agricultural and manufacturing counties in the late 1970s and early 1980s, Seneca County watched its economic base erode. The nonagricultural unemployment rates from the end of 1982 through the first half of 1983 ranged from 9.6 percent to a high of 13.8 percent. When the Philips television plant was partially closed in 1981, 402 local jobs were lost, and the 1983 closing of Comtec Corporation meant another 120 losses. Other, smaller businesses also closed or relocated.

The 1980s were generally a difficult time nationwide for small-scale farmers like the ones in Seneca County. National farm policies, trade embargoes, and poor weather conditions drove many family farms out of business, especially in the Midwest, where farms that had been worked for generations by a single family were lost to foreclosure. In Seneca County, according to the Seneca County Cooperative Extension office, the situation was not so desperate. The county led the state in soybean production, corn exports, and hog marketing, and was fourth or fifth in milk production. In addition, by 1987 there were twelve hundred acres of grapes growing at thirty-three vineyards, and eleven wineries were in operation, giving a boost not only to agricultural production but also to tourism.

Farmers in Seneca County traditionally experience only a 2.5 to 3 percent return on their crops. When weather conditions are poor, as they were in 1983, marginal farmers, including many who want to continue farming, are forced to sell out. But unlike those in the Midwest, most farmers in Seneca County remained financially solvent, according to Cooperative Extension, because they were able to sell their land for a good price. Amish and Mennonite farmers, who had begun emigrating from nearby states in the late 1970s, had been purchasing farms and driving up the prices and value of the land. Thus Seneca County escaped the plunge in land prices that devastated the midwestern states.

Outside of agriculture and industry, the Seneca Army Depot and the state psychiatric hospital at Willard were the largest employers. The *Re-*

source Handbook published by the encampment contended that "Many of the civilian jobs require a high level of skill or security clearance and are filled by persons who are brought to the depot from outside the Finger Lakes region. Many of the low skills jobs are filled by family members of military personnel stationed at the depot. The end result of this employment situation is that only a small percentage of all the jobs at the depot are open to local people" (*Resource Handbook* 1983:5). Nevertheless, the Seneca Army Depot employed approximately eight hundred civilian workers during 1983, and a national trend toward increased defense spending contributed to the depot's image as a strong and stable employer (even though the number of civilian employees had been steadily decreasing). The depot's public information director stated that the depot puts $33 million per year in salaries and contracts (including pay to the military personnel) into the regional communities. Although it is difficult to measure how much of that money actually made its way into the local economy (the salaries to military personnel, who had base housing and shopping, were not necessarily spent locally), certainly some of it contributed to Seneca County's economy. The loss of the depot as a source of steady money would have been a blow to the county.

Yet the Seneca Army Depot, as residents would readily state, was not an unambiguously positive economic asset to the local community. The depot is just one of several federal projects that provide needed jobs and services but also bring in unwelcome "outside" influences and take extensive areas of land off the county tax rolls. Local residents often view the SEAD—along with a state park, a wildlife preserve, a national park celebrating women's history, the psychiatric center, and a federal land-use area (failed farms purchased by the government and set aside for cattle grazing and now for recreation)—as yet another sacrifice to be borne by a county that has given more than its fair share of resources to the state and federal governments (12 percent of the land in Seneca County and 33 percent in Romulus and Tyre townships is government owned). Yet even as a mixed blessing the depot was generally seen as a sign of the possible economic survival of Seneca County in difficult times.

It is ironic but not inconsistent with their actions that many regional residents not only didn't lose jobs or money because of the encampment but in fact made money providing goods and services to the thousands of protestors, reporters, and curiosity seekers. Extra civilian guards hired by the depot were drawn from the local population, and local restaurants and hotels fed and housed the extra police called in for the large protests. The $195,000 tab for the extra county security services was reimbursed within a year by the federal government after lobbying by area politicians. Representative Frank Horton and Senator Alfonse D'Amato argued that the lengthy protests had put a special burden on a rural county that was unable to bear it. The Department of Justice agreed and offered to reimburse the county for security expenses. According to the county budget director in 1984, all but about $84,000 of the bills of 1983 had already been paid with unanticipated extra sales tax revenue; a good portion of the federal money would therefore be counted as additional revenue for the 1984 budget year (*Finger Lakes Times*, January 11, 1984). Thus the county actually made a profit on the events of 1983.

In a market economy, economic activities are seen as more important than "merely" cultural ones and usually as distinct from them. But the "economic" discourse surrounding the events of 1983 should be widened to include issues beyond money, profits, employment, and taxes. The activities of that summer could easily be thought of as what Georges Bataille calls an "unproductive expenditure" (1985:118), which, like pleasure and unreproductive sexual activity, is assumed to be wasteful and antisocial. Alternatively, these activities could be seen as part of a network of social exchange which is absolutely necessary for the definition and continuation of the social world. Economic discourses are always intricately interwoven with seemingly noneconomic ones to create the idea of the "economy" as a "ground where self and society both define and confuse ethical and material values," according to Wallace Martin (1986: 19). As Marshall Sahlins reminds us, the economic basis of a society is also a "symbolic scheme of practical activity" (1976:37), a way of judging and classifying value, functionality, utility, importance, and meaningfulness. When people talk about the economy, they are using one of commonest measures in our society for indicating changes in status, identity, social standing, and values. In her study of rural poverty in upstate New York, Janet Fitchen (1981) has pointed out that changes in the rural economy are often strongly associated with major shifts in the social context; neither is the determining force, and each informs us about the other.

The protests were a compelling social as well as economic drama about which everyone—depot employees or not—seemed curious. As one man explained:

> I went down to watch them because I'd never actually seen a protest in person. . . . I went down there [to the depot main gate] and watched. And I just kept watching and watching. . . . yeah, it was weird, I was just transfixed; took my wife out there on the motorcycle, and she got into it

because she was sort of a rebel anyway, being in college and all. But like I said, it was the first time I ever seen anything like that, and I just stayed there for like hours and hours and hours, just watching. . . . That was quite a learning process for me, trying to figure out what they were doing.

Some local residents used the analogy of "coming out to watch a fire to explain the interest in the encampment protests." At a fire everyone wants to know whose house is burning, who discovered the fire, did the fire department respond quickly, was anyone hurt, how much damage there was—questions that build the fire into a human drama that contemplates the nature of social relations and the condition of human beings in an uncertain world. The encampment protests were something that, like a fire; they provided people with the opportunity to confirm, protect, and expand their definition of themselves as members of a community and a world that was both precarious and stable. A combination of curiosity and a desire to be a part of a community event, the wish not to miss out on shared information and activities, certainly could be compelling.

The people watching the antinuclear protests were not necessarily depot workers or relatives of workers out defending their jobs. One active counterdemonstrator who did work at the depot actually lost his job during that summer, and according to his claims, it was precisely because he was counterprotesting and being interviewed in the newspapers that he was laid off. Another prominent counterdemonstrator worked not at the depot but for the local radio station, and he was nearly fired for his vocal protests and visibility at demonstrations. What attracted depot workers and nonworkers alike was a sense that the community was under attack and needed to be defended on all fronts. The events of 1983 provided people with a ritualistic means of contemplating and witnessing exactly those things that could tear their society apart and then those things needed to put their society right again. Like the man who went out to watch, "trying to figure out what they were doing," people were trying to give meaning to what they saw. That meaning was always a combination of the social, the political, and the economic.

4

Introductions

Late in the 19th century, many thousands of gypsies came to America. . . .
They were nomads, always traveling. Many came through Waterloo, often
making camp outside of the village. . . . Some were good musicians, handing
down to later generations the folk songs and proverbs which preserved their
tribal customs, the laws by which they were self-governed. Local store-
keepers and housewives maintained cautious watch of their properties while
the gypsies were in town.
— Sign on exhibit in Waterloo Historical Society

The history of Seneca County provides discourses in addition to the
economic ones that helped organize the interpretations of the summer's
events. Local histories, folk descriptions, and tourist guides have often
depicted Seneca County and the Finger Lakes region in general as an
upstate Garden of Eden, a place of natural beauty, abundant resources, and
peace. The first white European inhabitants of this Garden of Eden were
the patriotic soldiers of the American Revolution, who had been mobilized
with a promise of land as compensation for their services in lieu of pay
(Zinn 1980:85). One and a half million acres of this promised land were
located in the rich, enticing Finger Lakes district, which was cleared of its
Native American, British, and loyalist inhabitants in the Sullivan-Clinton
Campaigns of the late 1770s and early 1780s. In 1980 this action came
back to haunt Seneca County when the Cayuga Indians filed a lawsuit
laying claim to sixty-four thousand acres in Seneca and Cayuga counties.
When the encampment opened, the county was already considering the
possibility that it would have to relocate seven thousand property owners
and pay $350 million in damages if the Indians won their case.

After it was cleared of inhabitants in the eighteenth century, this land was divided into twenty-eight townships, each contains one hundred lots of six hundred acres, which were given classical and mythological names: Ovid, Romulus, Hector, Virgil, Aurelius, Marcellus, and Ulysses. The plots were randomly distributed by lottery in Albany in 1790. Each soldier received six hundred acres, and officers received more (Patterson 1976:19). Records indicate that few of the soldiers actually settled in the area and most of the plots were sold to land speculators. Nevertheless, the area is still home to a few of the descendants of these original Revolutionary War soldiers.

Throughout the next two centuries, Seneca County experienced cycles of economic prosperity and significance in regional history. The great postrevolutionary westward expansion was facilitated in the Finger Lakes by navigable waterways, and transportation was later enhanced by a series of transportation projects: the turnpike of the early 1800s, the Erie Canal system of 1825–1870, the railroads beginning in the 1830s, and the post–World War II highways (called the Erie Canal of the Atomic Age and designed to ease troop movements in future wars and as a means of escape in the event of an atomic attack). Cities located on transportation routes grew, while those that were bypassed faltered. Since successive modes of transportation followed new routes, Finger Lakes towns went through boom-and-bust cycles.

Ever-improving transportation made possible the movement not only of people and goods but also of ideas. In the early nineteenth century, the Finger Lakes region was called the "Burned-over District" because of the many reform movements and religious revivals that were prevalent there, including women's rights, abolition, millenarianism, Mormonism, spiritualism, utopianism, and temperance. The area was indeed "burned over" as one spiritual or social fire after another swept through the area in waves. They were local manifestations of the social reform associated with religious revivalism that was extremely influential in changing the larger American scene at that time.

The temperance movement began earlier than the religious revivals, was fueled by them, and in a sense has not yet ended (Cross 1950:211). The anti-Masonics had supported temperance early on, but soon the famous evangelical preacher Charles G. Finney in Rochester combined temperance with revivalism. For the first time, according to Whitney R. Cross, "use of intoxicants became a sin instead of a mere departure from decency and expediency, and the existence of intemperance in American society came to be considered the major hindrance to the revival of spirituality which was to introduce the early millennium" (1950:211). Alcohol, the preachers insisted, was keeping people from salvation and preventing the millennium (Christ's thousand-year reign on earth) from coming. Intemperance was a convenient sin for most itinerant preachers to dwell on, but for some it became the most important religious and social issue. By 1855 thirteen states had prohibition laws and in the 1860s work on a constitutional amendment began.

Like the temperance movement, abolitionism was intimately tied to religious revivalism in the Burned-over District. The goal of millenarianism was to create the perfect society by eradicating every source of sin. Accordingly, some revivalists defined slavery as sinful and demanded its elimination. When these ideas reached the Finger Lakes, "The Burned-over District seized leadership in the abolition crusade, and the consequent influence of this region upon the enlarged antislavery agitation of the forties and fifties and upon the Civil War itself, constitutes the most important single contribution of Western New York's enthusiastic mood to the main currents of national history" (Cross 1950:217).

The women's rights movement can, if it chooses, also trace its history back to the Burned-over District and religious revivalism. Temperance, religious revivalism, and abolition all had significant effects on the roles of women in American society. The majority of the converts of the Second Great Awakening were women, and they were involved in all the related social reform movements. These organizations gave women experience in public speaking and public self-presentation at a time when the "cult of true womanhood" was beginning to require middle- and upper-class women to be domestic, maternal, religious, idle, subservient, and restricted to the home sphere (Griffith 1984:15). Revivalism promoted the idea that women as well as men were redeemable individuals, and as Glenn Altschuler and Jan Saltzgaber remark, "Since the dynamics of religious enthusiasm denied feminine passivity, revivalism served as a training ground of women activists" (1983:77).

Elizabeth Cady Stanton and Susan B. Anthony, two major figures in the American women's movement, both lived in the Burned-over District. Both also experienced frustration with the way women were treated within the social reform movements. It was this problem in part that led to the development of the women's movement, which Stanton helped organize and into which she drew Anthony.

In 1840 Stanton and Lucretia Mott met at the London World Anti-Slavery Convention where they were both angered by the convention's refusal to admit them. Stanton and Mott later organized the first women's rights convention in Seneca Falls, New York, in 1848. The convention attracted three hundred participants and passed a series of resolutions about women's rights. One of the resolutions, which Stanton had proposed, demanded the vote for women. It passed despite heavy opposition from participants who considered it too radical. Ironically, suffrage later became the leading issue for the movement, but Stanton's radicalism, partly derived from her religious revivalist activities (she wrote a revised, feminist version of the Bible), eventually led to a split in the women's movement. Stanton's organization, the National Woman Suffrage Association, broadened its goals to issues beyond suffrage. It was opposed by Lucy Stone's American Woman Suffrage Association, which was more conservative and limited itself to suffrage only, believing that all other social reforms would fall into place if the vote was won. These activities by reformist women of the Burned-over District, particularly those residing in or near Seneca Falls, provided the basis for the suffrage movement of the 1920s and the later resurgence of the women's movement in the 1960s and 1970s.

In some ways this rich and mixed military and social reform history of the region could be considered the basis for the events of 1983, for both the depot and the encampment could claim their legitimacy through local history. In the late 1930s, as the threat of war became more apparent in the United States, the federal government began planning the Seneca Ordnance Depot, as it was then called, which would be used for munitions storage and preparation. Seneca County was chosen for several reasons: it was inland and thus safer from enemy attacks; it already had a railroad, which was essential for transportation; and its historically patriotic residents were considered "All-American," presumably making the project safe from sabotage (Watrous 1982:8).

Early in 1941 the government announced that construction would begin in July. The site would be an 11,500-acre tract of land on the eastern shore of Seneca Lake, which was then occupied by 150 farm families. These people got thirty days' notice to vacate their homes. Newspapers celebrated the chance for county residents to do their patriotic duty but also lamented the loss of land that in many cases had been owned by the same families for many generations.

The immediate effects of the project on local communities were devastating. By the time construction was going full-force, approximately fifty-seven hundred new workers, some with their families, had relocated to Seneca County from New York City and from eleven states. This sudden population increase stretched the resources of the county. Housing could not be found for many workers, who ended up living in tents and trailers.

The population of nearby Geneva increased by three thousand in the first year of construction. The roads became clogged with workers, and access to the area had to be controlled. The higher wages of the federal government compared to those paid locally led to price inflation and lavish spending by workers seeking food, housing, supplies, and recreation. Black workers couldn't get housing at all and were resented for taking jobs away from white residents. A scarcity of clean water threatened health, and epidemics were feared. One newspaper editorial of the day contemplated the situation:

> In other periods, this locality has escaped the full extent of such trends and life has never gone to extremes. We never had the booms in the twenties that the cities had, and we never had the bread lines of the depression that these cities also had. This project will certainly bring Seneca County and its villages an unprecedented boom. If this war-time project is going to be an economical windfall to our community, let us make the most of it to build a better community for the peace-time era that we know will follow. If it is going to mean sacrifice for the defense of our nation, let us make that sacrifice without losing the character and qualities that have made this a good town for over a hundred years (*Waterloo Observer*, July 18, 1941).

The depot cost $11 million and by the end of 1941, seven thousand people were employed on the project, both local and imported labor. After the December 7 attack on Pearl Harbor, the construction schedule accelerated, and military control of the entire southern part of the county increased. Even as construction continued, work within the munitions storage facility began. Three thousand people, many of them women taking over traditionally male jobs, found employment at the depot. In the meantime, other local industries could not fill all their vacancies, even with the influx of female workers.

After the war, the depot was expanded to store and process the munitions left from the war and produced in the subsequent cold war. In the 1950s, the weapons storage area was extensively renovated, reportedly to store nuclear weapons. A 1981 report by the Center for Defense Information, an independent research organization under the direction of retired military officers which monitors military spending, disclosed that the depot was a storage site for nuclear weapons, probably including the neutron bomb. To inquiries about the rumors about the storage of nuclear weapons at SEAD, Defense Department representatives reply that it is the policy of the Department of Defense neither to confirm nor to deny the presence of nuclear weapons or components at military installations.

The Seneca Women's Encampment for a Future of Peace and Justice opened in 1983 within a year of the initial discussions about developing a women's peace camp in the United States similar to the ones that had begun operating in Europe. The best known of these European camps was the one at Greenham Common, a Royal Air Force base that under North Atlantic Treaty Organization agreements is used by the United States Air Force. NATO's 1979 decision to locate ground-based nuclear weapons in Europe spurred the growth of the European peace movement and the development of the Greenham camp in 1981 (Cook and Kirk 1983:5). When it was proposed that ninety-six of the European-based Cruise missiles be placed at the Greenham base, protesters gathered to oppose their deployment. A group of men and women staged a 125-mile walk to the Greenham Common base in August and September 1981. Afterward some of the women in the group who wanted to continue publicizing the nuclear issue set up the peace camp. These women also organized a large demonstration in December 1981, when thirty thousand people "embraced the base" by holding hands and completely encircling it. The Greenham Common camps are located on military land and are subject to constant harassment and violence from both the military police and local people who do not want the protesters there.

The Greenham Common camp and others like it in Italy and the Netherlands were well known to the women who met in New York in June 1982 for the largest U.S. antinuclear demonstration to date (with half a million people participating) and for the Conference on Global Feminism and Disarmament that preceded it. The organizing process for the development of a women's peace encampment involved women active in various peace and feminist groups including the Women's International League for Peace and Freedom, Women's Pentagon Action, and the Upstate (NY) Feminist Peace Alliance.

Several women at the meeting suggested the Seneca Army Depot as an appropriate site for the first U.S. peace encampment. These women, members of the Upstate Feminist Peace Alliance, living in Rochester, Syracuse, and Ithaca, had been involved in an unusual protest at the SEAD that year which had gained some attention within the movement and got the participating women invited to the New York City conference. They had staged a "Miss Missile" contest at the base, a takeoff on the Miss America contest. The women dressed as various nuclear weapons and tried to convince the "judges" they should be "Miss Missile" by reciting the "vital statistics" about their ability to cause destruction and death. Other groups, especially the Finger Lakes Peace Alliance (FLPA) and a group of Catholics from Rochester, had been protesting regularly at the depot in the early 1980s, but the depot was certainly not a nationally known staging area for antinuclear protests (the Griffiss Air Force Base in neighboring Rome was better known). As one organizer explained, when women from upstate New York proposed the SEAD site at the New York conference, "nobody had heard of it."

The organizers, however, thought they saw several advantages, both practical and symbolic, in the Seneca County location. The depot was located in a rural area where some organizers felt there might be more local support for peace groups. The Finger Lakes region also contains land that is claimed by Native American groups. Some of the women saw the American Indians as being in opposition to the same militaristic and patriarchal forces of the U.S. government that the women themselves were protesting. Some of the women hoped that locating the encampment near this Native American land claim would emphasize the connections among all oppressed groups.

The depot was also "consciously chosen" because it fit the idea of conversion (which the women wanted to promote), the theory that facilities presently being used for military production should be not closed down but converted into factories that would produce peaceful, nonmilitary products. The SEAD, some of the women would emphasize, could easily be converted to such peaceful production. The SEAD also gave the women a simple, concrete issue to focus on—the planned shipment that fall (1983) of nuclear missiles from their suspected storage place in Seneca County to U.S. military bases in Europe.

Perhaps most significant, however, was the location of the depot and the proposed encampment in an area that had a well-known and lengthy history of women's rights and women's peace activities. This historical connection was important to the organizers when they were initially looking for land in Seneca County and was later used extensively in the encampment's promotional material. For example, the cover of the encampment's *Resource Handbook* (see figure 1), establishes a tradition of women's resistance in upstate New York.

The tradition of women's activism in the area was said to have begun with a gathering in the late 1500s of women from the Iroquois Confederacy who demanded an end to the war among the Indian nations. It continued with the events of the mid-1800s, when Seneca County and other upstate New York communities were involved in the Underground

Figure 1. Cover of the *Resource Handbook*

Railroad, which moved slaves from the South to freedom in the North. Harriet Tubman, a "conductor" in this network of abolitionists, resided near the present site of SEAD and was later honored by an encampment march that visited her home and gravesite. The best-known contributions to women's rights history in Seneca County occurred about fourteen miles from the encampment, in the town of Seneca Falls, site of the first gathering of American women demanding equal rights. Feminists consider Seneca Falls the birthplace of women's rights and the contemporary women's movement. It is now the location of a national park devoted to the history of women's rights, and the 1848 convention is commemorated by the Convention Days celebrations held every year in Seneca Falls. A Women's Hall of Fame, which commemorates famous women who have contributed to women's rights struggles, is also located in Seneca Falls.

This continuity in time and space with other women's peace and civil rights activities provided a compelling argument for locating the encampment in Seneca County. In fact the encampment often became confused with Seneca Falls, and some called it the Seneca Falls Peace Camp. Although most of the participants were undoubtedly not familiar with all these details of women's history, the general aura of women's historic activism in this area provided the 1983 encampment with the sense of validation derived from invoking tradition. As Eric Hobsbawm explains, the "attempt to establish continuity with a suitable historic past" provides a group with the "sanction of precedent, social continuity and natural law" which makes the group and its activities appear all the more inevitable, legitimate, and compelling (1983:1–2).

Feminists have been revaluing and re-membering such aspects of history, creating in turn "herstories," or stories not controlled by the patriarchy, to challenge standard histories that have systematically excluded the lives and deeds of women. These patriarchal histories are seen as denying women a past and defining and confining knowledge in such a way as to make women's present-day situation seem natural and inevitable. This use and creation of history by the Seneca encampment subtly subverted the predominant discourse that says women lack a history of activism, cooperation, and political power.

This power of tradition and re-membering of history enabled the encampment participants to employ historical precedents in their efforts to make the antinuclear/antipatriarchal protests appeal to a wide range of women. Since the organizers were hoping to draw feminist and peace activists as well as women who had never been involved in either movement, they needed a focus of protest to which many women could connect their interests. They also needed some element, a "glue," that would unite these diverse women and enable them to work together.

The depot itself provided an adequate target for the varied antipatriarchal, antimilitaristic, and antiviolence themes of the encampment's protests. For feminists it was a suitable representative of the patriarchal establishment whose threats could easily be defined and illustrated through its role in the promotion and storage of nuclear weapons. But it was less satisfactory in connecting peace activism to feminism. It was far from apparent to some participants and to many nonparticipants why it was necessary or desirable to restrict the encampment to women or why nuclear activists should be concerned with feminism or how simply invoking the unknown, albeit provocative, entity of the Seneca Army Depot would address problems with the patriarchal society. Finally, it was the theme of women working together for peace and justice, as local tradition showed they have been doing for decades, that was just the attractive binding force needed. The glue designed to connect all the issues and all the women was the notion that nuclear weapons, the violence of patriarchy, and women's oppression all affected women, as women, deeply and personally and negatively. Women who came to the encampment would, according to this approach, be participating in the long tradition of women's activism when they recognized that they needed to work with other women to change social conditions.

5

Circle for Survival

We invite you to the Seneca Army Depot, the U.S. point of departure for nuclear weapons to Europe. Stay for as long as you can, part of a day or several weeks. Bring your dreams, ideas, skills, resources and creativity to make the Encampment a powerful witness and a strong community. The Encampment will be our own creation. Join us.

—*Resource Handbook*

One of the crucial tasks as the planners set out to organize women for a summer of protest was somehow to make other women see value in spending time at the encampment. The problem was not just a matter of publicity and advertising, of getting the word out. Well before the encampment opened, news of its development had spread throughout the extensive nationwide network of feminist and peace groups. Instead, the problem was how to define and present the encampment so as to appeal to the diverse interests and concerns of these potential participants. Those already involved in antinuclear protests and peace activities had used a wide range of strategies (from prayer vigils, singing, and marching to civil disobedience and violent, destructive actions) toward a wide range of goals (from simply eliminating nuclear weapons to overthrowing the patriarchy) that were not always compatible. Moreover, many men were involved in these groups, and the decision to limit the encampment to women could be expected to create some antagonism. And despite talk of a "women's movement" as if it were a unified entity, there was no one group and no one set of principles and positions universally accepted by women who identified themselves as feminists or political activists.

The decision to limit the encampment to women came early in the planning, but it was not made easily. The debate on this issue illustrates some of the fundamental differences among the various types of women involved in the organization of the encampment. In one early meeting organizers discussed the role of men in the encampment, the definition of feminism, and the reasons for making the encampment a women-only action. They could not come to any consensus. Some argued that defining the camp as feminist might be more exclusionary than just calling it a women's camp. They were concerned that a lot of attention was being focused on the exclusion of males rather than on the development of something positive for women. Some women clearly did not want to exclude men completely and worked to have a separate public space on the encampment land where supportive men could gather to talk and provide help. One supporter, in a long letter, expressed her dismay, shared by many others, that male children over the age of twelve were to be excluded. "Dear Friends," she wrote,

> It is a crystal morning in the mountains. Every green plant in the sun gleams iridescent and those in the shade sway gently, shaking off the lush dew. I fathom the message of the morning, gather a primrose, happy with its perfume, rub the wounded stem and pick some clover I will admire in the window before I dry it for tea. And I cry, for the earth I love so, angered that human beings have dealt with and are dealing so badly with her—and each other.
>
> I have been an active, enthusiastic and creative participant in the group of Greater Burlington women organizing to support the Women's Encampment for a Future of Peace and Justice.
>
> It was my idea to emblazon our leaflets with the words: "SEND MOTHER TO CAMP." I never expected the corollary to be: "But don't let her children visit her there—if they are boys."

The woman went on to explain that her two teenage sons, ages fifteen and nineteen, had been active in antinuclear protests since they were young, and the fifteen-year-old had been looking forward to coming to the encampment.

> Jeremy cares very much about peace. Like many kids his age he wonders often out loud—if he has two minutes left—as part of life on earth. He's a teenager now, but his male hormones haven't persuaded him to bare his teeth and take guns. I'd like you to meet him. . . . He was so excited about Seneca. He thinks peace activists are his friends. And now he understands, there is nothing on earth he can do in some women's minds to be considered a friend. And that is sexism, not women's liberation.

I never had a harder thing to say in my life than to tell him he wouldn't be allowed to visit me at the Women's Encampment. I told Jeremy a lot of women are afraid, that boys over twelve rape.

Jeremy offered to get a hundred letters saying he is absolutely opposed to violence of any kind. Would that do it?

. . . I raised my sons to be brothers in the work for peace and they are.

Unless males are raised this way, there will be no peace. Peace cannot be the issue for only part of the species, and the millions of young men around the world who resist the draft testify to this. The more than 60,000 ex-GIs who committed suicide after returning from Vietnam testify to a raping of their lives as well.

I close this letter, but not my mind, in the hopes that you haven't closed yours to the idea that sons and brothers can visit the WOMEN'S ENCAMPMENT FOR A FUTURE OF PEACE AND JUSTICE. (June 29, 1983)

The encampment eventually agreed to define itself publicly as a women-only activity and space. Men were not involved in the organization of the encampment or in the purchase or physical preparation of the land. When the encampment opened, men were allowed only on the front grounds; they were encouraged to support but not actually to participate in the protests. As the encampment proceeded through its first summer, this became even more of an issue for some of the women who were not involved in the initial discussions. As one woman explained in a letter she wrote after she returned home,

The march yesterday was invigorating, emotionally, spiritually and physically. Your courage and commitment is an inspiration, enough so that my husband and I attended the march. While I am committed to the same ends that you all are, I must speak to the issue of separatism that seems to have influenced so much of what you are doing

It is undoubtedly true that men have manipulated events that have led humanity to this point of confrontation and confusion and have per- petuated a reprehensible crime on the planet in spreading the horror of nuclear arms, but there is a new generation of men, and Sam [her husband] is one of them, who do not want to be "like their fathers," who are trying desperately to break free from the enslavement that the traditional male image implies. If we in our struggle for equality and freedom relegate our brothers to the position of "nigger," then what have we gained? Yet another oppressed class. By alienating those who wish to help and who have as much a vested interest in the outcome of the issues as we have, we will make the opposition stronger and will insure our own defeat.

Man and son in encampment front yard

Please give thought to this question of segregation. Let's not put more people "on the back of the bus," but let's work together to guarantee our sons and daughters a future worth living and neighbors worth loving. (August 2, 1983)

The encampment was meant to be conceived as a safe place where women could work together without the physical, emotional, or mental stress that some considered inevitable in the company of males. Nevertheless, this foregrounding of gender as a major issue in the critique of the militaristic-patriarchal-nuclear establishment caused difficulty for many women who became involved in the encampment, particularly those who had close ties to men through marriage or motherhood, or whose political beliefs did not tolerate exclusion or separatism.

Many Encampment organizers and participants, however, believed that there are indeed substantial differences between male and female spheres of activity and interest and that women must provide solutions to the problems created by the male-dominated society. In the *Resource Handbook*, published as an orientation guide, several women explained their reasoning in a section titled, "Why a Women's Peace Camp?" (36).

An action of this length without men . . . allows for creativity and community unique within the American peace networks with the possibility of a totally new direction emerging from the acknowledgement of women's experience.

—Terry Faatz

It is a vast statement that no longer will women sit back and allow men to make the decisions alone which affect the entire globe.

—Rebecca Linsner

Throughout history, in all the world's warring, feminist process has never been used for conflict resolution.

—Helene Aylon

In this view, history and previous personal experience had shown that women needed to work apart from men to be most effective. The idea that men and women occupy different spheres has been debated in the women's movement for over a century (Bernard 1981). In recent years it has reemerged in feminist thought under the rubric of a "woman-centered" approach. Feminisms in the late 1960s and early 1970s were generally based on the recognition of gender differences, but these differences were seen as the source of women's oppression, and they were ascribed not to some psychological, biological, or social inevitability but rather to the patriarchal social and political system that relied, says Hester Eisenstein, on "the exaggeration and the maintenance of women's otherness from men" (1983:45).

The path to the successful resolution of this problem was seen as twofold: to deny the significance of these differences and to eliminate the notion that women were significantly different from men by providing women with equal opportunities and rights. This solution was thought possible through an approach that supported androgyny, "in which," Gayle Rubin writes, "one's sexual anatomy is irrelevant to who one is, what one does, and with whom one makes love" (1984:169). The new rights and opportunities this approach promised were supposed to enable women to show that sexual differences were insignificant for determining what a person could become.

By the mid-1970s, many feminists were questioning this approach, in part because of new research in psychology, anthropology, history, and literature and also in part as a result of the direct challenges of feminist activists and lesbian feminists to heterosexism and patriarchy. In history, literature, and the arts, interest arose not only in evaluating the patriarchal representation of women in texts and visual works but also in revising the canons in these fields so that they included the contributions of women. These corrective measures relied on uncovering information about women's contributions and also necessitated a revaluation of the standards by which such contributions are judged. Literary critics debated whether there was such a thing as "women's writing" or a "women's style," challenging, if not reconstituting, the criteria by which literature was analyzed and judged (see Eagleton 1983; Moi 1985).

The interest in the previously excluded realm of women's lives fit well with the new focus in history, which began to turn from the study of great events and famous men to the study of the everyday lives of common people (Gies and Gies 1978; Ferguson et al. 1986; Ginzburg 1982). In the art world, art by women became better known and feminist contributions began to challenge artistic canons and art history (see Broude and Garrard 1982; Hess and Baker 1973; in film: Kuhn 1982, 1985; de Lauretis 1984).

In anthropology a similar trend manifested itself in cross-cultural research that focused on women. Women's activities in the "private," domestic sphere were shown to be as complex, meaningful, and significant as the male activities in the "public" sphere. Ideas about women's universal symbolic connection to nature and men's to culture were considered and discarded, but not before they influenced a large body of work that helped reveal the worlds of women (see Rosaldo and Lamphere 1974; Reiter 1975).

In psychology rereadings of Freud and other reconsiderations of psychic and sexual life (see Garner et al. 1985; Mitchell and Rose 1982) and female development (Chodorow 1978) led to a reevaluation of the specifics of women's lives and how they differed from men's. Psychologist Carol Gilligan investigated the features of this proposed female sphere of difference and has defined what she feels is a unique female moral sensibility that has developed in our culture. According to Gilligan's analysis of women's development and values, women have a strong sense of obligation to others which develops out of their social role as caretaker of the family. This enables them to understand the needs of others and consider their point of view; their caring and concern for other people makes them aware of the great emotional cost of success achieved through competition (1982:15–16). Unfortunately, they develop these qualities in a society that places value on just the opposite behavior patterns. As a result women are caught in a contradiction between what they have come to believe and value, and what they are told is worthwhile. It is just this contradiction that a woman-centered approach hopes to diffuse.

Like Gilligan, many feminists were emphasizing the differences between men and women rather than dismissing them in the late 1970s and 1980s; they were interested not in minimizing these differences but in understanding and defining them. Eisenstein explains, "Instead of being considered the source of women's oppression, these differences were now judged to contain the seeds of women's liberation." Rather than "a form of inadequacy and a source of inferiority, this view considered these differences to be a source of pride" (1983:xi, 46). Women's activities are to be valued as highly and studied as seriously as men's. Moreover, women's particular strengths, values, and ideas are seen as a superior basis for the organization and execution of social activities. A woman-centered approach requires that society change to accommodate the women's sphere rather than that women accommodate themselves to the world as constructed by men.

The peace encampment organizers actively employed this woman-centered approach with its unique male and female spheres and its privileging of women's contributions to social, cultural, and political life. The same values that Gilligan identified as "female" were considered the basis of the alternative world toward which the encampment was striving. As a result, in the "official" position of the encampment, feminism was to be defined as being woman centered:

> Feminism is a value system which affirms qualities that have traditionally been considered female: nurturance of life, putting others' well-being before one's own, cooperation, emotional and intuitive sensitivity, attention to detail, the ability to adapt, perseverance. These traits have been discounted by societies which teach competition, violent conflict resolution, and materialism. Feminism insists that the qualities traditionally considered female be recognized as deserving respect and manifesting great power. These qualities need to be emphasized more so as to create a balance with the traditionally male attributes of assertiveness and effectiveness in the world. (*Resource Handbook* 1983:32)

The encampment was developed, then, as a place where these female qualities could be expressed and put into practice. Yet this seemingly straightforward attempt to define feminism as woman centered was the source of much internal dissension in the 1983 encampment.

Throughout the late winter and the spring, these issues were debated at large monthly organizational meetings in upstate New York cities and in New York City and at smaller satellite meetings throughout the North-

Encampment woman in front of painted barn

east. The meetings focused both on the logistics of setting up the camp—buying or leasing land, raising funds, advertising, physically preparing the camping space—and on more philosophical issues related to the purpose of the camp, the development of a vision statement, and the refinement of a political agenda.

The farmland on which the encampment eventually came to rest was located in the winter of 1982–1983. Some saw the circumstances surrounding the purchase as a good omen. The land was a worn-out farm that had been on the market for quite a while priced at about $45,000. A woman from Rochester told the encampment organizers about the parcel, and some of them visited the owners, two women who had inherited the land from an aunt. The owners had already refused to sell the land at a reduced price to other potential purchasers, but the organizers were able to convince them that the "educational" camp they wanted to open would be worthwhile. The land was purchased for $37,500 on May 23, 1983, with money raised from donations and personal loans provided by concerned activists. Women began preparing the land in the spring in anticipation of a July 4 opening.

Like every group trying to mobilize masses of people, the encampment needed more than just a shared space and a formal organization; it needed a way of referring to itself as an entity. In order for members to perceive themselves as a group, they needed to share an identity that was supported by symbolic constructs and interpretive discourses. The encampment needed to create itself as an "interpretive community" whose shared strategies would organize the group's approach to meaning and action and define what was reasonable to say and do in that community.

The early encampment organizers did not necessarily see themselves as a nicely unified, coherent group that could easily explain itself to others. On the contrary, the monthly organizational meetings were making clear the divergent thinking, conflicting value systems, and varying hopes and expectations of those involved. Yet the women recognized the need to decide on an image or representation of themselves in order to communicate with others. This representation would influence not only the decisions about the running of the encampment and the development of protest actions but also all the verbal and visual information the encampment created, including T-shirts, posters, books, songs, and press releases.

It is the job of every organization to create a representation of itself that through repetitive use comes to seem a mirror of that group's actual constitution. This representation becomes the group's identity only if it gives some assurance of reflecting the real world; the representation created about and by the encampment was assumed to reflect the inner workings of that group. It was also designed to persuade other women to identify with this representation enough to attend the encampment and become actively involved in its promotion.

Representations, whether they are created by totalitarian agencies or feminists devoted to equality, are not disinterested images but powerful political tools that in a sense become more real than reality itself (Kappeler 1986:3). Representations are the currency we use in social exchanges; they stand in for more complex, contradictory, and inaccessible things. If a representation is to appear coherent, if some type of communication is to be successful, and if the discourse is to be controlled, representational forms must be simplified and edited. Thus any representation of a group necessarily involves the repression of difference within it (Jacobus 1986: 117; Meese 1986:84).

This issue is quite problematic for a feminist group. On the one hand, feminism is guided by the principle that every woman should speak only for herself, that patriarchy has repressed important differences based on race, sexuality, ethnicity, politics, and religion, which women must now be allowed to voice. But difference is the greatest threat to representation because it brings up the possibility that the representation does not accurately reflect a stable reality. When a woman rejects the possibility of representation, when she says that it is impossible to state definitively who she is and how she should be interpreted, she certainly rejects authority (which is a positive outcome for feminism), but she also loses the possibility of taking a political stance. This failure to create a specific political agenda could not be permitted at the encampment, and any hesitations about the construction of a representation had to be put aside to allow for political action.

What is interesting, then, about the encampment's representation of itself is not whether it accurately reflected the makeup of this women's group but how it was employed for political purposes both within the encampment and with outsiders. In describing the content of the self-representation this group created, therefore, I am more interested in understanding the representational process itself. The analysis and interpretation of the meanings of this specific representation are of interest only insofar as they enable us to consider the process and politics involved in the construction and use of that representation throughout the first summer of the encampment.

The encampment constructed a representation of itself through three means. The first means was the development of a name. During the early organizational meetings, the organizers referred to the encampment as the Women's Peace Camp or Women's Peace Encampment. They settled on a formal name at an April 1983 meeting in Albany. The Third World Women's Caucus, a group of women concerned about women of color in "underdeveloped" nations, suggested that the word "justice" appear in the name in order to show that the encampment was concerned not only with peace but also with the social transformations necessary to create a peaceful world. The women debated whether to say "peace with justice," "justice with peace," or "peace and justice." One woman suggested Women's Peace Camp for a Just World without Weapons, but the participants finally decided on Women's Encampment for a Future of Peace and Justice.

The second means of developing a self-representation was through the drafting of a vision statement that would express the encampment's goals and philosophy. The vision statement, which was to appear in all encampment literature and publicity, needed to be concise and straightforward. At several meetings the women discussed their hopes for the encampment. Many drafts were prepared, discussed, and edited before the following statement was formulated:

> Women have played an important role throughout our history in opposing violence and oppression. We have been the operators of the Underground Railroad, the spirit of the equal rights movement and the strength of the peace movement. In 1590, the women of the Iroquois nation met in Seneca to demand an end to war among the tribes. In 1848 the first Women's Rights Convention met in Seneca Falls giving shape and voice to the 19th century feminist movement.
>
> Once again women are gathering at Seneca—this time to challenge the nuclear threat at its doorstep. The Seneca Army depot, a native American homeland once nurtured and protected by the Iroquois, is now the storage site of the neutron bomb, and most likely the Pershing II missile and is the departure point for weapons to be deployed in Europe. Women from New York State, from the United States and Canada, from Europe, and, indeed, from all over the world, are committed to non-violent action to stop the deployment of these weapons.
>
> The existence of nuclear weapons is killing us. Their production contaminates our environment, destroys our natural resources, and depletes our human energy and creativity. But the most critical danger they represent is to life itself. Sickness, accidents, genetic damage and death, these are the real products of the nuclear arms race. We say no to the threat of global holocaust, no to the arms race, no to death. We say yes to a world where people, animals, plants and the earth itself are respected and valued.

The third means by which the encampment created a self-representation and presented it publicly was through the use of symbols. Symbols provide the means by which an organization can be "seen" (Kertzer 1988:15). The anthropologist Victor Turner has shown in his work with symbolic systems that for any social group we can identify the dominant or focal symbols that "make visible, audible, and tangible beliefs, ideas, values, sentiments, and psychological dispositions that cannot directly be perceived" (Turner 1967:50). These focal symbols are multivocal, that is, they stand in for many different things and are thus "economic representations of key aspects of culture and belief" (ibid.). Although we should be aware of the dangers in assuming that symbols possess more uniformity in use and meaning than is possible with social beings, they are nevertheless a useful means through which to study how a group attempts to conceptualize and present itself.

Symbols have a great deal of work to do in a social group: they must maintain order, provide a social identity, and categorize people and ideas (Bolton 1988:7). In order to fulfill these needs, the peace camp organizers successfully employed two symbolic constructs, the circle and the web. These two focal symbols provided a consistent framework for the alternative, woman-centered world being developed and later acted out at the encampment. The peace encampment did not completely abandon the meanings of these symbols as they have been constituted by the dominant discourse. Instead, the women expanded and revalued these meanings as they applied the symbols to this alternative setting.

The circle was the first symbol borrowed from the dominant discourse for revision and use at the encampment. The encampment accepted the dominant discourse's technical definition of the circle and also employed the archetypal definition of the circle as the natural way, according to followers of C. G. Jung, for westerners to represent the self or psyche, a central place, wholeness, and the universe (Jung 1964). In Western discourse and social life, says Jung, this symbolization is played out most publicly in art, architecture, and the designs of cities—all of which employ circular patterns dependent on these meanings. The circle is also commonly used to represent cyclical, endless movement as in the movement of the sun and planets; it can also be seen as a circuit that eventually brings things back to their point of origin.

The women of the encampment greatly expanded the implications of these meanings of the circle in their efforts to define a woman-focused world. The circle was used to represent the female essence on the most basic, "natural," elementary level: it was the womb, the inner-oriented core of the female world. Many encampment organizers believed that all women possess this inner orientation, not just as a result of women's biological makeup but as a spiritual connectedness that all women share even if they are not yet aware of it.

Many of the encampment women had read the work of feminist philosopher Mary Daly, who has stated that sometimes when women first meet they feel that they have a psychic, spiritual connection (Daly 1978: 371). This uncanny experience confirms for the believer the notion that all women are connected simply by virtue of being female. Inner orientation

Circle at beginning of March from Seneca Falls through Waterloo.
Photo by Pam Quiggle

is seen as the source of womanpower, "the power-from-within . . . a power based on a very different principle from power-over, from domination" (Starhawk 1982:3). This shared inner orientation that defines the essence and power of femaleness is thought to bind all women together.

This approach is often critiqued as essentialist, that is, as promoting the idea that *all* women share a particular essence, or basic characteristics. Some feminists see this essentialism as dangerous because it duplicates the oppressive strategies of the patriarchy, which lumps all women together by claiming that all share a flawed nature. Nevertheless, some of the planners used the essentialist argument when they tried to explain why so many different kinds of women were moved to participate in the encampment. One woman explained:

A lot of women are more concerned with the world and the world's going to blow up and I think it struck a deep inner core. I can remember being in Ithaca and being out to dinner . . . hearing this couple [at the next table] in their late forties or early fifties talking and arguing about the peace camp. And the woman was defending the peace camp and understanding the issue of why we had to be so rowdy to attract the press or why it was an all women's camp, the man just having no concept. And obviously the woman had never been there and never really had any direct contact but just from the media presentation she on a gut level understood. And I think it was that kind of inner place that the peace camp touched in women who had never thought about the issues or never thought about going to an all-women's space.

This statement certainly reflects this essentialist notion of shared womanhood, but essentialism was also used in another, more intricate way at the encampment. As Teresa de Lauretis (1990:5–6) has explained, many feminists use this idea of a female essence not to describe reality but as a utopian, idealist project that "re-visions" the world. *Woman* is defined not as a set of immutable characteristics but as a locus where different effects come together. The female body, together with particular dispositions developed through living as a female in a patriarchal culture at a specific historical point, forms women who are both similar and different. Perhaps the essentialism of the encampment should not be condemned as simpleminded and restrictive but should be celebrated for employing this utopian definition of female potential. The truly challenging as well as frustrating nature of the encampment was that it claimed it was possible to alternate freely between these aspects of essentialism.

The encampment came to be seen in the larger feminist-activist communities as one of the centers of women's activities and energies, as a protecting womb that, as one organizer stated, "everything comes from and grows out of." The life-protecting aspect of the womb/circle parallels the peace-keeping activities that all women are said to find a "natural" part of their lives. As the encampment *Resource Handbook* explained: "For the last 10,000 or so years, women have generally served society as peacemakers. Women have cleaned up after manmade wars. They have tended the wounded, comforted and cared for the widowed. They have been the peacemakers within the family, and within the community. Women have raised and trained the young, formed and staffed the charities, healed the sick, assisted at births and tended the dying. Women have enriched and enhanced the living-out of human lives, in all ages and in all regions of the world" (30).

That the circle-as-womb was a particularly powerful representation of this inner orientation and all-female connectedness can be seen in an event that took place to advertise and celebrate the peace camp. At the 1983 Michigan Women's Music Festival, an annual summer gathering that celebrates women's (particularly lesbian) "culture," a symbolic space was created to represent the women's encampment, which was taking place concurrently. The place created at the music festival consisted of pillowcases decorated with women's dreams of peace, hung on lines to create a secluded enclosure, a protective, womblike structure made of dreams. This same ritual space representing the encampment was later transported to New York City and set up on a sidewalk. According to one of the organizers, "The women all slept inside of this little womb that they made for themselves out of these pillowcases and that was their only protection from the outside world."

This space was used in Michigan for "centering", a process that is supposed to establish a sense of location, to place a person spiritually, physically, and emotionally. Centering is an important concept for the woman-focused world, both for the individual and the group. As one organizer explained: "It is important no matter what kind of organizing we do to immediately establish what the center is, because the center gives protection. It is where the gathering happens for support, for healing, for nourishment . . . and on land that we go on we try to find the center of that land . . . [so as to] draw energy from that physical space."

The encampment contrasted its use of such concepts as the circle, centering, the womb, and circular movement to the use of the line, phallus, and linear movement by the dominant, patriarchal discourse the women were opposing. The line is used in this discourse to represent the path of a moving point, of progress or movement away from the point of origin. In common everyday usage, time is generally seen as linear, not cyclical, and the ideas of power and progress derive from linear, hierarchical organizations, not circular ones. The circle indicates uncertainty, indefiniteness, a lack of direction. For example, people who fail to progress toward their goals are said to be "going around in circles" instead of "making a straight line" for something; "walking the straight line" indicates a sense of purpose, direction, and sobriety. A cogent argument has a "line of thought" backing it, whereas an incoherent one is based on "circular reasoning." A circle of friends is a casual, egalitarian group, but a line, ladder, or chain of command differentiates people by power, wealth, or status.

The encampment considered the line a phallic symbol and associated it with the power exercised and controlled by males. The circle was seen as a more generalized female symbol associated with cycles (of menstruation and the moon); with the vagina, womb, and breasts; and with softness and roundness. (We can note in continuing the analogy that a circle is never hard, but a "hard line" can be taken in an argument; also that hard women are masculine and soft men effeminate.) Linearity and masculinity, along with the concomitant feature of differential access to power and authority, were used as a foil by the encampment as the focal symbols expressing the essence of patriarchal discourse.

Police line with counterdemonstrators. Photo by Pam Quiggle

Surely not all the women who came to the peace encampment believed in the ideas behind these symbols or were even familiar enough with them to decide whether they agreed with their use. But because many of the organizers claimed all women naturally shared an affinity with this symbolic orientation to the circular, they developed an entire community around these ideas, and any woman coming to the encampment could not help but be exposed to this view. The model based on the circle was played out for general consumption in several ways at the encampment. For example, it was used as the organizational principle for the meetings held as a regular part of encampment activities. Ideally, participants sat in a circle, all of them face-to-face, speaking to one another as members of the same community. The meeting circle had no leader, only a facilitator who moved the meeting along but did not dominate the discussion.

The entire alternative model represented by the circle was also exemplified by the attempt to base decisions on consensus rather than majority rule. As it was phrased in the *Resource Handbook*, "The fundamental right of consensus is for all people to be able to express themselves in their own words and of their own will. The fundamental responsibility of consensus is to assure others of their right to speak and be heard. Coercion and tradeoffs are replaced with creative alternatives and compromise with synthesis" (42). Consensus, then, was seen as an active step toward a new approach to dealing with other people, one that rejected aggressiveness and coercion and advanced cooperation and mutual support. During the exchange in which consensus is sought, discussion proceeds around the circle as the participants attempt to come to mutual understanding and agreement. Although in reality decisions were often made on the basis of who could survive the longest in meetings that stretched on for hours or days, the ideal of consensus guided policy making.

One direct expression of the belief in the protecting powers of the circle is found in a song called "Circle for Survival," which was sung at many protest actions throughout the summer. Based on a song by Linda Hirschorn, this version was circulated by the encampment women on mimeographed sheets.

> *Chorus*
> Circle for survival, circle for the right
> not to disappear into the everlasting nite
> Circle for survival, circle for the right
> not to disappear into the everlasting nite
>
> Circle all the bases, circle day and nite
> enclose them in a wall of sacred strength and sight
> let the people see them for what they really are
> let the people know they threaten our home star
>
> *Chorus*
>
> Circle all the strip mines, circle day and nite
> Circle all the people, lend them all our might
> Circle all the rapists, the men and their machines
> Circle all the ones who take away our dreams
>
> *Chorus*
>
> Circle all the pueblos, keep them safe from harm
> Circle native people with hearts and minds and arms
> They're fighting for their homelands, what little they have left
> It's up to us to help them rectify the theft
>
> *Chorus*

The circle is our weapon, the circle is our tool
The circle is our heartspace, the circle is our school
the circle is our kiva, the circle is our truth
the circle is our power against the ones who rule

Chorus

While singing this song, women would form a circle, their arms around one another. The circles they formed during ritual protests at the army depot often provided a striking visual contrast to the lines of military personnel also present. Ritual circles held at the encampment itself were used to create a sense of community and tranquillity, especially after long and difficult meetings. Circling was also used during depot protests as a means of protection in confrontations with violent or bothersome males. A group of women, to diffuse the confrontation and separate the problem male from the other women, would form a circle around the man while attempting to talk to him and move him away from the area. The circle both protected and empowered the women and helped to contain the dangerous male force. During several confrontations with local residents, encampment women sat on the ground in tight circles that showed their unity and also protected them. Circles of women were even used to form a privacy screen for women who needed to urinate during long protests in areas that had no restroom facilities.

The use of the circle as a focal symbol by the encampment made sense for many reasons, most notably because it was easily opposed to what was seen as the patriarchal mode of linearity, hierarchy, and power-over. It should also be noted that the circle is an important aspect of feminist spirituality rites, and many women at the encampment, especially camp organizers, embraced and practiced these religions to varying degrees. The circle, explained Starhawk, a feminist writer who defines herself as a witch and priestess of the Old (Goddess) Religion, helps define a ritual time and space, setting the participants apart from everyday life. Casting a circle "is the formal beginning of the ritual, the complex 'cue' that tells us to switch our awareness into a deeper mode" (Starhawk 1979:58). The circle is also considered significant because it is an "energy pattern that contains whatever power we raise so that power can be focused and concentrated. It protects us from intrusion, forming a barrier to any unwanted forces" (ibid.). The ritual circle, then, like the encampment itself, was a means of participating in an alternative world with an out-of-the-ordinary set of rules.

The web was another focal symbol developed and used at the encampment. Its popularity in feminist circles is at least partly attributable to the Spider Woman stories of Native Americans, which some feminists take as proof of women's power in other times and places (see Mullett 1979). Like the meanings of the circle, the web's particular meanings in the dominant discourse were transferred to the encampment and revalued in the process. The most common referent for the web in the dominant discourse is the spider's web, which acts as a trap to capture insects. The spider is often associated with the female because of its weaving and spinning. The habit of some female spiders of devouring their mates after sex also has developed as an element of our common discussions of spiders. A web can refer to the complex machinations of the mind or imagination, as in a web of lies or a web of intrigue, but the symbol does not seem to have been used this way at the encampment. The term web is also gaining popularity as a way of referring to networks of people or organizations in both the feminist and nonfeminist worlds.

At the women's peace encampment, the symbol of the web elaborated upon the alternative cultural model represented by the circle and was the means by which the influence of the circle's model was extended. Nevertheless, although used to construct and support the same "culture," the two symbols do not duplicate each other. The circle is the local organizational principle, whereas the web is the operationalization of this principle, the extension of the circle into the larger world.

The factors tying the second symbol of the web to symbol of the circle derive from the physical properties of the spider's web. The circle forms the center of the spider's web but does not share its physical properties; it is only the beginning, and the web, not the circle, keeps growing bigger, extending far beyond the center. This process was seen as analogous to the organizing of the encampment, which was carried out initially by a core group of hired staff who eventually gave over the responsibility for the operation to a more diffuse group called a work web. One organizer explained,

> Well, you have a circle in the center of the web. The web came to the Encampment really early. . . . When we were burnt out and needed some kind of help and guidance, a group of women came and set up a work web . . . so that the center, the center being the hired staff, did not have to bear the full brunt of the responsibility. The center was rapidly becoming like the center of a spider's web and losing its core and you have an empty circle. But in a spider's web, the circle does not support the rest of

the web. By the time the encampment opened, we as the circle core could not support the rest of that web, and then the work web started to function and started to feed nourishment into the circle once again.

A further analogy with the spider's web involves the function of the web as a means of getting women involved in the issues represented by the circle. This worked in a positive sense when women became "captured" or "engulfed" by the web of the encampment experience: "That happened a lot at the Encampment. Women were going to the Encampment for a weekend, and they went for a weekend and stayed for a month. Or they went for a day and stayed for a week, or they would continuously come back. . . . There was a woman who was a therapist who went home and told all her patients to come to the camp, that they didn't really need her. Closed her practice, has never practiced since and came to stay at the Encampment all summer. . . . She's still there every now and again."

The web also functions as a less benign trap when dealing with the "enemy," those elements that threaten the web and refuse to participate in its process: "The way women build webs. . . . I'm thinking of an enemy coming into the web and getting stuck, then the spider comes and eats that enemy. . . . you just eat them, get the web around it, eat it up." This concept was visualized in the encampment *Handbook* (1983:18) by an illustration in which President Reagan and his nuclear weapons are captured and controlled by the web of feminist and peace protests (see figure 2). The actual constitution of the web also provides protection from these outside enemy forces because, one organizer said, "every part is connected to another part, and even if one part is taken out the web still exists. . . . it can become fragmented but still maintain its strength." She visualized the entire women's peace movement this way—at times it may appear fragmented but all the connections are still there, ready to be put into action. These ties were described as invisible: "Lines [were] coming into the encampment, getting ready to take off and once it took off, all these invisible links went back out to new people and changed lives," expanding the web in the process.

The web provided another explanation for and unifying image of the large number and diversity of women who came to or supported the encampment. According to one of the planners, women were "organizing in communities thousands of miles away without ever having had any contact with us, just that they heard this encampment was happening." One story told by the organizers stressed this connection to groups of which they were not even aware:

Figure 2. Image of Ronald Reagan in a web

There was this nursing home and these women couldn't go [to the Encampment] so they got together and had a sewing circle and made a peace lamb. [Other] women [from the same community in Minnesota] went on August 1st to the big demonstration and they had this lamb that they were carrying because it was from their community. And they got to the fence [of the army depot] and it came time to climb the fence and everybody got so excited that they threw the lamb over the fence. And when these women in the nursing home heard this, they got so excited they were clapping their hands and squealing and said, "We did it, We did it," that they themselves had sent a representative to the base and it had gotten thrown over the fence and they were ecstatic over the whole thing. This was a symbol of their efforts and their community work and they just loved it. And they never went to the encampment, they just heard and sent their proxy sacrificial lamb.

This story points to some of the same concepts of connectedness with the web that are also emphasized with the circle—that all women have natural ties to one another that will express themselves given the chance. These ties can be demonstrated when women weave ritual webs, con-

Women joined by yarn web during protest. Photo by Pam Quiggle

structed by groups of women, each of whom holds a piece of yarn or string which they weave randomly, interlocking and overlapping the yarns to form a weblike structure. These webs can be quite small or can cover extensive areas, and often they are made as part of a larger ritual. The women do not plan the web out ahead of time but use their "spiritual ties" as a guide. Women perceived these connections as both intellectually understood and emotionally felt.

The web, like the circle, also was used at the encampment to represent an organizational process that takes its strength from what participants believed was women's unique approach to the world. The web again endorses a nonlinear approach. Several of the organizers interviewed expressed this concept. For one, the web represented "a different way of structuring things. It is not like planning how to build a pavilion [a building being constructed on encampment land], put one board here and one down there. It comes out a different way." Another continued: "The spirit leads to the building of it, as opposed to some kind of mental plan. . . . when we're doing a web and we connect, we don't know if we are going this way or that way. But no matter what way you go, it is part of it and that just encompasses all the different realms that women are coming from." Another added: "[That is] the one thing that being involved in the encampment has taught me. I've always heard people say, 'You have to trust in the Goddess.' But it really felt with the encampment that if you do what you're supposed to be doing, things will fall into place and it may not be until one second before absolute calamity but usually someone pulls through at the right minute."

The web not only connected physical beings, it also provided a symbol for tying together all the issues that were seen to stem from a patriarchal, male-dominated society. The idea was that none of the issues—the nuclear arms race, child care, poverty, battering, rape, or racism—were separate. They were all related to the power relationships set up by patriarchal institutions. In a chapter titled "Everything Is Connected," the encampment *Handbook* addressed many of the economic, social and racial issues related to militarism, stating that "past anti-war movements [i.e., male-dominated ones] have failed to address patriarchy as a premier cause of militarism" (1983:19). The press release announcing the opening of the encampment also made this point, indicating that, "The Women's Peace Encampment will not only make a statement against the Pershing II missiles and other nuclear arms, but will also make a statement against the military buildup in general, which is irresponsibly taking away from human needs." One of the participants in a workshop at the 1983 encampment expressed the same concept: "If we're women and we're thinking holistically rather than linearly, then we have to see that they're all connected and we have to work on them all at once because they're all connected."

The web, like the circle, had physical and visual manifestations at the encampment. A yarn web was woven on the back of the main house and a large web was painted on the side of the barn behind the main house. During protests, yarn webs, often incorporating personal possessions, photographs, and memorabilia, were woven into the fence around the Seneca Army Depot. The personal possessions and photographs were indications of things that a woman did not want to lose in a nuclear war—often the pictures were of children and friends. This type of web symbolism was inspired in part by a ritual that took place at the 1980 and 1981 Women's Pentagon Action, a protest against expanding militarism in the United States, and by a protest at the Vermont Yankee nuclear power plant. In both places women wove yarn webs across the entrances to these sites to close them symbolically.

Work at the encampment was organized by "work webs" in which each woman was expected to participate. These webs not only were the organizing principle of work crews but were also promoted as a way for women to get involved with the other women at the encampment. Women

Encampment meeting in front of web painting

were expected to sign up daily for "webs" that involved three hours of labor in the areas of security, garbage recycling, child care, food preparation, dinner cleanup, reception, gardening, healing/emotional support, office/clerical work, general maintenance and construction, and media work.

These two interrelated symbols, the circle and the web, provided part of the self-representation created by the women's peace encampment. Both were successful focal symbols that had multiple applications in the visual, rhetorical, organizational and ritual activities of the camp. Taken together they helped form and express the alternative world that the encampment was striving to develop and live out, a world that was woman centered rather than male dominated. Its major metaphors were circular rather than linear, and it was seen as egalitarian rather than hierarchical. It proposed to celebrate the life-giving womb, peace, protection, cooperation, and caring rather than the phallic patriarchal world of destruction, war, violence, and competition.

This new world was not being proposed through a complete redefinition of dominant discourse symbols. As we have seen, the meanings of the circle and web in the dominant discourse were quite similar to the meanings employed by the encampment women, who attempted to revalue femaleness conceptually without changing the definition of femaleness and female qualities, as had been standard feminist practice in the past. Rather, the symbols of the circle and the web were used to present an alternative view that did not entirely contradict dominant discursive notions of male and female but instead put more value on qualities perceived as female in the dominant discourse. Because the circle and the web were marginal, not focal, symbols in the mainstream culture, their meanings were flexible enough to be used successfully to revalue the female sphere in an innovative way. Yet they were familiar and accessible to most women without extensive education, and they fit well with the representation the encampment organizers wanted to create—a picture of women working together naturally to better the world.

The development of these meanings of the circle and web certainly contributed to the establishment of a basically unified identity for the encampment. Such stable signs help establish group identity and a workable representation by creating shared meanings. Yet at the same time the use of symbols can be seen as conservative and somewhat unfeminist in that they tend to suppress difference and plural interpretations. The female circle with its connections, continuities, and equalities represents a world that is supposed to be in direct contrast to the linear, patriarchal world of hierarchies, dominance, and inequalities. Yet the privileging of such terms as "center," "source," "meaning," "holism," "origin," and "unity" suggests a repetition of the desire for coherence, unity, and authority so severely critiqued when they are used in patriarchal discourses. Symbols often play a conservative role in discursive battles as each faction tries to articulate its own positions and those of the other positively and clearly. Symbols can be the first and last line of defense in self-definition, but they also lock one into a stance that denies or ignores important differences and dissenting views. Donna Haraway (1985:73) has suggested that speaking from such a position—one in which shared group identity has been so specifically and perhaps rigidly established—can be a poor political strategy for women because it merely reproduces the essentialist categories and static representations that women now suffer.

But political necessity often seems to dictate that feminists not question their own discursive practices when they attempt to dismantle those of the enemy. The encampment was caught in this trap, forced to negotiate between utopian idealism and practical political action while experimenting with new theoretical possibilities. The use of the web in conjunction with the circle perhaps represents an attempt to avoid all the pitfalls of representation, for the web, which opens up meanings and makes connections that might seem unthinkable, tempers somewhat the essentialism and erasure of difference promoted by the circle. It is only through the intertextuality suggested by the circle in conjunction with the web that the encampment had the possibility of acting out any deconstructive feminist goals.

A third symbol, the labrys, a double-bladed ax (see figure 3), was introduced early into the encampment representation, but this one, unlike the circle and web, was neither well known nor well accepted. Mary Daly in her "metadictionary," which attempted to uncover words hidden in "patriarchal dictionaries," defined the labrys as "the symbol of gynocratic power in Crete as it was among the Lycians, the Lydians, the Amazons, the Etruscans, and even the Romans . . . found in the graves of Paleolithic women of Europe, buried 50,000 years ago" (1987:142). The labrys was seen as a sign of women's power, especially the power derived from association with other women.

For many of the encampment organizers, the labrys was a familiar and welcome symbol used by lesbians. As one organizer explained about the labrys and lesbian identity, "If someone was wearing a labrys and you were in a totally strange city, you would know that woman was a lesbian. One of the things that happened with the camp was that a lot of the women who were straight women who had never been involved with lesbians or with feminists before became exposed to lesbian symbols and have begun to incorporate them into their own reality." When the labrys—a symbol one woman suggested sends the forceful message "Don't mess with me!"—was put on an early encampment sign, several women felt it would provoke violence from the local community. It was, however, the association with lesbianism that made the labrys unacceptable for the women creating the early representations of the encampment and for those who came to the encampment later.

Lesbianism became a controversial issue. It was the focus of much of the antagonism between the encampment and the community and among encampment members themselves. Many women at the encampment considered lesbianism an important aspect of their alternative, non-patriarchal world. Since the encampment was designed to be a physically, socially, and spiritually safe place, women were encouraged to express all aspects of their femaleness freely. For many women, identifying as a lesbian was the most important feature of this revised identity. The encampment *Handbook* provided this explanation:

> The Women's Encampment is meant to be a place of safety for all women, a place where women can gather strength to protest the nuclear

Figure 3. Labrys, the double-bladed ax

threat. Women of all races, classes, religions, ethnic backgrounds, sexual preferences, are encouraged and expected to participate. It is with this in mind, that we briefly discuss the issue of homophobia (fear or discomfort of lesbians and/or gay men) as it pertains to lesbianism and as it relates to the visions of the encampment. One vision of the encampment is that it will provide an environment where women are free to be themselves. For lesbian women, this means a place where lesbians can feel safe and unself-conscious about their sexual choices, a place where lesbianism is appreciated as one of the many life choices that women make. Another vision of the encampment is that it will be a model for ways that women can work together, a place where women can share plans for a peaceful world. In such a world, all would be welcome; lesbians would not have to hide. (12)

This public acknowledgment and acceptance of lesbianism as simply a variation in the spectrum of women's behavior focused much attention on issues of homosexuality at the encampment. The encampment, by setting up a community where "lesbians would not have to hide" was challenging the invisibility of lesbians and gay men that was demanded by patriarchal discourse. The images of homosexuality that predominated in the patriarchal discourse were seriously attacked by encampment lesbians who wanted to replace patriarchal representations with their own interpretations of lesbian life.

Homosexuality, explained Vito Russo in a study of the representation of gays in mass-media films, is viewed in the dominant discourse as "something you 'do' in the dark and like a bad habit it can be broken" (1981:91). Until 1974 the American Psychiatric Association listed this "bad habit" as a mental disorder, an imbalance in the mental and physical condition, "a failure rather than a variant of sexual reciprocity, an asymmetry which disrupts what are held to be immutable categories" (Watney 1987:126). Many churches, particularly those associated with fundamental Christianity, still condemn homosexuality as unnatural and sinful. Most communities have refused to pass ordinances banning discrimination on the basis of sexual preference, although most states have at one time or another proposed such laws.

In 1977 the battle over one such community ordinance became national news, and during this time the discourse about homosexuality was articulated nationwide. The spokesperson for the dominant discourse was Anita Bryant, a former Miss America contestant, orange juice promoter, and self-proclaimed expert on homosexuality. In January 1977, the Dade County (Florida) Commission enacted an ordnance that would ban discrimination against gays in housing, employment, and public accommodations. It was the first gay rights ordinance passed by a southern city, and within weeks Bryant's group was working for its repeal (Shilts 1982: 155). During the fight against the ordinance, Anita Bryant came to symbolize the country's conservative attitude toward homosexuality, which she labeled as evil, sinful, and deviant, "a cancer on the soul of society" (Bryant and Green 1978:125). When Dade County voters repealed the ordinance in June 1978, Bryant said, "Tonight, the laws of God and the cultural values of man have been vindicated. The people of Dade County—the normal majority—have said, 'Enough, enough, enough'" (Shilts 1982: 157).

The discourse on homosexuality has been further articulated more recently in relation to Acquired Immune Deficiency Syndrome. This AIDS discourse didn't have extensive nationwide dissemination until the death of homosexual actor and leading man Rock Hudson in 1985. In 1983 the disease was just beginning to be recognized. Nevertheless, the basis for this discourse was available long before Hudson put AIDS on the front page. This representation of homosexuality and AIDS "fastens on what is most frightening and alluring in the other—for example, gay men's fantasized freedom from sexual and family constraints—and projectively makes it the sole marker of identity" (Grover 1987:24). Thus homosexuality represents the body, social contracts, sexuality, morality, the self, and reproduction in crisis (Beaver 1981:99), and AIDS is interpreted as the result of challenging the natural and legal order.

Lesbians have the additional difficulty of being subsumed under a category that takes the gay man as its reference point. As Jan Zita Grover (1987:25) explains in discussing the perceptions of lesbians in relation to

AIDS, lesbians are lumped with gay men, blacks and Hispanics, and intravenous drug users. Like these known "risk groups," they are designated as "essentially and socially different from the 'general population'" and so are believed to be AIDS carriers, even though as a group lesbians have among the lowest incidence of AIDS.

The discursive representation of lesbians is not as definitive as that of gay males. In a sense, lesbianism is unthinkable in a patriarchal society because gender identification not only is the proper identification with one's biological sex but also "entails that sexual desire be directed toward the other sex" (Rubin 1984:165). Gay males are thought to enact this scenario, according to the dominant discourse, by taking on stereotypical male and female roles, but lesbians, because of their greater invisibility, have not had these precise representations constructed about them yet. Lesbians are an unwritten text onto which any number of scenarios can be projected. Lesbians, according to Anita Bryant are "anti-male, antiwhite, antifamily, anti-church and anti-American from start to finish" (Bryant and Green 1978:124). When they do appear, lesbians consistently serve as a foil for the "normal": "In a society so obsessed with the maintenance of sex roles and the glorification of all things male, sissies and tomboys served as yardsticks for what was considered normal behavior" (Russo 1981:63).

But the lesbian also presents a different kind of threat from that posed by the gay male. The male homosexual can be neutralized by the claim that he maintains the patriarchal system of sexual and interpersonal relations (despite the shift in the sex of his partners) because gay male relations are thought to duplicate the male-female relations of patriarchal society (Shilts 1982; 1987). Lesbians, however, can be seen as more threatening not just because they break out of the culturally constructed gender categories that specify proper female and male relations but because they challenge the heart of that categorization—the acceptance of the male as normal and the standard against which all others are measured. The result is an unacceptable confusion not just of gender roles but also of power relations, and a violent reaction against these threats is often attempted by the patriarchal society.

Underlying the privileging of lesbianism at the encampment was the concept of the lesbian as being woman centered. As Hester Eisenstein explains, lesbians "escaped from, and indeed, renounced, the definition of 'woman' as secondary, derivative, or second-best to men. That is, they accorded to one another that primacy and importance that most women accorded only to men" (1983:52–53).

Lesbianism has been used within the broader feminist world (although with much disagreement) as a symbol of this orientation of all women who are woman centered, even if they are not sexually involved with other women. According to lesbian writer Jill Johnston, "The word [lesbian] is now a generic term signifying activism and resistance and the envisioned goal of a woman committed state" (in Eisenstein 1983:48). Adrienne Rich has also expanded the meaning of lesbian and lesbianism beyond "clinical" definitions to include "the sharing of a rich inner life, the bonding against male tyranny, the giving and receiving of practical and political support" (1984: 417).

The difficulty with these expanded definitions of lesbianism within the peace encampment (as in the larger feminist community) is that not all women, heterosexual or lesbian, could agree on how to employ this concept. For some separatist lesbians, it was unacceptable to apply the term lesbian to women who continued their social or sexual relations with men. For feminists who were homophobic or who did not want feminism to be narrowed to a discourse on sexual preference, this association of the encampment with a lesbian identity was also unacceptable. When women publicly displayed affection to each other or otherwise engaged in what the local community defined as lesbian behavior, the public message was that lesbianism was condoned, or even promoted by the women's encampment. Yet the encampment itself could not agree on just how to work lesbianism into its self-representation. The labrys, then, as a third symbol of the encampment's operations and philosophies was problematic partly because it was basically unfamiliar and also because the encampment participants could not generally accept it as representative of all of them.

Participants developed and reworked the encampment's self-representations throughout the summer of 1983. The circle and web remained important aspects of that representation in 1983 and for years afterwards; the labrys became an accepted symbol after the first summer, when the encampment became more of a lesbian community. Not surprisingly, the local communities often misunderstood or disapproved of how the encampment represented itself, and the symbols of that representation became weapons in the discursive battles that ensued.

6

Who Goes There

As for knowing whether nuclear arms are stored at Seneca Army Depot or not, it is none of their damn business. It is enough that the persons entrusted with the defense of our Country know where these armaments are stored. It is not and should not be public knowledge.

—Editorial, *Pennysaver*

The women's peace encampment, some Seneca County residents would later say, was the biggest thing to happen to the county since, well, the drought of 1918, according to one resident, or the closing of the railroad station in 1950, as one newspaper claimed. "It was the hottest thing to hit here since the Civil War!" exclaimed the head of the county health department. "Nothing like this has ever happened here in two hundred years," said a local judge who had to preside at the arraignment of some encampment women, "and I hope it never does again." As a major event in an area that claims it doesn't have many, the peace encampment became the center of attention in 1983, the subject of seemingly endless newspaper and television stories, and the topic of many summertime conversations.

There certainly was a lot of talk in 1983, explained Doyle Marquardt, the chief of police in the town of Waterloo, and all of it seemed to him very negative. Whether you were sitting down for a meeting, getting your hair cut, or standing in line in the supermarket, everyone was talking about it. In the Waterloo coffeeshops, where you could hear all the local gossip, the talk that summer was about the women at the so-called peace camp.

People got most of their information about the encampment, from the local newspapers, the chief believed. In what became a community-wide ritual, people dropped what they were doing at 2 P.M. ("We did it at the police station," he said) to read the latest about the encampment in the local paper. By midsummer, the local papers were featuring stories on the encampment, usually on the front page, nearly every day. Regional newspapers also had extensive coverage, usually on the front page of their regional section and often put on page 1 of the entire newspaper. At first the national papers didn't cover the story, and the television stations came only in for the big events; so the local newspapers, with their continuous coverage and their letters-to-the-editor sections, provided an ongoing forum for the summer's discussions. People would say, "Did you see what was in the newspaper today?" and that would be the topic of conversations all around town.

It's not that the Seneca County residents and neighbors were in any way pleased with the local reporting on the encampment. In fact, by the middle of the summer, the local people were quite dissatisfied with the coverage, feeling that the stories did not report their point of view and distorted the importance of the encampment. As more than one person said, if the women didn't have the publicity, they would just fade away. Many saw the encampment as what Daniel Boorstin (1985) has called a "pseudo-event," not spontaneous news that occurs "naturally" but a planned activity that is designed and staged primarily to capture attention and coverage. The news media coverage actually takes over as the event, and the desire for additional coverage becomes the reason for sustaining the life of the event.

The local people were perceptive in this assessment, but their negative judgment of the encampment's use of the news media to serve its purpose assumes that the media are supposed to function only as a system for providing accurate and correct information about spontaneously occurring events. The mass media (television, radio, motion pictures, newspapers, magazines, advertising) have traditionally been viewed this way, as a "neutral delivery system" that is part of a network of formal and informal information communication in a mass society (Meyrowitz 1985: 13). This communication model assumes an objectivity according to which the reporter tries to get the who, what, when, where, and why of a story, to be accurate without self-involvement (Manoff and Schudson 1986:3).

More recent approaches to the analysis of the process and effects of mass media suggest that this view is naïve and represses information about how news is created rather than reported, together with the important ideological implications of this creation of news in a mass society (Meyrowitz 1985; Manoff and Schudson 1986). In this revised view, the mass media do not report reality, they invent it (Parenti 1986). The media, whether local or national, play an important role in our process of "worldmaking" (Goodman 1978), which structures for us how we interpret the media we are exposed to and how we transfer these interpretations to the lives we actually experience. The mass media are a primary source and creator of the representations that we use to structure these interpretations. And because the news media and their audiences assume that news has a privileged relationship with reality, media representations and interpretive frameworks take on an authority derived from their perception as truthful, natural, and inevitable (Manoff 1986: 225).

According to film theorist Dudley Andrew (1984:113), the media contribute to world organizing. They help each person in a particular cultural world be "at home in his world by insisting first and foremost that his world is in fact the world, the natural order of things pre-ordained by God and physical laws to be just the way it is." The media construct these ideological versions of the world through representations of that world— representations of the people who are supposed to populate that world, representations of the actions possible in that world, and representations of the likely outcome of any acts or utterances in that world. Through these representations, these images of who, what, when, where, and how, the media constrain and guide interpretations and consequently the social action based on those interpretations.

The important question to ask of the news media in Seneca County in the summer of 1983 is not, then, whether or not they reported the news about the protests accurately. More significant is how the news media, particularly on a local level, contributed to the sea of representations that were floating around during that summer, representations that helped structure the summer's events and interpretations.

The peace encampment did not come onto the scene as a fully developed, well-defined entity. The gradual release of information on the encampment (and by the encampment) allowed for construction and testing of a representation of it by and for local use. The primary means of fleshing out this representation during the crucial early period of the encampment's existence (April to June 1983), as Waterloo's chief of police pointed out, was the coverage by the local press. Few people other than reporters and some county officials had contact with the women at this time, and in fact, relatively few would have direct contact throughout the summer.

Most people, then, got their information about the encampment from newspaper stories, and they developed opinions about these stories and about the women of the encampment in relation to the representations formed in these stories. But these representations, we must remember, were not complete, stable images that were wholeheartedly accepted; rather, they were argued and negotiated, rejected and supported in conversations and arguments that developed in the beauty parlors, the VFW post, schools, clubs, restaurants, parties, churches, or local grocery stores. Through news stories and the resulting conversations about them, representations of the encampment were put into circulation and this had significant consequences for the events of the summer.

The chief sources of printed news in Seneca County are the daily newspapers: the Rochester *Democrat and Chronicle* and the Rochester *Times-Union*; the *Post-Standard*, and the *Herald-Journal*, both of Syracuse (morning and afternoon editions of basically the same paper); the Sunday *Herald American* in Syracuse; the *Finger Lakes Times* out of Geneva; *The Citizen* in Auburn; and the *Ithaca Journal*. Other papers, from Elmira (the *Elmira Star-Gazette* and *Sunday Telegram*) and Utica, are available in certain parts of the county as well. Also available are weekly newspapers including the *Reveille*, published in Seneca Falls, and the *Trumansburg Free Press*, the *Ovid Gazette*, and the *Interlaken Review*, all published by the same company in southern Seneca County. Finally there were local weekly shoppers' papers with grocery store ads and local announcements. All the newspapers based in the large cities featured regional news in a separate section.

Local officials were alerted to the plans for a peace camp by a newspaper article that appeared in February 1983 in Buffalo, New York. By early March 1983 local county and Seneca Army Depot officials began coordinating their efforts to deal with this as yet inconclusively defined entity. In a March 18 letter to Seneca County sheriff Ken Greer the SEAD security officer, Major Wilford Sorrell, explained the need for the "military and civilian community" to work together:

> Colonel Wilson, Commander, Seneca Army Depot, has directed that I arrange a meeting between several law enforcement agencies and his staff to discuss a matter of mutual concern. As you are probably aware, a number of female organizations throughout the northeast are planning a major demonstration in our area this summer. The enclosed article, which appeared in a recent issue of the Buffalo News [February 10, 1983], indicates to us that the Encampment will probably be well-organized, lengthy in duration, and potentially disruptive. We would like to discuss the problem as it effects both the military and civilian community. The meeting is scheduled for 1PM, April 19, 1983, in the command conference room, Building 101, Seneca Army Depot.

Editorial cartoons from the Auburn *Citizen*, August 3 and 19, 1983

Local residents learned of the Encampment soon afterward. The *Finger Lakes Times* ran one of the first local articles on April 8. It was followed by an article in the Auburn *Citizen* on April 28 and another, in the *Finger Lakes Times* on May 6. In these articles we can see some of the themes that recurred throughout the summer's coverage of the encampment, beginning to develop, themes that were important in the early attempts to create a coherent representation of the newcomers.

Editorial cartoon from the Auburn *Citizen*, August 23, 1983

The April 8 *Finger Lakes Times* article was titled "Women Plan Summer Camp to Protest Nuclear Weapons." A summer camp, in this area well known as a vacation destination, usually refers to a place for children to spend the summer out-of-doors or to a summer vacation home, usually on one of the local lakes. Both summer camps promise a refuge from the summer heat and the everyday world of work and problems—camps, after all, are for vacations, and vacations are a time-out from more serious aspects of life. By designating the encampment a "summer camp" and then questioning whether the encampment can live up to this designation (because it wants to deal with the serious issue of nuclear weapons), the article, even in its title, calls into question the seriousness of the activity.

Concentrating on its rumored controversy, the article problemized the upcoming peace encampment by emphasizing all the worries the organizers had and the difficulties they anticipated. It did not do so, however, by defining specifically what the encampment would do or what its activities would be. The article began with a statement that gave no hint of the controversial nature of the women's "camp": "Women opposed to nuclear weapons hope to attract thousands of other women to a peace camp this summer near the Seneca Army Depot, which they claim is a storage site for atomic weapons." Without further explanation of the women's intentions or plans, the story established the controversial nature of the as yet undefined activities by quoting an encampment organizer, who explained that it would be difficult to rent property in the area because "not many people are interested in renting something they think will be controversial." Because the nature of this controversy was not explained, readers were left with the assumption that the controversy was self-evident. Another encampment organizer, quoted later in the story, said: "We want a place where we can't be kicked out, a place where we can't be arrested. . . . We don't want people to risk going to jail just because they've chosen to join us." Since there was still no indication in the article what the women intended to do that would expose them to arrest or eviction, this danger again seemed to be inherent in the development of the encampment itself.

Halfway through, the story specified some of the worries of the organizers. The writer noted that the encampment was to be limited to women and then immediately defined this limitation as a problem, albeit the lesser of two evils. "It would be more of a problem if the camp was mixed. The media would have a ball with that one," an encampment organizer was quoted as saying.

The article anticipated awkward relations with the local communities (the women had not yet even purchased the encampment land), quoting organizers who expressed concerns about these relations and who charged other, outside organizers with inadequate consideration of the issue. The article legitimated and confirmed this problem by quoting a local woman who said she was a "peace activist" but refused to give her approval or endorsement of the encampment. Instead, indicating that there were going to be some negative reactions to the (undescribed) activities which she did not want to deal with, she noted, "I have to stay here and work after they're gone. The jury is still out for me."

The problematic nature of the encampment was also emphasized in the other two early articles, which reported on the plans county officials were developing to deal with the encampment. Meetings between army and county officials were reported, as were canceled vacations and leave for the Seneca County sheriff's deputies (reports that were denied by the sheriff but confirmed by a deputy). Also reported was the installation at the main entrance of the depot of a "200 foot chain-link fence with two gates" (*Finger Lakes Times*, May 6, 1983). Although an army official denied that the installation was related to the upcoming protests, its inclusion in an encampment story firmly connected it to the emerging plans to defend against the peace encampment. A April 28 Auburn *Citizen* article reported, "One estimate is that 200,000 protestors are expected," without providing any source for the information. The figure became the basis for much of the rest of the article, in which the encampment women disputed the number and the local officials used it as a basis for worry.

It was not the encampment itself but the vagueness of the plans, the refusal or inability of the organizers to predict exactly what would happen that summer, that seemed especially worrisome to both army and local officials. In the April 8 article the depot's public affairs office withheld comment about preparatory plans until the army received more specific information about it,' and county officials expressed concern about the lack of direct information about what was planned. One member of the county board of supervisors was quoted: "It kinda scares me in a way because I don't know what could happen."

Army and local officials put this reported lack of information to good use, suggesting that this secrecy should make people suspicious of the peace camp intruders. Only those charged with safeguarding "national security" could harbor secrets and withhold information; secretive citizens in a "free society" should be considered dangerous (see Rogin 1987). The holding of secrets threatens and challenges established interpretations and authority by suggesting that some information can rightly be withheld from such authorities. Any threat to the establishment's right to control information is unacceptable. That the local residents supported this right of the established order to hold secrets can be seen in their repeated comments that the government had the right not to tell them if weapons were stored in the depot and that it was none of their business what went on there. Despite the popular rumors about the bizarre white deer (said to be radiated mutations) that roamed the depot land, few people saw fit to question the depot's agenda.

The representation of the encampment organizers as possessed of secret plans and withholding vital information continued even after the women held a press conference on May 23. During May and June, the news media portrayed them as vague on specifics and depicted this problematic aspect of the encampment. May 15 in the Syracuse *Herald American* and in the April 28 Auburn *Citizen*, SEAD public affairs officer Robert Zemanek had claimed that "all we know about the camp is what we read in the newspapers." This statement not only legitimated the newspapers as the authoritative source of information but also suggested that the lack of information was serious because the rightful authorities were not informed.

Plans based on the anticipated peacefulness of demonstrators might, it seemed, have to be reevaluated. The Syracuse *Herald American* quoted Zemanski: "Demonstrations in the past have been relatively peaceful. We hope they stay that way" (May 15, 1983). The sheriff's department, in the same article, reiterated this point: "If they're peaceful, we're placid." On May 20 the *Democrat and Chronicle* specified this uneasiness in its headline: "Seneca Edgy over Protest at Army Depot." Although it modified the menace with a subheading that read, "Some Fear Unruly Crowd, but Others Aren't Worried," the article guided the reader to question the intentions of the protesters and to disbelieve those officials who said they weren't worried. The first two paragraphs set up the issue:

> A nationally publicized women's encampment for peace outside Seneca Army Depot in Romulus this summer has made some local officials nervous about crowd control and the possibility of an unruly demonstration.
> But other officials say they believe camp organizers who tell them they intend the demonstration to be peaceful, with modest-sized crowds.

The view of these unworried officials remained qualified throughout the article and ended up reinforcing the message of the headline, that everyone in the county was "edgy." The officials who were not worried were reported to have only the word of the encampment women that they "intend" to be peaceful. One of these unworried officials, Romulus town supervisor Ray Zajac, commented, "They assured me that they want the people of the community to know them as friends." Sheriff Greer also qualified his statement, saying, "Hopefully this will turn out to be a small demonstration." Greer praised the efforts of the group to keep the officials informed: "I was impressed with the people I talked to. I feel this particular group wants to cooperate and keep the lines of communication open." His praise of their openness was negated, however, by the next line in the story, which stated, "Efforts to reach the organizers of the Encampment were unsuccessful." Seneca County Board of Supervisors chairman Stuart Olsowske also called into question the intentions of the women to communicate and cooperate: "I wonder if (the organizers) are keeping their estimates low just to throw us off track." This comment came immediately after one by Ray Zajac, who expressed doubt about the crowd estimates that ranged to 200,000 people. Thus every moderating comment by an unworried official was countered by a statement from a worried one. By the end of the article all the reader's own uncertainties would have been exacerbated by the contradictory comments of local officials. Neither the worried nor the unworried ones were providing a stable and reassuring story.

The press conference of May 23 marked an increase in the coverage of the encampment and an elaboration of some of the early motifs of reportage. Most of the local newspapers covered the press conference in their May 24 editions in stories headlined, "Depot Foes Buy Land for Summer Vigil," "Peace Camp Workers Reveal Summer Plans," and "We'll Be Good Neighbors." Despite the information revealed at the press conference, the stories continued to emphasize, through their content or their choice of phrasing, the uncertainties surrounding the encampment. The May 24 *Finger Lakes Times* focused on unanswered questions with no explanation of why the "necessary" information might not be available or might not fit in with the women's approach to organizing. The story alternately depicted the women as unorganized or evasive—perhaps deliberately. The proliferation of indefinite and conditional words and phrases (such as "if," "but," "hope," "plan," "would," "should," "expected," "either . . . or," etc.) created a sense of ambiguity and uncertainty:

> Organizers . . . say they hope the camp will be a good neighbor. . . . The camp is expected to focus on the presence of nuclear weaponry. . . . But the organizers would not say what form the protests would take or how many people they would involve. . . . The organizers said they plan to work with the County Health department and police officials. . . . Campers should register. . . . Water either from a well on the property or from outside sources will be provided. . . . The organizers said they are uncertain how many women will camp there. . . . no large scale events are planned for the opening. . . . The general purpose of the camp is to increase awareness of nuclear weapons. . . . "If we had any specific goals they would be education for ourselves and others." . . . Ms. Reale said no blockade of the depot or similar protest is planned. But she would not rule out such a possibility. . . . The organizers do not plan to interfere with depot employees. . . . local officials said after the briefing they are willing to cooperate with the camp organizers but are anxiously awaiting more specific information about their plans. . . . "A lot remains to be seen, about how the camp will run."

The article ended with a paragraph that stated: "Romulus Town Supervisor Raymond Zajac also said he wants to know more about the activities planned for the camp. 'If they want to have a peaceful demonstration, that's fine,' Zajac said."

The article leaves the reader hanging and the inconclusive ending reiterates the message of the rest of the story—that the reader should be uncomfortable because the narrative storyline cannot yet be conclusively determined. The "lack of information" about the encampment, the inability or refusal of the organizers to outline the events in advance, was taken as a sign of the frightening impossibility of defining, understanding and predicting the plot line of the story. This lack would become compelling as the story developed, and in many ways it propelled the events of the summer and the narratives about them.

From the start, in addition to edginess and nervousness among local officials, the newspapers reported negative reactions among local residents. In this early stage the residents tended to be quoted anonymously, with the significant effect of making the speaker seem to speak for the whole community. The Syracuse *Herald American* (May 15, 1983) quoted an anonymous local resident as saying that the women were unrealistic in what they were trying to achieve (headline: "Romulus Protestors 'Unrealistic'"). The story described the residents of "everyday Romulus" as collectively "less worried by the bombs than by the looming encampment of protestors from out of town." It said that the residents (again anonymous) were afraid that the "radical groups" coming into their communities would "conduct noisy and violent protests" and would drive the depot away, causing a loss of jobs. In its May 24 report on the encampment's first press conference, the *Ithaca Journal* predicted that the protesters would number in the thousands and "might not get a warm reception from some of the 4,064 Romulus townsfolk." They based this conjecture on rumors that residents either reported hearing or seem to have been creating themselves during the press conference. Without investigating the bases of these stories or examining their implications, and without attribution, the newspaper reported generalized local fears that the women were troublemaking hippies left over from the 1960s, drifters who planned to sign up en masse for welfare, or exhibitionists who intended to strip naked during protests.

Just as representations were being created by and about the encampment women, so the local people had to construct and hold a representation of themselves as a coherent, identifiable entity. They came to define themselves as a community, as a group of people who believed they shared something with each other. All communities larger than small, isolated villages, explains Benedict Anderson, are "imagined," that is, the members of the community "will never know most of their fellow-members, meet them, or even hear of them, yet in the minds of each lives the image of their communion" (1938:15). With thirty thousand people in Seneca County, many more in the entire Finger Lakes region, and at least several thousand each in the smallest towns, the community calling itself "Seneca County" or "the local people" or "the people around here" was very dependent on this imaginative construct.

I have been referring to the neighbors of the women's peace encampment as the "local residents" of Seneca County, but the term is a bit of a misnomer when it is applied to the people who opposed the peace camp. Those who complained about or actively protested against the encampment actually came from all over the Finger Lakes region. But the term "residents" was often used locally to refer to people who were perceived as having the legitimate right to be in the area. Other people—tourists, transients, visitors, and the women of the encampment—were just passing through and were seen as lacking a good basis for commenting on or protesting against local conditions. As residents, many of the people living in and around Seneca County claimed never to have even noticed the eleven-thousand-acre SEAD, never mind been bothered by it; the outsiders were simply sticking their noses into someone else's business.

The way to distinguish communities, Benedict Anderson asserts, is by the style in which they imagine themselves. The encampment, for example, imagined itself as a united group of women with spiritual, political, emotional, and physical bonds built on a foundation of common womanhood. The local residents in and around Seneca County saw themselves as one cohesive, uniform group of simple, conservative, peace-and-quiet loving people living in the typical rural small town in America where dramatic occurrences are rare, people are friendly and helpful, and outsiders are rightly viewed with suspicion. The local residents confirmed this image for one another in a variety of ways, most effectively through comments to newspaper reporters and letters to the editor. Statements by local officials usually helped reinforce the image. One judge, presiding at a hearing for some arrested encampment women, began his session by saying, "This whole thing has disrupted the peace and quiet of the community, and threatened the safety and welfare of the community" (Rochester *Times-Union*, August 4, 1983). Even a letter that supported the Encampment confirmed that "in our small, quiet community, unaccustomed to political protests, the demonstrators may seem like troublemakers bent on disrupting the peace of our towns."

Local newspapers often used this theme of outside intruders on local tranquillity in their stories. One editorial (*Democrat and Chronicle*, August 1, 1983) said that the local people "resent the rude interruptions of quiet rural ways." The Auburn *Citizen* (July 10, 1983) printed an article titled "Sleepy Town Awakens to Protest," in which the reporter wrote, "The countryside around the Seneca Army depot and its summer neighbor seems so calm and peaceful. Harmless, like a stick of dynamite that hasn't been lit." Romulus was said to be "used to the sleepiness of a town that is basically a four-corners and a few mobile home parks." It is as if the huge weapons storage depot did not even exist in the town or as if criminal activities and disturbances of the peace were unknown in the area. Yet the eighty-seven hundred or so complaints that are reported to the sheriff's department every year suggest Seneca County is no different from any other community its size.

The fable of the quiet, idyllic community, disrupted by outsiders was very popular in the stories that were published or broadcast far from Seneca County. One story in the *Miami Herald*, titled "Ladies' War on War Ruffles Town" (July 23, 1983), stated:

> This is a rural and Republican town of 2,414 residents, three churches, a youth center, a gas station and a single soda machine that stands in front of the old Romulus Hotel, which, despite its name, is no longer a hotel but one of two restaurants in town.
>
> A neighborly spirit prevails in Romulus, where the town supervisor is married to the town assessor and also runs the J&C Superette in nearby Willard, and where the town beautician is a volunteer fire fighter who just happens to be married to the town barber, who drives the school bus.

The article portrayed what it called the "Norman Rockwellian character of Romulus" and conjured up ideal images of prototypical America, where everyone knows and is related to everyone else, where people help one another (by volunteer fire fighting and driving the school bus), where people are compatible (husbands and wives have complementary jobs), where life is simple (only one gas station and soda machine and two restaurants, so that decisions about where to eat, drink, and refuel are not difficult), and where people are religious and care for their children. A *Detroit Free Press* reprint of the same article is subtitled "Town Is Disrupted by Women Fighting U.S. Nuclear Arms" (July 25, 1983). In a July 11, 1983, *Canandaigua Daily Messenger* article, Romulus is described as the "archetypal image of small town America," a "quiet place where people enjoy the cool summer breezes from their front porches, and men hang out at the local gas station," where "children were fairly free of restrictions and are used to roaming at will throughout the countryside before the encampment." This idyllic tranquillity was threatened. The encampment was now signaling "an end to life at a slow pace."

This image of small-town America as a quiet haven from the worries of the world is not a purely local construction, no matter how accurately it seemed to reflect reality for the local people. Rather, it is a representation shared and practiced widely in the United States. As Leo Marx has shown in his analysis of the theme of pastoralism in American social life and history, America has been seen, from the early days of its "discovery" by Europeans until the present, as an untouched land of promise and wealth, a pastoral retreat, "remote and unspoiled," an "abundant garden" that as a "permanently rural republic" would offer its citizens "escape from the terrible sequence of power struggles, wars, and cruel repressions suffered in Europe." As Marx explains, "To depict America as a garden is to express aspirations still considered utopian—aspirations, that is, toward abundance, leisure, freedom, and a greater harmony of existence"—and the image embodied the "timeless impulse to cut loose from the constraints of a complex society" (1964:36, 138, 43). The image of a garden of peace, leisure, and pleasure in Seneca County, being spoiled by the urban, political forces of the complex outside world is one of the shared images of American social life.

That this image of the small town as paradise and retreat was not a local interpretation of actual events can be seen in the repetition of this motif in newspaper stories about other events in rural and suburban areas. The depiction of nonurban areas as isolated from unusual, disruptive, unpleasant occurrences is clear, for example, in a *Finger Lakes Times* article about murders committed in the post office at Edmond, Oklahoma, in 1985 (August 21, 1986; reprinted from the *Dallas Times Herald*). "For most of its nearly 100-year history," the article stated, "Edmond was a place in which fear and uncertainty were strangers, a place where residents figured tragedy could always be relied on to happen elsewhere." The editor of the local newspaper was mystified: "There's no way to explain something like this happening here." The small town as immune to outside influence and unchanged with the passage of time can also be seen in a *New York Times* article about a Maryland Island threatened with development (November 8, 1987). Following the headline "Discovery Jolts an Island Where Time Stands Still," the article begins: "For most of the three centuries that people have inhabited this marshy island in the middle of Chesapeake bay, daily life has been governed by tide, wind, season, isolation and the Methodist church. This is a place of God-fearing watermen. They work hard crabbing and oystering and fishing, and they pray hard, three times on Sunday." In another *New York Times* article (June 13, 1983), a "riot" in the New Jersey town of Perth Amboy was depicted as an unexpected, uncharacteristic event that shattered local peace. The small city was described as quiet, "within spitting distance of New York City but imbued with an air of suburban calm that shows in the tidy storefronts and well-kept homes that line romantically named streets like Catalpa Avenue and Wisteria Place," where "elderly women chat on park benches in the late afternoon sun and children skitter after pigeons along a tiny beach." The article quoted a resident, who exclaimed after the riot, "It shook us up. We thought we were never going to see that here."

This representation of small-town tranquillity and isolation served several important purposes in Seneca County during the antinuclear demonstrations. First, it negated the rationale for staging the protests in this location. As one Auburn *Citizen* article stated, "The countryside is almost too peaceful for any kind of confrontation" (August 2, 1983). The gardenlike natural landscape was inappropriate for such conflict:

> Route 96A, south from Waterloo to the Seneca Army Depot, is a perfect blend of rural life, typical of Upstate New York. Wheat fields are ripening in the mid-summer sun, and corn is "as high as an elephant's eye." Cows graze in the pastures dotted with tiny ponds and farmers are taking advantage of the sun which followed the morning rain to begin baling hay.
>
> Just a few mile from the Women's Encampment for a Future of Peace and Justice, a Mennonite mother, trailed by her toddler, hangs dozens of snow-white diapers on the line. At another farm, a single kite flies high above the head of its youthful handler.
>
> The scene shifts dramatically at the corner of Yale farm road, where sheriff's deputies congregate at the town of Varick Highway Department. From then on, traffic is slowed at every major intersection by deputies and volunteers, checking and guiding the cars.

Throughout the summer residents insisted that it was unnatural to hold protests in their peaceful little county, often jeering at the women to take their demonstrations to Washington or Moscow.

Next, this representation provided a way of placing responsibility for the local protests on outsiders who did not share local standards. If the small towns were seen as timeless, they could not also be seen as the source of any agitation for change. The local residents thus claimed for their communities an impossible stability: Seneca County did not change; it maintained traditional values in the face of radical social challenges. These communities were a Shangri-La, a mythical haven from war and outside forces. Here residents maintained primeval American habits that elsewhere had been lost to the exigencies of modern life. The rural landscape was seen as a paradise of harmony and urban areas as dangerous places that bred discontent and chaos. Thus, change and disruption were seen as the products of city life, and isolation from this urban upheaval was considered possible and preferable. As one Seneca County resident said, "We're away from the city, far enough so that it doesn't rub off much."

This motif also made political activism and dissent seem unusual. When normal, everyday activity is said to consist of sitting on porches or walking through golden hayfields, any kind of protest seemed not only counterproductive but also absurd. How could there be anything to protest in towns where everyone helped everyone else and life was epitomized by quiet and peace? The protesters could only be mentally unbalanced "kooks" if they didn't understand that there was nothing to complain about.

The peace camp also subscribed to this representation of the local residents as all members of a uniform community, though it used the image for its own end. The encampment promoted a stereotype of the simple, isolated, uneducated farmer as a way of contrasting themselves and their goals to those of the local residents. In a section of the *Resource Handbook* titled "Rural Organizing," two antinuclear activists from Wayne County (north of Seneca County) described what they saw as the makeup of the local farmers:

> Unlike an urban area where the influx of new ideas happens at a fast rate, change and exposure to new concepts is slow to happen. People's priorities are much more centered around their local community. If you haven't been further away from home than Rochester, it's difficult to be concerned about the rest of the US much less people across the ocean in Europe. . . .
>
> An important thing to remember is that there is a country way of talking that could easily lead one to think of people as slow or stupid. Be careful of this and listen carefully to what is being said. The sentence structure and concepts may appear to be simple—in fact they probably are, due to lack of outside exposure—but the feelings at the base of these ideas are profound and come from life experiences of the people. They are going to know when someone is being straight with them and when they're being given a line. . . .
>
> If you come from a large urban area, your way of life is totally foreign to life in this area. Farmers, in particular, have to work extremely hard.

They, more likely than not, don't know about cultural affairs, haven't read very much and haven't traveled. However, they do know how to grow crops, read the weather and fix just about anything. They often don't have time to work on "causes" as they certainly don't have 9–5 jobs. (7)

Despite the disclaimer in the article that "the aspects of rural vs. urban lifestyles have been characterized in an attempt to make a point; no one anywhere fits into a strict mold," this representation of the local communities outraged many local people, who resented being portrayed as slow-speaking, slow-thinking farmers who never left town or their farms. As one man explained, "They don't know that most of the farmers are going to Florida every winter, or the Caribbean, or California, or somewhere, you know." He noted that the encampment women had left a copy of their *Resource Handbook* off at the local beauty shop and those who came in to get their hair done read the offending passage. "Some of them got mad," he said, and went across the street and made photocopies of it, which they then circulated in town. The passage was eventually revised after many letters and complaints from local residents, but not before they came to associate the peace camp women with these unfortunate stereotypes.

The representation of the local residents (by themselves and by others) as peace-loving small-town folks was negotiated and revised often as the local people tried to define their relationship to the encampment. Some elements, however, remained consistent throughout the summer. For example, one theme was to present the innocent town of Romulus and the defense-oriented depot as being under military attack from the encampment women. The use of military language to describe the women's plans and the depot's response set up a warlike, confrontational scenario for the events to come. One local resident later described it, "This was a battle and this [the Depot] is a fort here that was being besieged. . . . this is essentially a fort and it was being attacked by the peaceniks."

Newspapers also employed this military discourse throughout the summer. Headlines described the depot as the "target of women's peace protest" (*Ithaca Journal*, May 24, 1983) and as "bracing for nuke protests" (*Democrat and Chronicle*, May 25, 1987) from "depot foes" (Syracuse *Herald-Journal*, May 24, 1983). When five women entered the depot undetected and walked around for four hours, the Syracuse *Post-Standard* (July 11, 1983) defined it as a "raid," and the *Buffalo Evening News* (July 11, 1983) said the women "infiltrated" the depot. Other papers directly identified the women's protests as a war. Recall the *Miami*

Herald headline (July 21, 1983) "Ladies' War on War Ruffles Town." The *Detroit Free Press* ran the same story under the title "Small War over Peace." The idea that the women were "training" protesters (headline: "Peace Group to Train Near Seneca Depot" [*Democrat and Chronicle*, May 24, 1983]) also fit the military-oriented discourse.

Putting these two groups into a war scenario and discourse set up certain expectations, for example, that expensive and extensive preparations would be necessary to protect the local people and the depot from this outside force. Three newspapers ran stories on May 25 describing the depot's preparations, which the army now admitted were in direct response to the encampment. "Seneca Army Depot Beefing Up Security Force" (*Auburn Citizen*) and "Seneca Army Depot to Beef Up Security Force" (*Finger Lakes Times*) were two headlines on stories describing the hiring of additional security guards.

This military discourse also fostered the assumption that any interaction with the women, with the enemy, would be violent. Before the encampment opened, *The Reveille* (June 1, 1983) stated, "County Joins SEAD in Hope 'Peace Camp' Stays Peaceful." After the opening, *The Finger Lakes Times* observed, "Romulus Protest Gets Off to Peaceful Start" (July 5, 1983) and "Protesters Hold Orderly Vigil" (July 13, 1983). After Waterloo, any contact that was not accompanied by violence was noteworthy because it was unexpected: one newspaper headline said, "Protest Comes Off without Violence" (*The Citizen*, August 2, 1983), as if most protests were not usually nonviolent. Another headline, in the Rochester *Times-Union* (August 4, 1983), noted, "Peace Returns to Depot Area," only after most of the several hundred women who had participated in a weekend protest had left the encampment. Reporting on the large August 1 demonstration, *The Reveille* headline announced, "Aug. 1: Not So Peaceful, but Bloodless" (August 3, 1983).

The military discourse supported by these stories bolstered the perception of the encampment as potentially violent. It is important to remember, however, that the war was being fought not by military units armed with guns and bombs but by communities with different identities and different strategies for interpreting the world. It was a "war of signification," the kind of war that enables communities to define themselves. This is the contest that underlies much American conflict.

7

The Plot

The detective story, no doubt, was acceptable because in it something was definitely done, the "what" being comfortably decided beforehand by the author.

—Harriet Vane

The "edginess" that residents and local and army officials expressed can be seen in textual terms as the desire to know, to set the plot of the developing story of the Seneca Women's Encampment for a Future of Peace and Justice in Seneca County in the summer of 1983. The attempt to fix this story by trying out already-known motifs (small-town peace disrupted by outsiders; hippies attacking American society; the perpetual battle between town and city) points to the importance of knowing the plot for battles of signification.

What, first, is a plot and why is it important for a story? A plot is the "structure of relationships by which the events contained in the account are endowed with a meaning by being identified as parts of an integrated whole" (White 1987:9). The plot is the outline of the story, the direction in which the narrative will go, the design and intention of the narrative (Brooks 1984:12). Knowing the plot is knowing the discursive framework it fits into, and this knowledge allows control of what is said, who can say it, what it can mean, and what people can do about it. As a guiding discursive framework, the plot allows us to take seemingly disparate or random elements and make sense of them; a plot poses an explanation of how the elements relate to each other in "logical" and chronological order.

This type of explanation is not scientific (that is, it is not proof that these things must go in this order) and it is not predictive; rather, it is literary: it organizes the telling and the comprehension of events, people, thoughts, and actions (Veyne 1984). According to Peter Brooks, the word *plot* has four basic meanings:

1. (a) A small piece of ground, generally used for a specific purpose. (b) A measured area of land; a lot.
2. A ground plan, as for a building; chart; diagram.
3. The series of events consisting of an outline of the action of a narrative or drama.
4. A secret plan to accomplish a hostile or illegal purpose; scheme [that is, a scheme to control the narrative] (Brooks 1984:12)

A plot, then, is a way to organize information, to mark (things) off and to categorize. The fourth meaning seems in some ways to oppose the other three, for its intention—to accomplish hostile purposes—would threaten the order implied by the other three. Brooks points out, however, that this is not a contradiction but an often overlooked aspect of the plot—that it is an organizing structure produced by intention, "goal-oriented and for-ward-moving" (ibid.). Plot organizes elements in a specific order, its own order, and this jealous ordering of things is a form of discursive control. As Edward Bruner points out, "Narratives are not only structures of meaning but structures of power as well" (1986b:145).

Steven Marcus notes that "human life is, ideally, a connected and coherent story, with all the details in explanatory place" (85:71), but of course, life is never perfectly ordered. When life as it is does not match life as we imagine it should be, we seek or create narratives to explain why and to guide actions that we think might remedy the undesirable discrep-ancies in our lives. This desire to create coherent guiding stories with identifiable and controllable plots is a compelling task of all imagined communities.

Narrative constructions are not limited to strict reliance on events that have taken place; they are also influenced by the choices of the commu-nity, what it remembers, emphasizes, treasures, or even invents. In trying to make sense of events that are happening in the present, a community draws on past narratives whose ends and interpretations are well known. Thus narrative, in a sense, proceeds in reverse, with the anticipated or desired end necessarily affecting the interpretation of events being fit into the story. How actual events are structured and interpreted depends on the plot lines available to a particular interpretive community.

We can trace this tendency to structure a story according to a particular plot, regardless of the "facts," through the transmission and interpretation of one of the rumors about the encampment women which spread through the local community. Rumors that the women had appeared nude in public were persistent and widespread. Nearly every person interviewed about the encampment had "knowledge" of these alleged transgressions:

> They just came in here and they took right over, go to the car wash and stripped down and hosed each other off.

> Some of the women went up to the laundromat, took off their clothes, threw them in the washer, and proceeded to make love while their clothes were washing.

> There was a lot of frustration over nudity, like when the women would strip or not wear [under]pants and sit spread-legged in places, or strip when the guys were getting off the post.

> They go down to the laundromat and take a shower, you know.

> They come down to Geneva and they go right in the car wash and take showers and not even have any clothes on.

One resident was aware of the constructed nature of these stories but nevertheless did not dismiss them: "They used to say they'd go down to the car washes and they'd take a shower.... I heard those stories, but not ever seen it myself. But then at the time it happened I think anything that was said about them anybody would believe." Many people did believe the stories and interpreted them as true indications of the type of women at the encampment and their behavior. Yet the owner of the laundromat in Ovid, where the women supposedly waited in the nude while washing their clothes, suggested in a newspaper article that what "really happened" and how it got interpreted and spread around were two different things:

> One of the most persistent rumors surrounding the peace camp has been the story that some women disrobe in laundromats to wash their clothes.
>
> Dave Terry, who owns the Ovid laundromat, snorted as he moved through the chicken barbeque line at the Ovid Fire Department carnival last weekend and tried to explain its origin.

"I'll tell you exactly how that story got started, and then I'll tell you what really happened," he said, balancing four chicken dinners in his hands.

"A couple of girls from the camp came in to do their laundry, took off their jeans and tossed them in. Once. I don't know whether they had bathing suits underneath or what, but I have campers coming in all the time and doing worse."

By the next morning, he said, "the story was all over town" that the women were completely disrobing. Said Terry's wife, Marge, "We've had guys come up to us complaining, 'I've gone in there twice a week for the past month and they're always fully clothed.'" (*Democrat and Chronicle*, August 14, 1983)

The point of the laundromat owner's account is not that the locals constructed a false or incorrect story but that they had already available in their community a plot that could have been used to interpret whatever it was that the women had done. They could have classified them with other tourists who did such things all the time but were rarely seen as a problem. Instead, the local people "chose" a different plot that allowed them to classify the women's behavior as deviant and unacceptable by local standards.

Akin to the need to plot the story is the need to define and categorize the actors or characters in the developing narrative. Each community categorizes and labels persons, and such categories are socially useful (even if not always ethically desirable) for making quick judgments and establishing normal expectations about people. It was very important, therefore, for the local community to define and describe to itself who these encampment women were and where they came from. For the Seneca County officials, the inability to identify these women "properly" threatened a loss of control over the narrative events that were developing around them. Stuart Olsowske, chairperson of the board of supervisors, expressed their discomfort: "I feel very uncomfortable even with the idea of 1,000 people [coming to the encampment] when we don't know who those people are" (*Democrat and Chronicle*, May 20, 1983).

The characterization developed by local officials and newspapers emphasized that the organizers of the encampment were outsiders: from Rochester, Ithaca, and Albany (*The Citizen*, April 28, 1983); from "peace and women's groups around the country" (*Finger Lakes Times*, April 8, 1983); from "women's peace groups from the Geneva, Ithaca, Rochester, and Syracuse areas, as well as women from similar groups in Albany, New

York City, Boston, Mass., and Philadelphia, Pa." (*Herald-Journal*, May 25, 1987); or from specific, nonlocal, organizations: "A group called Women's International League for Peace and Freedom is planning the Encampment, together with several other local and national organizations in the peace and anti-nuclear movements" (*Democrat and Chronicle*, May 20, 1983). Even when local women were identified as active participants (thus potentially calling into question the label "outsiders"), they were not seen as controlling figures:

> Four camp organizers, Seneca County residents Julie Reinstein of Hector, Harlene Gilbert Karsten of Varick, Barbara Reale of Geneva, and Rochester resident Kris Eberlein, told a press conference yesterday that the encampment organization is controlled by Women's International League for Peace and Freedom and numerous other groups throughout the Northeast including Catholics against Nuclear Arms and the War Resisters League, Women's Strike for Peace, Women's Pentagon Action, Rochester Peace and Justice, and the Upstate Feminist Peace Alliance. (*Democrat and Chronicle*, May 24, 1983)

Although the groups involved are specifically named, their goals, philosophies, and membership are not described. Thus, they remained basically unknown entities despite what appears on the surface to be an abundance of information about those who were organizing the encampment. One article, the only early in-depth analysis of the peace camp structure, called the encampment, "a European, feminist, leaderless" organization (*Democrat and Chronicle*, May 29, 1983).

A significant strategy for identifying the women was to look for leaders who could speak for the group. This strategy has been well documented by Todd Gitlin in his study of the mass media and the coverage of leftist politics. He explains that "from the media point of view, news consists of events which can be recognized and interpreted as drama; and for the most part, news is what is made by individuals who are certifiably newsworthy. Once an individual has been certified newsworthy, he or she has been empowered, within limits, to make news" (1980:146). Since the encampment refused to allow the designation of either leaders or permanent spokespersons, however, it presented a dilemma to the institutions that required the individual leader/celebrity as the legitimate source of information. Newspaper reporters would often try to speak to the same women each time they came to the encampment and to create identifiable personalities by publishing individual photographs, names, and background information in newspaper articles. The encampment, for its part, resisted because this strategy was in conflict with its self-representation as communal and cooperative, rather than hierarchical. At one point, when it began to seem that one woman was being consulted and quoted too often, the women decided that she should no longer make herself available for statements to the press and that other women should take on more visible roles.

Local and army officials also tried to insist that the women designate representatives who could deal consistently with the officials. As one official explained later, "There was no authority there. There's got to be a chain of command there; like I told them, if something serious happens out there, what are we going to do?" The designation of leaders is important in narrative structuring in general because a leader provides an authoritative voice that can be used to guide the creation of the narrative and provide essential and reliable information and direction for the plot. When the women refused to appoint leaders, the idea of leaderlessness at the encampment became another significant motif in the narrative developments, a worrisome motif for officials.

It should be clear that presently occurring events make sense to the participants only when they are understood through a narrative structure involving a known plot and stable characterizations. Without the plot, events appear random and unrelated, statements illogical and irrelevant; without the characters, events seem disembodied and unmotivated. It was in precisely this situation that Seneca County found itself in late May of 1983 before the encampment opened. The available information didn't yet seem to fit any known or desired story outline, and plot development seemed stalled, as if the local community had a kind of social "writers' block." The direction for this story was not yet clear, and so people's past and potential actions didn't quite fit yet. Seneca County at this point was not so much following a plot as searching for one.

Having to acknowledge their inability to categorize the encampment participants and place them in a known story put Seneca County authorities in a vulnerable position. On a practical level, lack of a narrative structure made it impossible to prepare for all the actions the women might take. No one knew what equipment to have ready, what and how many personnel to employ, what tactics to use. On a more theoretical level, it threatened to expose the fragility of the system authorizing their command. Textually, control and authority are thought to belong to the author of the text or narrative that is being constructed; loss of the power to author the text is frightening, for it means one does not control the discourse and the end of the narrative. Since the end is what makes sense of the entire narrative and provides the motivation for actions and words, a knowledge of it is essential for narrative control. One letter to the editor July 17, 1983) articulated this failure to maintain control. Several women had been able to sneak onto the base and wander undetected for hours. The letter writer commented, "The women already have shown the government that they got caught with their nuclear pants down" (*Democrat and Chronicle*, July 17, 1983).

A series of essays in a local newspaper early in the summer promised to provide the needed plot outline. The essays, by local writer Alice Larsen, appeared in the *Tri-Village Pennysaver*, a weekly shoppers' newspaper published in the southern part of Seneca County. Larsen insisted that the women were simply communist dupes being used by the Russians to control American peace movements. On May 11, 1983, in one of the first local responses to the news of the peace camp, she commented, "There are some who feel that Seneca County is more in danger from the 'Peace' movement than from nuclear weapons at the Depot." The fear, she said, was that the protesters would draw "known activists and/or terrorists" who would threaten American individualism and freedom.

Larsen's arguments were supported in print and from the pulpit by Father Albert Shamon, pastor in 1983 of a Catholic parish in Waterloo. According to Shamon, only two types of people got involved in peace rallies and other such activities: "There are dupes and there are dopes." The dupes are well-intentioned people who are fooled or taken advantage of; the dopes are people who are just not able to make intelligent decisions based on facts that are right in front of them, especially facts about the communist threat. The threat was eminently clear, he thought, to those who were willing to recognize it. By this logic, therefore, anyone who did not ardently stand up to communism was a dupe, a dope, or probably an active communist, directly involved in evil, anti-American deeds.

Shamon's dupe/dope characterization and Larsen's communist plot were echoed throughout the summer to explain the women's behavior. One letter to the editor explained that "the encamped ladies at the Seneca Depot, plus others now protesting American nuclear armaments, are insufferably ignorant and stupid in their assessment of Russian methods and goals" (*Elmira Star-Gazette*, July 25, 1983). Another called the dupes "useful idiots of the peace movements" who are "hastening the Iron Curtain's progress" (*Elmira Star-Gazette*, August 2, 1983). One resident adopted the dupe characterization: "Most of them are just followers. They don't have a mind of their own."

Communism was seen here as a contagion of ideas, a disease whose spread results from a weakness of will and intellect; a belief in American ideology was seen, on the other hand, as a sign of mental and social health. Communism was also defined here as an international conspiracy to overthrow the American government, an idea that has been widely used at least since the late nineteenth century, when the communist threat to American life was perceived as originating in the burgeoning American labor movement (Rogin 1987:72). Belief in this international conspiracy, Michael Rogin says, "divides the world between the forces of good and an empire of evil and traces all troubles at home and abroad to a conspiratorial center" (ibid.:8). Rogin calls this conspiratorial search for a convenient "other" an example of "political demonology" because it turns "political difference into absolute struggles between good and evil" (ibid.: 58).

For countersubversives, those who perceived themselves as fighting this communist conspiracy, pluralism is not a positive characteristic of American society but a dangerous weakness that could lead one into the arms of more threatening demons. The goals of countersubversive strategies, Rogin says, are contradictory. On one hand, they attempt to eliminate any pluralism that might suggest that America is not a stable, unified society: "To win, in the countersubversive tradition, is to be an English-speaking white man. To lose is to fall back among the undifferentiated masses of aliens, women and peoples of color. Countersubversives desire the submergence of separate identities within an ideal America" (1987:279). On the other hand, eliminating pluralism would theoretically equalize all people, and this "boundary collapse" seems even more frightening to the countersubversive. Creating the ideal life for all people might produce the kind of "undifferentiated masses" that are a feared result of communism. Yet, the desire to maintain differences of power and privilege conflicts with the American ideal of equal access to power and privilege. The "paranoia" of American countersubversive politics stems from this conflict in priorities and possibilities.

Rogin suggests that the political demon in the form of the communist threat does not so much reflect real differences between the two systems (especially since the changes in Eastern Europe) as express our own fears about ourselves and our ambivalence about the system in which we live. The communist has faithfully served as the "other," that necessary foil who confirms our own, constructed identity. Since communism is by definition alien to American ways, it must be kept outside the boundaries of American life. At the same time, the communist alien other "comes to birth as the American's dark double, the imaginary twin who sustains his (or her) brother's identity" (Rogin 1987:284). This other thus does not stand for differences between one entity or one system and another; rather, it emblematizes the differences *within*, which must be repressed if identity is to be coherent. The "alien preserves American identity against fears of boundary collapse" (ibid.), and it also reflects those aspects of American identity that cannot be readily admitted.

The effectiveness of an idea of a threatening other depends for Americans on the complementary idea of the innocent self. The Soviet Union, according to Alice Larsen, was trying to make the United States appear "falsely as the 'aggressor' and as the world's greatest threat to peace" (*Pennysaver*, May 11, 1983). An editorial in the *Pennysaver* admonished the encampment women for trying to "intimidate a peaceful nation" (June 1, 1983). In local discourse the United States was consistently depicted as having nuclear weapons for defense, not offense, and the Soviet communists were identified as known aggressors.

Peace demonstrators, in this discourse, were seen as naïve about defense issues, and local residents often accused the encampment women of wanting to weaken the United States. One longtime local resident, a direct descendant of the early settlers of the area, related a story:

> You know, the Quakers were opposed to violence, and there'd be a knock on the door, the Quaker would open his door and hold out his hand, and he would say, "Peace," and the Indian would bury his tomahawk right there. . . . A society can't survive that way but our people here [the encampment women] seem to think that the way to have peace with the Russians was to give them what they wanted. I don't happen to believe that and neither does anyone else around here. We just don't accept that. We've had enough fighting down through the years to know that that's not the way human beings settle things.

Apparently, this man, and many of his neighbors, believed that working for peace was a foolish way to try to preserve American society.

8

Oh Say Can You See

Hello! Remember me? Some people call me Old Glory, others call me the Stars and Stripes; also I have been referred to as the Star-Spangled Banner. But whatever they call me, I am your Flag, or as I proudly state, the Flag of the United States of America. There has been something that has been bothering me, so I thought I might talk it over with you. Because it is about you and me.

—Opening section of essay read by
Representative Nichols of Alabama in Congress on Flag Day, 1967

Emerson Moran, a Seneca County resident with media access and savvy, subscribed to Alice Larsen's and Father Shamon's theories about the peace camp women. "I think," he said, "that a lot of American women were duped; I think they were infiltrated by forces that were subversive to their main cause." The proof of infiltration was the method they used: "Their method definitely was tied in with an international movement which everybody knows was sponsored and encouraged by the Russians." If he began from the starting point Larsen and Shamon supplied, however, Moran moved past it, devising additional elements of plot and characterization that clarified and solidified the developing narrative. What is significant about Moran is not that he had remarkable personal influence over the events of the summer but rather that he made possible the implementation and circulation of a stereotypical but very desirable generic plot line.

In 1983 Emerson Moran was seventy-three years old, a retired business-man who had recently moved back to Seneca County after leaving it in his youth to work for nearly fifty years in the meat-processing industry. A few years before the encampment developed, Emerson (then sixty-seven) had been relieved of his responsibilities as the general manager of the Los Angeles plant of the Vienna Sausage Manufacturing Company. Although promoted to the position of West Coast vice-president, Moran lost much of his meaningful decision-making responsibility and became, as he called himself, "pitiful," or, according to his wife, "a doleful mess."

Carolyn Moran, his wife, was concerned about her husband's melancholy, but she also had a practical consideration: she knew, as he reminded her, that she needed to "find something to keep you busy after I'm gone, something that is going to bring in a little money" (Moran and Moran 1979:3). Thinking that she lacked marketable skills because most of her work had been in her home and in volunteer activities, Carolyn saw the solution in opening her own business. She decided on a mail-order jewelry business that she and Emerson named Moran Power, which, they said, expressed "the strength of our little branch of the family of God" (ibid.: 19). They sold jewelry based on a helicopter part called the Jesus nut, which keeps the rotor blade attached atop the helicopter. The Morans wrote a joint autobiography titled *Grandma, Grandpa, and the Jesus Nut* to explain the significance of this jewelry/helicopter part.

Despite various technical, physical, financial, and bureaucratic difficulties in getting the business going, the Morans persevered and today sell about forty different versions of the Jesus nut as tie tacks, key chains, rings, pendants, cuff links, and money clips. The Jesus nut is not a charm, the Morans say, but a reminder that there is a source of meaning, a way to make sense of the trials we all have to face. It does not solve problems; it just represents the idea that there is someone—Jesus—"holding the whole thing together." It is a symbol that instills a confidence that problems can be faced and dealt with creatively if one only trusts and believes in that "other power" which does not reside in and is not controlled by the individual human being. The Morans believe that many problems originate precisely in the unwillingness of the individual to recognize and obey a higher authority. Once people accept this authority, they achieve a confidence that enables them to find the cause of a problem and thus to understand its meaning. Understanding provides a sense of security even if the problem is not solved. One at least is on the right track and the solution may eventually be uncovered. This approach seemed to serve Emerson Moran well in all his dealings—business, religious, and personal.

The Morans left California in 1982 and settled in Romulus, Seneca County, New York. Because they would be able to bring Carolyn's business with them and also be closer to treasured East Coast relatives, they saw the move as most logical:

> It all makes such sound common sense that we should have thought out our old-age program by ourselves, starting with the miniature Jesus Nut and Moran Power two years back.
>
> It always looks that way after the Lord says, "Do," and the Lord says, "Go," and we answer, "We will!" (Moran and Moran 1979:128)

Emerson Moran followed the motto "What is right must be done" in making these decisions, and he carried this motto into his interactions with the women's peace encampment in 1983. What had to be done when Emerson Moran first heard of the upcoming peace encampment was to find out "just what sort of folks were moving in down at old Art Mc-Grane's place." The "natives were anxious" about the camp, Moran said, and so he made several attempts to acquire the means of judging the women's character and motives. Moran was able to contribute to the characterization of these women through several encounters he initiated in June and through later letters to the editor and interviews on television and radio and in the newspapers.

Moran first met the protesters when he visited the encampment in early June. He brought over a list of local churches and "undertook to invite them to attend church services in the area." In an interview broadcast on WSFW-FM, Seneca Falls, on July 29, 1983, Moran explained:

> I have made two gestures towards the campers. On the day following the announcement of the purchase of the old Art McGrane place I wrote to nine churches in the area requesting their permission to list them on an invitation to the campers to attend worship services with their neighbors. I spent several hours over a two week period preparing the invitation, which included a scale map of the county on which the churches were located with the distance of each from the camp. Several women reported to have accepted the invitation—I know two have attended the same church as do Carolyn and myself. We also spent over fifty dollars for the printing.

The maps read, "Come summer campers to worship with your neighbors at the Churches nearby." As Moran described, the maps showed the churches and asked, "How far is it to church?" The thousand or so map invitations seem to have been used, for Moran reported that the encampment requested more in July.

Moran's second gesture was the offer of an American flag. On June 9 he visited the encampment and spoke to some of the women:

I don't really know how I got into this but apparently it had occurred to me that I could get some kind of statement from the women if I went down and offered to give them a flag if they'd put it up. So I did, I went down, and I had a meeting in the yard there with three of the girls, and told them what I wanted to do, give them a flag. Two of them thought it was a great idea; third one thought, well, we have to take this up with the national committee.

Moran sent a note the next day confirming his offer. "Dear Ladies," he wrote,

This is to confirm my offer to Michelle yesterday at the campsite to provide you with an American flag for display on the porch of your house.

My reasons for the offer were discussed with Michelle and others during my visit. I'll procure the flag immediately on receiving your acceptance of my offer.

As he explained later, what he said to them was, " 'I want to give you a flag,' and I said, 'If you take it, why, I've already arranged for a press photographer to come and take pictures of it being put up, and if you don't take it, why, I'm gonna tell the people you wouldn't take it, period.' " He waited for their reply.

By this time the focus of activities for the peace encampment organizers had shifted from Philadelphia, New York, and Geneva to the peace camp land itself. Three of the organizers (Jody, Shad, and Michelle) in a 1985 interview recalled their early encounters with Emerson Moran and the American flag. They had perceived Moran's two "gestures" as hostile tests of their legitimacy:

Michelle: Eventually meetings started to shift to the hub [the peace camp land in Seneca County] because we wanted to centralize the activity, it had always been at New York or Albany or around, and this was going to be the first meeting at the house itself on the land. I believe it was June, the beginning of June. Up to that point a few of us had been doing outreach in the community, going to the fire station, eating dead bird [a derogatory term for chicken], and singing *God Bless America*.

Jody: In our best voices mind you. Because we're the representatives who are at the encampment, the only ones there, so we have to go because the fire chief had been by twice to invite us.

Michelle: So we were doing this kind of outreach to public meetings and there emerged this guy named Emerson.

Jody: Emerson Moran.

Michelle: Emerson Moran.

Jody: Now this goes back to what Shad was talking about, having to discuss the fact of agents and spies and the FBI and all those, being set up—because we get set up all the time.

Shad: I'm sure this is a classic example.

Michelle: So Emerson Moran starts dropping by. We had set the house up, where the front room would be, where the pamphlets were, and we encouraged community people to come and ask us what was happening. And good old Emerson was always pulling up in his big old eight-cylinder car and getting out of his gold whatever, and Emerson Moran was about fifty-six years old and patronizing as hell and he'd come out to see what we girls were doing. And we would spend countless hours talking to this man, I mean in a really nice way.

And we have women from Philadelphia who are in like corporate America, we have women from New York City in War Resisters League, we have a broad range of types sitting in this circle. We explained to him that this operates through consensus and he just happened to come at a time when everybody was represented at the encampment and our process was to bring it to the circle, talk about it, consense about it, and that would take us a day or two and we would get back to him. He said to us "Well, I really hope you take the flag because if you don't everybody's going to hear about it."

Jody: "I'm going to tell the media," laughing as he drives off. And he had never said more true words. Ever.

Although the organizers did not agree with all the things the flag traditionally symbolized, they felt it would be politically wise to accept and fly the flag. They took the issue to a group of women who met for several days in order to create a policy. The women discussed the symbolic content of the flag. They mentioned the association with violent and militaristic nationalism that they found unacceptable as well as the idea that the flag stands for the good things about the United States. Some women felt that an international peace camp should not fly the flag of just one nation; other women suggested flying the flag upside down as an international symbol of distress. Since the women could not reach consensus, they could not decide to accept Emerson Moran's offer. They did decide that any women coming to the encampment could create any kind of flag the size of a pillowcase and hang it on clotheslines on the front lawn. Throughout the summer participants made flags covered with drawings, words, and symbols. Some women flew pillowcases that were painted to resemble the American flag. The flag decision became a part of the encampment's "respected policies," but the issue was periodically raised at evening meetings that summer and for years to come.

Some of the organizers who were living at the encampment when Emerson Moran made his offer were frustrated that the consensus procedure had prevented acceptance of the flag:

> *Michelle*: The group would not let us take the flag and of course they all go home and we were stuck with having to write him a letter, why we don't want to take the flag when we really wanted to take the frigging flag. But we wrote him a letter saying all the reasons why we couldn't take the flag, and sure enough the next day in the *Pennysaver* is this big article about how we didn't take the flag.

> *Jody* [as if reading headline]: "Romulus women refuse flag."

> *Michelle*: Which of course meant we were commies, right? And it escalated from there and he went out and bought three thousand little miniature flags and gave everybody in town a flag. So when the opening day came it was twilight zone with all these flags, and women would call and say how do we get to the encampment and we'd say just come and go down and when you get to a house that doesn't have a flag, that's us (laughter).

The formal reply to Moran's flag offer came in the form of a letter signed by six of the Encampment organizers:

On behalf of everyone involved in the Seneca Women's Peace Encampment, I would like to thank you for your gracious offer to donate an American flag for the encampment. We have been greatly encouraged by the show of support we have received from you and other citizens of Seneca County, and we wish to continue a friendly and supportive relationship. For that reason I'm writing to explain why we will not be able to accept your donation and fly the flag.

Like many symbols, the flag means different things to different people, so that there was a wide diversity of opinion on this issue. Some of the women at our national meeting this week-end expressed that the flag symbolized to them their love of country, and therefore they supported flying the flag. Some women felt that to fly the flag would communicate to everyone that we are loyal United States citizens expressing our constitutional right to influence the decisions of our government.

Other women felt that there were other symbols that more accurately portray what the Peace Encampment is all about. The women who did not wish to fly the flag said that national flags are often a symbol of military victory, a symbol of conquest. Since we have a message to communicate to the whole world, and since our encampment is a gesture of support to the women's peace camps in England and other European countries, some of us expressed that the American flag is not an appropriate symbol for the work we are doing.

Much of the decision not to fly the American flag was based on the spirit and tradition carried on over the centuries by many respected religious and secular groups. There is a tradition within the peace movement to use international symbols of peace and justice rather than national flags, which emphasize boundaries between people.

I hope that you will accept our refusal of your donation in the spirit of American political dialogue. We believe that our actions here speak strongly for our concern and commitment to America: our openness about decision-making process, the hard work we are doing on the land, our participation in local town gatherings, our eagerness to comply with all local and state codes and regulations, our commitment not to interfere with the rights of other citizens, and our expression of our constitutional right to protest.

This letter was addressed and sent to Emerson Moran directly; it did not appear in local newspapers, but Moran responded to it with an open letter that was published in the last week of June in several newspapers:

This is an open letter to the Women's Encampment for a Future of Peace and Justice, located in Romulus:

Your letter of June 13 in which you refuse my donation of an American flag to fly over your encampment stares back at me from my desk. It takes more than one reading to begin to understand the reasons, to me specious, for spurning the flag as a suitable symbol of peace and justice.

You write that the rejection was by committee. The majority obviously grew up alongside a knee different than did we. Here at our house we fly the flag daily. Do you think that it is [our] symbol of militarism and conquest? No!

Our reason for flying the American flag is expressed in two quotations. One is from Abraham Lincoln's Second Inaugural Address:

" . . . the last best hope of earth. . . . The way is plain, peaceful, generous and just—a way which if followed the world will applaud forever and God must forever bless."

The other is included in the Pledge of Allegiance:

" . . . the Republic for which it stands, . . . under God . . . with liberty and justice for all."

Your decision to turn your back to your flag does not advance your cause. The real world that you come to influence begins at your doorstep and your decision has placed you at odds with your neighbors who believe that their country truly is the last best hope of earth.

Yet you write that you have more appropriate symbols of peace and justice. We at your doorstep will be interested to see the banners under which you have intruded among us.

We will watch especially for your international symbol guaranteeing the phrase with which your rejection ends—"our constitutional right to protest"!

Emerson Moran's careful response to the encampment's "rejection" letter helped set up more guidelines for interpretation of the women's actions and words. His claim that "it takes more than one reading to begin to understand" what the women were saying about the flag signaled the reader of his letter that the women were not really being open and forthcoming about their intentions. If something took several readings to understand, apparently it was not being presented honestly. Moran called the type of language and argument used in the women's letter "specious," suggesting that although the words might sound good, they were actually wrongheaded.

Moran also referred to the women's rejection of the flag as a "spurning," a term that indicates emotional contempt, not logical decision making. This emotionalism fits with a representation of the women as not living in the real world—the world they "came to influence." The women were seen as functioning outside the bounds of logic in an imaginative world often associated with women and children. In the real world people believed that "their country is the last best hope of earth," not an advocate of "militarism and conquest." Obviously these women could not be from this "real world"; in Moran's ironically poetic words, they "grew up alongside a knee different than did we."

Moran's letter introduced the important question of difference into the developing narratives. As the women themselves stated, "like many symbols, the flag means different things for different people." This was a serious point of contention for Moran because from his point of view the flag had very specific meanings for people who were *not* different, and these meanings were thought to remain stable over time, despite changes in context and challenges to those connotations. No interpretation of the flag was allowed under this scheme: its meanings were set and always would be. Rejection of these meanings, these well-known and widely accepted connotations, was a sure sign that something was, indeed, "different" and therefore wrong.

This position—that the flag should be taken literally as a sign for all that is good and true about America and that it be interpreted only in this light—was not new or unique to Emerson Moran. Indeed, as many Seneca County residents would note, this flag incident seemed similar to the last major national confrontation over the flag, which had also involved the question of who had the right to determine the content of this symbol. During the antiwar protests of the 1960s and 1970s, the American flag became a central symbol through which to express the disagreements of the era. These various stances seem to have been inspired in May 1966 when, it was reported, an American flag was burned during an antiwar demonstration in Central Park in New York City. Reaction was swift and widespread in the media and among the general public. One's relationship to the flag became a measure of one's patriotism. Construction workers, proclaiming their loyalty to America, began to wear flag symbols on their hard hats while antiwar activists and antiestablishment protestors criticized, ridiculed, and manipulated the image by utilizing it in clothing, body decorations, artwork, and bed sheets. In 1979 the district attorney in New York City closed an art show called the People's Flag Show, in which well-known artists used flag imagery for political criticism, and several artists were arrested for flag desecration. For the artists, Lucy Lippard explains, the main issue was "the extent to which the state can compel veneration of a state symbol and compel it to be treated as a sacred object without violating the First Amendment" (1972:51). Years later, in 1989, an art installation titled What Is the Proper Way to Display a U.S. Flag? caused a furor in Chicago because it included an American flag placed on the floor.

The United States Congress reacted to the 1960s flag "desecrations" by passing a federal law in 1967 that would make such acts punishable by imprisonment and fines. The proposal was debated for hours as every politician took the opportunity to make a statement about patriotism and the American way of life. Some of the comments in these 1960s House debates included:

> Mr Kuykendall [Tennessee]: Those Americans who have engaged in trampling the flag, burning it, spitting upon it, fail to realize the significance of their actions. Throughout the history of nations the flag has been the symbol of the principles upon which the particular nation has been founded. The very act of despoiling the flag threatens the foundations upon which the nation is built.

> Mr. Hall [Missouri]: In a land composed of all races and creeds from every corner of the earth, the "Stars and Stripes" are a single unifying force, representing the ideals and principles which bind so many diverse people together.

> Mr. McClory [Illinois]: The flag is the Government—it is all of the people. It is comparable to the Queen of England.

> Mr Baring [Nevada]: As I stood to pay my respects to these fine young men in uniform who have given so much in their devotion to our country [during a Flag Day ceremony], I was deeply choked with emotion. But this emotion was turned to anger as a mental picture of those dirty, long-haired, Communist-led beatniks burning the American flag in Central Park flashed before my eyes. These flag burners were not burning a piece of cloth, they were showing their hatred for America and for everything this great Nation stands for. (*Congressional Record*, June 20, 1967)

After a Supreme Court decision in 1989 that declared laws punishing flag "desecrators" unconstitutional, Congress again attempted to institute national flag laws. Again, the debates focused on the flag as a uniform, unifying symbol of America. As Congressman Hutchinson (Michigan) had stated in 1967, "The flag is the symbol of the Nation itself, and contempt upon the flag is contempt upon the United States themselves" (*Congressional Record*, June 20, 1967). If the stability of signs is supposed to be the hallmark of a well-ordered political system, as Terry Eagleton maintains (1986:1), their destruction must be an indication that the system is under attack.

Difference is precisely the issue and the problem here. If the women didn't understand or, worse, actively rejected these meanings, they had not properly learned why Americans fly the flag. Moran provided the women with a remedial civics lesson, explaining that the reason for flying the flag was contained in two quotations, one from Abraham Lincoln and one from the Pledge of Allegiance. The Pledge of Allegiance was used to support the idea that the flag physically stands in for the United States, that the flag functions as a literal sign of the nation and its way of life. In the Pledge of Allegiance, the flag is said to represent America as a nation and as a republic where the supreme power is ultimately in the hands of the electorate. In quoting Abraham Lincoln, Moran relied on a time-honored view of the United States as a special, unique nation with a "manifest destiny," to be a guiding example for the world.

This idea of a nation ordained by God has its roots planted solidly in the Calvinist ethos of the early New Englanders. They devised an origin story in which Americans are seen as God's chosen people, who have a compelling divine mission that must not be allowed to fail. This divine mission was not strictly religious, according to Sacvan Bercovitch, but "entailed a fusion of secular and sacred history" (1978:9). As Bercovitch explains, Americans read the country's destiny in its landscape and so, "despite its bewildering mixture of race and creed, could believe in something called an American mission, and could invest that patent fiction with all the emotional, spiritual, and intellectual appeal of a religious quest" (ibid.: 11).

This was not, however, the only interpretation of the American republic that has been important in American history. Arthur Schlesinger (1986) distinguishes this idea of America as a nation with a manifest destiny from the idea that it is a historical experiment. This idea derives from the notion that the decline and fall of the Roman Empire indicated that republics were doomed to fail. The founders were thus engaged in an experiment to test whether a republic could survive in defiance of history. Some feared the fate of Rome and "passionately ransacked the classical historians for ways to escape the classical fate" in which "time guaranteed decay" (ibid.:6, 10). This story of America as an experiment is also based in the

Calvinist ethos, but it emphasizes a different tenet of Calvinism, the belief that human beings are and must be constantly tested. The Calvinists believed that "life was a ghastly risk" (ibid.:6) and considered crisis the norm. In one sense the American errand or mission was always in process, always unfulfilled, always liminal, for its fulfillment would mean the end of history.

Schlesinger sees these two themes—America as a nation of divine destiny and America as an experiment with a questionable outcome—"in recurrent contention over the meaning of America" (1986:3). At present the divine-destiny theme seems to have cycled into ascendancy, and Americans perceive their country "as mankind's designated judge, jury, and executioner" (ibid.:16). Once the notion of the grand experiment functioned to "liberate its progeny from history," Schlesigner maintains, "history commenced on a new foundation and in American terms" (ibid.:16, 17). The new terms put aside historic determinism and gave America the status of "the elect nation, the redeemer nation," an indication of "God's effort to make a new beginning in the history of mankind" (ibid.:17, 19), to regenerate the world. Various contingencies of American and world history, which thrust the United States into a position of world power, "confirmed the hallucination" (ibid.:17). Whether Schlesinger has accurately traced its historical underpinnings or not, the notion of America as a nation of divine destiny is still important to national leaders. It is evident in President George Bush's rhetoric on U.S. intervention in Panama and Iraq, and in Ronald Reagan's remark in 1982: "I have always believed that this anointed land was set apart in an uncommon way, that a divine plan placed this great continent here between the oceans to be found by people from every corner of the earth who had a special love of faith and freedom" (quoted ibid.:16).

Emerson Moran echoed Reagan and other believers in "a divine plan" when he tried to explain to the women of the peace encampment the problem with their rejection of the flag: this nation must stand as a God-designated example for all the other nations of the earth. To question the most powerful symbol of this national destiny, the American flag, was to question both divine and secular order. America was not an experiment for Emerson Moran and Ronald Reagan; its destiny was not in question. As Moran saw in his own life, when the Lord says, "Go," and we answer, "We will," everything falls right into its proper place.

The notion of national destiny is a powerful doctrine that assumes an ordered and predictable universe, which is progressing, as the New England Calvinists would have been pleased to see, toward the perfected human being, the American. Even if we concede, as Bercovitch says we must, that this notion of destiny necessarily entails constant anxiety, unfulfillment, and liminality, it has nevertheless proven useful as an officially endorsed public myth. If the nation is seen as an experiment, however, it must be "perceived as one nation among many, liable like all others to angelic impulses and predatory lusts" (Schlesinger 1986:51). Moran logically read the refusal of the American flag as a challenge to the idea of a divine American destiny and the ideal of national perfectibility. For Emerson Moran, and later for his neighbors, to conceive of America as an experiment would be to admit into consideration "different" ideas and actions such as those of the peace encampment.

At some point while he was challenging the peace encampment women to fly the flag, Emerson Moran realized that his own neighbors were not regularly displaying Old Glory. This lapse was certainly not as serious as the rejection by the encampment, but it did present an inconsistency in the image of Americans that Moran was building. He decided that to maintain and strengthen the image he treasured, his neighbors would have to be gently reminded to fly their own flags. He took up the issue in a letter to the editor of the *Finger Lakes Times*, which appeared on June 14, 1983, and he sent copies of it to President Reagan, New York Governor Mario Cuomo, state and federal legislators, the Seneca Army Depot, and the American Legion and VFW posts of the area. After describing the potentially large crowds that might come into Seneca County for the summer's demonstrations, Moran asks his neighbors to envision the scene:

There is color in my vision of the scene—red, white, and blue. The citizens of the cities, villages, hamlets and farms have lined the streets and the roads with American flags. There isn't a house or business without our symbol of freedom. Here and there a flag flies from a barn.

So, there they go, carloads of demonstrators off to state their position in the summer ditches of Route 96, and waving back at them are our flags signaling our own message of belief. What a sight!

And what a thought! The real confrontation is within the heart and the mind. The dissidents may have some symbol of their fervent dedication; for sure we have ours. Let's present it, and proudly.

Come on! The flag is already up over our house. Unfurl yours. Go buy one. They are inexpensive and easy to find. Instead of a roadside debacle on Aug. 1, let us put on our fireside demonstration every day. Long ago they sang, "We will rally round the flag, boys, rally once again, shouting the battle cry of freedom." Let's do it!

Local residents at Waterloo bridge. Photo by Pam Quiggle

Moran had to exhort his neighbors in this way, he later explained, because it was not always easy for people to do what they should. But flag flying was not a criterion used to judge whether the local people were loyal Americans: their commitment to the American way of life was not being called into question. Perhaps the neighbors recognized, as Moran himself did, that flying the flag regularly was a difficult chore. Moran was sure his neighbors would show their true colors when reminded. Indeed, once they saw that flying the flag would make a point, his neighbors did not disappoint him.

Many took the opportunity to display the flag and their Americanism in a variety of ways in the next several weeks. *Finger Lakes Times* printed a July 4 centerfold of the American flag and encouraged local residents to put it up in their window. Flags started flying on businesses and residences and also showed up as decals in car windows. One resident who noticed the American flags on the beauty parlor, grocery store, and gas station in Romulus thanked the encampment women in a letter to the editor for reminding the locals to be patriotic. A visitor to the area, seemingly unaware of the controversy that had spawned the flag display, expressed her appreciation of the beautiful and omnipresent flags in a letter to the editor. The Waterloo VFW post donated to residents in Romulus about 250 of the little American flags that are used to decorate veterans' graves on Memorial Day. The residents used them to line the road from the peace encampment to the main gate of the army depot. Every time the women went to protest at that gate, they had to walk a mile or so down U.S. Route 96 between two knee-high rows of fluttering miniature Old Glories.

True to his word, Emerson Moran went to the press with the story of the women's "refusal" to fly the American flag. In print, radio, and television interviews, Moran explained the incident with great flourish. The stories accompanying the interviews tended to confirm the correctness of Moran's "test" by citing negative local reactions to the decision and by pointing to the flag issue as another ambiguity in the women's behavior. One article about the flag controversy, titled "Refusal of Flag Sparks Debate" (Syracuse *Post-Standard*, July 9, 1983), quoted Chet Todd, the owner of the barber shop in Romulus: "If we weren't a free country, they couldn't be doing this. If they were doing this in Russia they'd be shipped to Siberia. I imagine if you don't fly the flag, you don't have much love for America."

Accompanying the article was a photograph of Emerson Moran, shown handing out flags in downtown Romulus. The caption quoted Moran: "I told them the flag would communicate to the neighborhood that they aren't a bunch of crazy communist women, but Americans just like the folks who live here." Moran could point out, with undeniable logic, that his flag test had revealed the women to be just what he and his neighbors had suspected they were—bad Americans. As Moran later told the *Detroit Free Press*, "I put them on the spot. I made them declare themselves" (July 25, 1983).

Another article, titled "Flag Issue Raises Romulus Residents' Ire" (*Elmira Sunday Telegram*, July 3, 1983), showed a photograph of Emerson Moran with a flag sitting on his knee. The article quoted him. " 'It was a dandy flag... nice aluminum pole, with an eagle on top,' chuckled Emerson Moran, the erstwhile donor, 'and I sit here, flag on knee, waiting for them to change their minds and call and say they'll at least fly the flag on the Fourth of July.' " This article also suggested that the flag incident helped set the identity of these women: "The townspeople . . . say this only reinforces what some of them have thought all along: That some of the demonstrators are communists or are, at least, being used by communist forces." Other "evidence" in the article suggests the same thing:

And there was one more incident to add fuel to the fire. Moran was in the post office when one of the women came in and asked for stamps. He said the women didn't want stamps with the American flag on them.

"She said to the fella behind the counter, 'Don't you have something else?' And he gave a sheet with Martin Luther King but she wouldn't take the ones with the flags. Now, I can smile about that. But I also think that some of these kids are going too far in their thinking," said Moran.

What was interpreted as another damning bit of evidence came in the form of a comment from one of the peace encampment women on why she felt the flag had been rejected. In the first paragraph of the same July 9, 1983, Syracuse *Post-Standard* article in which Emerson Moran was shown handing out American flags, Dorothy Emerson, an encampment participant, was quoted as saying that the American flag means "terrorism, oppression, imperialism, economic rip-off." Although she was identified as only one of a hundred women at the encampment, her comments were taken as representative of everyone there and were used to justify local concerns. Many letters to the editor in the next several weeks responded directly to Dorothy Emerson's comments. "I was disgusted and particularly incensed," said one writer, "as were other veterans and just plain good American citizens, when I read the statement of one of the leaders of the supporters of the Andropov nuclear freeze plan whereby she states that the American flag means 'terrorism, oppression, imperialism, economic rip-off.'" (Syracuse *Post-Standard*, July 25, 1983)

Once Dorothy Emerson had spoken, the encampment women suddenly seemed to have a voice, an identifiable position that could be challenged and argued. Others took up the opportunity to address the encampment now that they had a recognizable enemy. In their letters to the editor and comments to the newspapers, local residents phrased more specific concerns about the encampment once they had a clear issue—the rejection and misinterpretation of the American flag—upon which to focus. For example, on July 25 the Syracuse *Post-Standard* ran a letter under the heading "Our Youth Has Lost Pride in Flag":

After reading the article, "Sparks Debate" July 9, I feel compelled to write in response. Dorothy Emerson was supposed to have stated that the American flag means, "terrorism, oppression, imperialism and economic rip-off." I can recall back in the early 1940's, as a young marine on Guadalcanal, Cape Glouster and Peleliu, seeing my friends and comrades give their lives, limbs, and life's blood fighting for that flag and our democratic way of life. At the age of 59 years, I still retain my nationalistic pride that makes my heart beat faster and my eyes water whenever I see our flag waving in the breeze. When they play the national anthem, I still feel so lucky to be living in the United States that my heart feels like it is about to burst.

Now I find myself thinking, maybe we were wrong after all. It seems that we were so busy to get back into the mainstream of life that we failed to instill in our children the pride in God and country that was our way of life in the good ole days. We didn't want our children to know the hard times, how precious a thing was when you had to work and sweat to earn it. We now find a generation of young who are used to the good life. If it feels good, do it. If you want it, tell Mom and Dad, they will get it for you. Forget the expense. Live for today. How can we expect them to be any different? They are what we made.

Our public officials have let us down mainly because we don't get involved. Let the other guy take care of it. Greed, corruption, passiveness, loss of respect for law and order have become a way of life. Divorce, abortion, rape, murder, child abuse, alcoholism, homosexuality, lesbianism—the list is endless. Our flag was not responsible for this. We did it ourselves. Now we must pay the penalty.

Until we decide to do something collectively to right these situations, we will have people like Dorothy Emerson damning our God, country and flag. As for me, I might be scoffed at, and no doubt will be ridiculed for my old-fashioned nationalistic pride; but until the day I die, and even on that day, I want my country's flag draped over my coffin. Yes I love my God, I love my country's flag, and above all I love my country for giving me the freedom to choose the other two.

One point that Moran and the women of the peace camp agreed on by the end of the summer was that the flag offer ended up being a test of the women's character. In a September 22, 1983, "open letter to Emerson Moran" (signed by six women with the disclaimer that they did not speak for the whole encampment), some of the women made clear their annoyance with Moran's summer-long accusations about flag desecrations at the encampment:

What was in your mind when you offered the flag to the women's peace camp in the first place? Was it truly a well-intentioned gift? Because your present seemed to be foisted upon the encampment as an attempt to coerce us—rather than given with kindness, out of a sense of friendship. By using a confrontatory manner and attempting to force us into a situation of acceptance, you have eliminated the purpose and joy of receiving, anything. If refusing to accept or acknowledge a present from an obviously unfriendly source with underlying motives (baiting and/or challenging) constitutes desecration, then pardon us.

The women concluded their letter with the question, "Next time, why don't you just send a pizza?"

9

Independence Day

Garlick's CHICKEN WINGS
served with Celery, Bleu Cheese & Crackers
Hot, Medium, Mild or Nuclear Hot
—Menu item in a restaurant
near the Seneca Army Depot

On July 4, 1983, some Seneca County residents decided to forgo the family barbecue, fishing and swimming in the Finger Lakes, or simply relaxing in their yards. They chose instead to spend the hot summer afternoon watching the opening day activities of the Seneca Women's Encampment for a Future of Peace and Justice. Several dozen residents, some sitting in lawn chairs, others leaning on cars and motorcycles, watched across the street from the main gate of the Seneca Army Depot on Route 96 in the southern part of Seneca County. Many said they had no interest in causing trouble or counterdemonstrating, but they were curious to see the women who had refused to fly the American flag on the Fourth of July.

At the encampment, the flag issue was still being discussed, and the opening ceremonies alluded to it, aptly illustrating the encampment's attitude. One woman led the five hundred or so women who had gathered there in a pledge of allegiance not to the flag but to the earth: "We pledge allegiance to the earth and the life she provides, one planet, interconnected, with beauty and peace for all."

Many of the local residents got their first glimpse of the protesters that afternoon. The women formed a column that spanned the width of Route 96 and walked the mile from the encampment farmland through Romulus

Opening day ritual at encampment. Photo by Pam Quiggle

to the main entry gate at the depot. As the column came into view of the gate, the onlookers saw that it was headed by a six-foot-six-inch-tall woman named Kim Blacklock, a resident of the nearby town of Geneva. Blacklock, though perhaps a familiar figure for some, presented an impressive sight as she led the marchers in her white sun dress and hiking boots. She was joined by a little girl wearing a sign that said, "Peanut butter, not bombs," and five hundred singing women who, when they got closer to the depot entrance, gave the local people their first taste of ritual protest.

Many of the women performed a slow-walk, twisting and turning their bodies slowly and almost agonizingly; the women took slow, heavy steps as they reached for and pulled each other toward the depot. The slow-walk looked painful but deliberate, restrictive and yet powerful as the women stretched their way down the road. All the while the women were singing, "All we are saying is give peace a chance," as Buddhist women who had walked to the encampment from Boston beat a regular rhythm on their flat drums. The women in the slow-walk passed two rose bushes—one red, one white—along to those at the front of the group who dug a hole near the depot gate and planted the two symbols of life. The hundreds of women gathered behind them cheered and held up their hands in a triangular shape (a sign called a yoni) that was coming to symbolize the women's resistance to the depot. Later, four veterans, some from the Vietnam era, came by and planted four little American flags near the bushes, saluted the flags, and walked away.

Women performing ritual slow-walk. Photo by Pam Quiggle

The rituals continued as some of the women tied themselves to the fence around the depot with ribbons and yarn. The women began "keening"— moaning, screaming and groaning—to express fear and anguish over the possibility of destruction by nuclear weapons. The entire crowd of women took up the keening, and cries and wails replaced the singing. Other women wove webs of yarn and ribbon into the fence and included in their webs pictures of loved ones and signs, including one that read, "My kids are growing up under a cloud of fear... and I am very afraid they may never grow up at all: Chris, age 10, Justin, age 8."

A woman called for silence and began the presentation of the encampment position statement to the depot. "I want to say that about a year and two months ago, about 350 women came to this army base and we made similar demands to the ones we are making today," she began. "They told us then to go home. We said, 'We're coming back, and we're going to bring our friends!'" She then read the prepared position statement:

To the Commander, Seneca Army Depot; the Secretary and Department of Defense; to the President
From The Women's Encampment for a Future of Peace and Justice

Encampment woman climbs SEAD fence and raises hand in "yoni" sign.
Photo by Pam Quiggle

Objects woven into depot fence. Photo by Pam Quiggle

We have gathered as women at the Seneca Army Depot to challenge the nuclear threat represented by the weapons stored here. We have come to stop their deployment. As first strike weapons, they lead us one step closer to planetary annihilation, by making nuclear confrontation and intervention more likely and by rendering a freeze impossible. As we speak today, our voices express the hopes and fears of women throughout the world. At England's Greenham Common and in many other places, women have gathered to protect [*sic*; mistake in written copy only] the deployment of weapons which turn communities into targets. Everywhere, we are struggling against tyranny and the madness of war—in South Africa, the Middle East, Latin America and elsewhere.

The increasing poverty of women throughout the world is directly and fiscally connected to military expenditures. As U.S. women, we have seen essential programs slashed in Food Stamps, Health, Education, Aid to Families with Dependent Children, Child Care and others. As workers, we also suffer from the channeling of national resources into military enterprises rather than into productive ventures that could create employment. Under this system, women of color suffer most by any measure, both here and abroad.

The militarization of the U.S. is supposed to be for our protection, but we question who is safe under this system. Certainly not us, not the earth, not our children who may never grow up. War against women is waged daily through rape and violence. What we experience individually is now magnified to a global scale where our very survival is in question.

Seneca has a rich tradition of women's resistance. In 1590, Native American women of the Iroquois confederacy gathered to demand an end to war among the nations. The year 1848 saw the first convention of women's rights advocates at Seneca Falls. During slavery, Harriet Tubman, a black woman, led her people to freedom along the Underground Railroad.

Today we come to Seneca again, in numbers, in strength, in peace. Like the women from Upstate New York who last year protested the storage of the neutron bomb, we come because we will not permit the continuing escalation of military violence with all of its consequences for us and our sisters and brothers. We will continue to act nonviolently in solidarity with women and men elsewhere, in keeping with our heritage.

—We demand to know what weapons are stored at the Seneca Army Depot, and to know what dangerous substances are transported through this community.

—We demand the dismantling of every weapon stored at SEAD, and the Depot's conversion to non-military purposes, providing jobs for the local community.

—We demand a halt to deployment of the Cruise and Pershing II missiles and an immediate freeze of all nuclear weapons.

We will continue to act, at Seneca and around the world, until we are answered. We bring bread and roses as a symbol of the alternative world we are working towards where both the body and spirit are nourished rather than threatened with extermination. The Army Depot's motto is Mission First, People Always; ours will be Our Mission is Always People.

A woman civilian depot guard came forward at the request of the encampment women to accept the statement and also the loaf of bread offered "as a symbol of solidarity." The encampment women themselves took more bread and passed it around, each woman taking off a piece for herself. The women then continued alternately keening, singing, and performing ritualized movements.

These ritual aspects of the protest were a significant feature throughout the summer. If the local people were expecting only the marches, speeches, and signs associated with the types of protests they might have seen on television, they must have been surprised at the elaborate, exciting, colorful, noisy, and often bizarre street theater that made up a good proportion of the protest activities. The ritualized behavior included Singins, dancing, masks and makeup, costumes, signs, and symbolic movements including actions like die-ins during which protesters lie on the ground like the casualties of a nuclear explosion. The protest rituals were performed for both pragmatic and symbolic reasons. In practical terms, the protests created the encampment as a witness to nuclear weapons storage in Seneca County. The rituals were designed to get attention for both local nuclear issues and global ones, and indeed they succeeded, for they made "good copy" for the news media. As the work of anthropologist Victor Turner (1967) has suggested, every society uses ritual to draw attention to a crisis and to resolve it or come to terms with it. Ritual thus does not separate people from "real" action; rather, it is the form much public human action must take if it is going to be meaningful to both participants and observers.

Pragmatic actions may be combined with symbolic ones in order to evaluate the crisis situation and restore the society to peace and order, or create a new kind of order. In symbolic terms, the ritual protests helped translate values, beliefs, and ideas into tangible sounds, visual elements, movement, tastes, and objects that are useful for the evaluation of individual and group life. Rituals provide the means of enacting the very conflicts that threaten to disrupt a community; they then attempt to resolve these conflicts symbollically in order to reintegrate the participants into the revised or renewed social world.

An example of one ritual performed during the summer illustrates the significance of ritual for these encampment goals. In July women from

Marching to main gate of SEAD. Photo by Pam Quiggle

Encampment women posing at the site of the first women's rights convention in Seneca Falls. Photo by Pam Quiggle

Massachusetts came to the encampment and planned and performed a two day "laundry ritual." One Saturday afternoon, fifteen to twenty of the women traveled to a laundromat in Seneca Falls that stands on the site of the Wesleyan Chapel where the first women's rights convention was held in 1848. Parts of the old chapel still exist in the rear of the building and a sign and a plaque mark the historic spot. The women went into the laundromat with their own laundry and while their clothes washed they hung up signs in the laundromat window which protested various women's issues. Each sign was headed "Dirty Laundry":

Dirty Laundry
1 out of 3 women will be raped

Dirty Laundry
I want to be a grandmother someday

Dirty Laundry
Women do ⅔ of the world's work and get ⅓ of the wages

Dirty Laundry
Women own less than 5% of the world's resources

Dirty Laundry
Women earn $.59 for every dollar men earn

Dirty Laundry
Women have been virtually unrepresented in Congress for 200 years

Dirty Laundry
The life we save may be yours

While their laundry was washing, the women argued with the manager of the laundromat, who demanded that they take their signs down. She said that the women were trespassing on private property and did not have the permission of the owner to put up the signs. The [protesters tried to persuade the manager to read the signs, and eventually she did so, but she insisted they take them down when their laundry was done because the signs would keep other customers away. The women sat on the sidewalk in front of the laundromat and composed and sang protest songs while their clothes dried. They also attempted to get the guard from the National Park Service down the street to clean off the plaque commemorating the Wesleyan Chapel, but decided it was better left with a patina of age on it.

At seven-thirty the next morning, the same group of women went to the army depot for the second part of their ritual. They took the same signs they had hung in the laundromat window and hung them on the depot fence, weaving them with yarn. Many of the protesters dressed as washerwomen, an idea they had borrowed from the Bread and Puppet Theater, which had performed at the encampment and the depot the day before. The washerwomen took tubs of clothing (mostly children's clothing) and ritually, in slow motion, scrubbed the clothes and hung them on the depot fence. The entire ritual was performed in silence until the laundry was completed. The women then sat in a circle, wailed and keened and sang songs. They created circles and spirals when they got up again and sang more encampment and patriotic songs. When the women felt the ritual had been completed, they headed to a local diner for breakfast.

This ritual, like many others, was more meaningful for the participants than the observer. For the encampment women, the two-day ritual combined practical activity (getting their dirty laundry done and visiting a historic women's site) with a highly symbolic ritual action and protest about women's issues. This combination reiterated the feminist theme that the personal is political, that the public and private spheres are not separate and unrelated entities. The ritual also served to affiliate the Massachusetts affinity group with other women at the encampment, especially when they reported about the ritual at the evening meeting.

The audience in Seneca Falls consisted of the people who came into the laundromat and those few people who saw the women sitting on the street. At the depot on Sunday morning, the audience consisted of the group of soldiers guarding the section of fence (not the main gate) where the ritual was performed, my own video crew, and a European film crew. A series of jeeps drove up to the area, and each soldier repeated into his radio to his commander the same description of the action: "There are 24 females and 1 male [an observer]. They are hanging laundry all over the fence, taking a lot of pictures, not doing much of anything." Soldiers on foot patrol called the women "lowlife communist trash," took down the American flag someone had put up as laundry, and banged the fence with the clubs they were carrying.

The encampment itself can be seen as a ritual event because its mere existence was a continuing cultural critique and a challenge to the established order. A ritual, especially as exemplified by the rite of passage, has three aspects: a separation from everyday life that leads to an evaluation of that life; a liminal state in which the rules of society are overturned; and a reintegration into a new or renewed social order. The ritual separation for the encampment women was accomplished in several ways. The remote, rural location provided most women, especially those from distant or urban areas, an immediate sense of ritual space. Women were also generally separated from their jobs and families and from the roles they played in everyday life. They had, for a day, a week, or a whole summer, new jobs to do and different roles to play. The encampment farm, called "the Land," was protected from outsiders, especially males, and was defined as a place to join with others who wanted to remove themselves from a nuclear-mad society in order to critique it.

The reintegration back into social life took place for most women when they left the encampment to return home. Some went back to lives that were essentially unchanged; others restructured their lives because of their encampment experiences; many got more actively involved in antinuclear protests and education. For many the experience was personally fulfilling and transformative as well. As one woman explained,

The thing that I left with in '83 was the realization that I'm an activist no matter what I'm doing. . . . I, inside of me, had this ability and need to work through some of the spirit of Seneca. It was that feeling people talk about sometimes, political circles growing like concentric circles, like throwing rocks into ponds and having concentric circles grow and intertwine until the whole lake is covered with circles. It's almost that feeling that I'm one of the circles myself, and when I left here I really felt empowered, that I was really energized, and really a legitimate activist and it became part of my identity.

Between the ritual processes of separation and reintegration, the encampment offered participants an opportunity to pass through a state of liminality as well, a state of transition and reflection. As Victor Turner notes, in the liminal state participants in ritual "are withdrawn from their structural positions and consequently from values, norms, sentiments and techniques associated with these positions. They are also divested of their previous habits of thought, feeling and action. During the liminal period, neophytes are alternately forced or encouraged to think about their society, their cosmos, and the powers that generate and sustain them" (1969:105). During this part of the ritual people seem to "be themselves" as they drop all the pretenses and rules of everyday life. At the encampment, women were encouraged to put aside the regular roles they used for life in the patriarchy and were asked to live an alternative life based on female principles. The women of the encampment, like all who are placed in the liminal state, spent much of their time in reflection about the system that had brought them to this place. This reflectiveness was encouraged through daily protests and discussions and through workshops on topics ranging from nuclear weapons production to nonviolence, herbal medicine, homophobia, and racism. Through these workshops participants could evaluate the established society and compare it to the alternative world represented by the encampment.

Because the liminal state places people "betwixt and between the positions assigned and arranged by law, custom, conventions, and ceremonial," those who are experiencing this liminal state are "necessarily ambiguous, since this condition and these persons elude or slip through the network of classifications that normally locates states and positions in cultural space" (Turner 1969:95). Turner has shown that in the liminal state, as opposed to the established social condition, people tend to experience equality. Status, rank, and property are absent; participants are either naked or they dress uniformly. Sexual distinctions are minimized and personal appearance disregarded. The hallmarks of the liminal are sacredness, spontaneity, foolishness, simplicity and unselfishness (ibid.).

A workshop at the encampment

The collective organizational principles at the encampment prevented the establishment of rank and status and fostered the sense of equality. All activities were nonhierarchical and participatory, from daily workshops and decision-making meetings to associations with the news media and the public. Although a staff took responsibility for certain of the camp logistics, all major decisions were made by consensus. Moreover, the simple communal camping conditions helped to minimize distinctions of property, rank, and status among the participants. Most of the women lived in tents (or an occasional wigwam or teepee) in a communal camping area. Simple camping arrangements were admired as much or more than expensive or elaborate ones; there were no motorized or electrified camping vehicles. The women were encouraged to participate in the maintenance of the camp by recycling all rubbish and by signing up for daily "work webs."

The symbolic equality of the encampment women was also reinforced by the similar physical appearance many of them adopted, a look unlike that traditionally associated with women in the outside world. Their casual, comfortable, and practical clothing, unstyled and often severely

Ritual die-in at SEAD main gate. Photo by Pam Quiggle

short hair, and shunning of makeup contrasted dramatically with the well-known media images of the ideal, successful, or acceptable woman. Indeed, the encampment women looked very different from the other women around them—local women, tourists, and other female visitors. Like others in the liminal state, they minimized sexual distinctions, most notably, perhaps, through the all-female construction force that built the camp and continued to work on it during the summer. The impression of sexual crossover from the unusual sight of women directing and participating in construction work was reinforced when the workers (and others) shed their shirts to cool off on hot days.

Individualism, the hallmark of the outside world, generally gave way to community concerns and activities even though women were still considered personally responsible for their actions. The practical and economic rationales for the regularly scheduled communal meals and gatherings are undeniable, but perhaps the most important effect of communal events was to reinforce the goals and political message of the encampment. The evening communal meal, for example, ensured that all would in theory have equal access to the same types and amounts of food; women who brought their own food were encouraged to donate it for sharing at this common meal. The regular evening meeting invited information sharing, and reports of daily protest activities praised the importance of working with others toward the goals of the encampment. Women planning protest actions at the army depot were encouraged to form "affinity groups" to provide "support and solidarity for their members" (*Resource Handbook* 1983:40). The *Resource Handbook* identified such groups as "probably the oldest and most ubiquitous form of organization by people seeking to make a better world" (40). The evening meeting also allowed for group decision making and a demonstration of the consensus process, and meetings often ended with a ritual circle.

The protest actions of the women of the encampment generally incorporated elements that tried to communicate these aspects of liminality to the participants and to the viewers. Liminal rituals would be expected to reflect contempt for the old social order and desire for the new, and so it was with the encampment rituals (and the encampment as a whole). They emphasized the importance of critiquing the established society instead of supporting it blindly. But it was the challenges to the existing social order that made the encampment seem so dangerous.

10

What Did You Bring?

Documentation of the encampment activities through written records and visual images was extensive and well organized. This documentation was used to legitimate as well as advertise the encampment and its goals. Women media producers and artists from around the world recorded the events, people, and processes of the summer of protest. The major video project was that of the Boston Women's Video Collective, which covered the peace camp from the initial planning early in 1983 to its official ending on Labor Day, 1983.

Since Boston was covering all the encampment's major events, my video partner (Nancy Zucchino) and I decided to cover the everyday lives of the women who had come to participate. Instead of focusing on protests, we recorded mealtime activities, women preparing their camping areas, camp maintenance, and other routine events. We wandered through the encampment and asked the women, "What did you bring with you to the encampment?" We asked this open-ended question so that they could say whatever they wanted about their reasons for being there, the encampment's activities, or the living conditions. Many women expressed surprise at the neutrality of the question, noting that it did not have the same political nature as the questions asked by other interviewers.

The following answers to our question were recorded on videotape during interviews conducted by Zucchino and myself in early July and late August 1983. The answers indicate the different types of women attending, their varied reasons for being there, their relationships with other women, and their expectations about the encampment's physical facilities and political activities.

> Woman: What a question! You mean physically or spiritually or just answer the question? Well I brought a real curiosity and interest and I brought some experience with the nuclear freeze and WILPF. I don't

know, I just came up here expecting to meet with people and learn some things and find some musicians. I'm a musician.

Woman: I brought with me a desire to see my daughter, who is here. And also a desire to share with other women some of their thoughts and views on peace and feminism.

Her daughter: And I brought all my worldly possessions. Which isn't much. I brought my cat, who lives with me in my tent, my mother who came to visit, and a willingness to put my self in a place where I really thought I could empower myself and grow.

Woman: I think in the abstract. A lot of garbage from the male chauvinist world that we're dealing with and talking about. And a lot of it that we weren't even aware of, that we're becoming aware of very quickly, and it's causing a lot of thinking. We just got here last night, but it's been a really already a very good mind-expanding experience.

Question: How long do you plan to stay?

Woman: We can only stay until Tuesday morning. So I guess we'll have to expand pretty fast [laughter]. But I guess that's the biggest thing I'd say on an abstract level. And a lot of interest in getting everything we can while we're here as far as experiences and broadening and more feelings about feminism and non-violence and direct action, and all that sort of thing.

Woman 1: Only what was absolutely necessary. You want me to be more specific? A tent and sleeping bag and a change of clothes and three books, in case I got bored with one of them I wanted to be able to read another. And my journal, which goes with me everywhere, and food. I forgot to bring a cup, a couple of utensils and a tin plate.

Woman 2: Can I answer that? Jill has forgotten to mention that she brought her lover and her friend with her which is obviously the first thing of importance, right? And her political co-worker.

Woman 1: And also, my bicycle. So that I could take off if I didn't want to be here.

Woman: What did I bring with me? A big desire to find out what the encampment was all about, to feel what it was like to be among so many women, that's what I brought with me, and a toothbrush.

Question: So, what did you find here?

Woman: I've never been in such a crowd of women, it's just been wonderful. There's a lot of solidarity and just this feeling of being encompassed by a very loving group. You know, noncompetitive, just a very loving group. It's been great.

Woman: I brought a lot of confusion. And I still have a lot of confusion, about exactly what the peace encampment is. I think it's confirmed my commitment to nuclear disarmament which is really good. I brought a lot of love. Got a lot of hugs. I had a great time last night; I was security until six in the morning with the walkie-talkie and that was great too.

Woman: Well, I've been traveling for about a week before I got here so my car is mainly full of dirty laundry. But I also have some books and particularly a book that I was reading to the people that I came with last night, a Margaret Atwood book. And some food, which I bought on the way down, because I heard that you couldn't buy food around here. And my cereal bowl.

Woman 1: Sleeping bags, and clothes.
Woman 2: Food.
Woman 1: Food, food, we brought a lot of food.
Woman 2: Artichoke hearts, cheese, salami, bread.
Woman 3: Only some of us eat salami.
Woman 1: Some of us eat salami.
Woman 2: A salmon salad.
Woman 1: We're going to donate it to the kitchen.
Woman 2: Yeah, whatever we have left over.
Woman 1: That's one reason why we brought a lot.
Woman 2: I brought a book.
Woman 1: And that's about it, all we brought. And each other.
Women in unison: Each other [laughing].
Woman 2: Like five of us.
Woman 3: And our car.
Woman 1: Our car.
Women in unison: Which we can't get into! [laughing].
Woman 1: Cause we lost the keys! So we might stick around for a little more time [laughing].

Woman: We're traveling for two weeks after this so we brought the kitchen sink. We brought the chairs, because we're going to a music festival. We brought food, we brought a mattress to sleep on, you know one of those inflatable ones that takes about ten hours to fill up. We brought a cooler with food in it, although the food is getting warm because the ice pack broke. What else is in our car? We heard it was going to go down to zero so I have my down parka. A little Sterno so that Judy can make her tea at night. And a lot of utensils to eat with, from Wendy's. Sterilized.

Woman: Spirits of love, and a lot of excitement. A real feeling of openness. A lot of support, for what's going on here. Sleeping bags, tent.
Her son (age 11 or 12): Well, obviously a car.
Woman: Lots of food. Actually we were going to bring a camera because my son wanted to do a mini-documentary and I was the one who left the film at home. Greetings from Syracuse, because there are a lot of women who are in support of what's going on here. Plus a map that was printed in the *Herald-Journal* to show us exactly how to get here.

Woman 1: I brought my guitar. Food, clothes. My sisters.
Woman 2: No, we brought ourselves.
Woman 1: No, I brought you. And a book to write in.
Woman 3: I brought a shitload of diapers. Oh, some clothes and food. I have this little baby.

Woman 1: I brought a book of Starhawk spells. I brought my basic food and water and books.
Woman 2: I brought some snacks because I knew there wouldn't be any here. I brought some books and a journal. It's really important to me to have that space and be able to keep in touch with all that, because I'm having a hard time doing that. That's another thing I should have brought with me was more time for myself.

Woman 1: I brought a desire to learn more from women of color, who are here, and who have been leading the struggles in this country for so many generations. I feel I have a great deal to learn from them.
Woman 2: Lots of physical stuff that I really needed. I was feeling a little burdened by that, by having to think about where it is and such things. But the other aspects, curiosity, since I really didn't know what to expect when I got here. I had some expectations, and some of them have been borne out and some not. And I also had a desire to talk to people about those expectations and I guess I'm finding my opportunities kind of limited. There are people who have said several times at orientations and general meetings that it's very easy to feel like a fifth wheel here and I haven't found that that feeling has gone away.

Question: Why is that?

Woman 2: Because it seems to me people who have been here for a while have already developed friendships and maybe don't take time to talk to people who are relatively new. And I just don't see very many people talking about things.

Question: Have you thought about bringing that up at a general meeting?

Woman 2: Well, I guess it could be done. I'm not sure, I've only had the experience of one general meeting, and it seems to be largely occupied with the mundane details of surviving here from day to day, and not very much occupied with any of the many reasons that we're here. I had been here almost twenty-four hours before anybody said anything at all about making a presence of some kind at the depot. I mean, granted it was a day that we had devoted to something that was very, very important; but I just thought it took quite a while.

Woman 1: I'm studying to be a rabbi, which is one of the reasons why I brought some [religious things]. I really want women to know that women can be rabbis and there are about sixty-five women rabbis in the world right now.

Woman 2: The first generation.

Woman 1: The first generation, ever, in history. So God willing, I'll be ordained in two years. It's a five-year program after a bachelor's degree. There was another woman here yesterday who was also studying with me, and it's great, it's really great to be here, and the women's community needs clerics and healers and lots of people so we'll all find our way to do it, but that's my way right now.

Woman: What did I bring with me? My cat. Well, you know, I can't leave home without my cat. My tent. And a lot of leaflets. And clothes and some food and my van, which is what I live in when I'm not living in my tent. A lot of despair, which has now been turned into hope. And myself. I thought this was going to be one of the political questions. I was all geared up to answer one of the political ones.

Woman 1: What did we bring with us? Tissues!
Woman 2: Materially or spiritually?
Woman 1: I brought tissues.
Woman 2: Did you bring enough for the whole camp?
Woman 1: I have two boxes. That's all.
Woman 2: Oh well. One sheet a woman!

Woman 3: Well, your usual basic tent, sleeping bag, clothes, towels, dishwashing coconut soap, tarot cards, three hundred T-shirts.

Woman 4: About thirty loaves of bread. We brought bread from Baba's bakery. Zucchini from the garden.

Woman 1: Oh no, not more zucchini.

Several women speaking at same time: Red Magic markers. We brought our spirit! We brought journals. We brought books, we brought flashlights that don't work any longer. Yeah, we brought extra batteries. We brought insect repellent. A cooler. We brought our friends and co-workers. Peanut butter, tahini, bread, Triscuits, fruit, granola bars, and cantaloupes and the cantaloupe is almost gone. Would you like a piece?

Woman: I brought hair-cutting tools.

Woman: Pass me a tissue?

Woman: I brought my artwork, my skills, and I have been creating structures here. Let's see, my motherliness; I like being in the kitchen and cooking hundreds, for hundreds of people.

Woman: I brought my tent, my sleeping bag, my fiddle, a book to read, my water bottle, rain gear, just a raincoat, shorts and a bathing suit, too many heavy shirts, in case I got cold, my towel, I always bring my towel, some handkerchiefs, a small first aid kit, some money, my passport, some incense and a little crystal thing from Betty. And I brought one pretty, long fluffy dress, in case we ever go dancing or something, and some music books because I like to do that. And my handbook from the encampment, and some plain thirteen-cent post-cards, in case I had to write to people and tell them I was arrested or something.

Woman: I brought a tent, and a bunch of camping gear, and a child and a friend, and her child, and some hopes for the future, and some ideas too. My ideas were that women could do something, that there was an upswelling movement for peace that was coming at the hand of woman, and I thought that we would all be here learning together what that looked like, what that meant.

Question: Have you seen that happening?

Woman: I've seen it a lot, I've seen a lot of women really dedicated to peace, and really giving it everything they had, to come up with ideas.

Woman: I brought a history of having become a little impatient with the very legal, accepted way of working, petitioning and lobbying congressmen. We even changed the congressman in our district because we didn't like his attitude towards the freeze. And the peace people and the environmental people changed our representation. It made us feel good for a while until we realized that we hadn't done anything about a single cutback in nuclear weapons production. And it became obvious to me that if I was going to respect myself as a peace worker I had to come here. I also brought three tents, a porta-pottie for the children's child-care area, a big cooler for the main kitchen, and my car which has been used by everybody and I feel good to be able to make positive, material contributions to the camp.

Woman: Oh, what did I bring with me? I brought some skills that I wanted to use, and I brought my guitar, and I brought this book that taught me how to make a wigwam and I did it. And I brought me.

I I

Innocents Abroad

Sharon said, when she came back, "I feel as if I was cheated. I was going there to meet people like you."

—Lucinda Talbot

The encampment invited women of all political, sexual, philosophical, ethnic, racial, and religious persuasions to join in the summer of protest. Since the encampment did not collect reliable information on the backgrounds of the women who attended, however, it is impossible to know the range of differences among them. Nevertheless, one incident suggests both that different kinds of women did indeed come to the encampment and that the encampment was not always able to deal with the significant differences that appeared in its community.

Early in July, Sharon Chapman and Lucinda Talbot, both from Elmira, New York, held an impromptu press conference on the encampment's front lawn to explain their reasons for leaving. Unlike most women, who came and went quietly and somewhat anonymously throughout the summer, announcing their arrival and departure only to friends and lovers, Chapman and Talbot gave the public news media vivid accounts of their encampment experiences.

By July 10 these two women, who had arrived for the encampment's opening on July 4 and had participated in encampment activities for the whole first week, felt strongly that they wanted and needed to leave. During the week following their departure, accounts appeared in several local newspapers about Talbot's and Chapman's experiences, in which the women explained that they had left the encampment because of their revulsion against the unpatriotic "lesbian-vegetarian-witches" there, who also desecrated the American flag. The *Ithaca Journal* article, which appeared on July 12 under the headline "Two Leave Romulus Women's Camp, Claiming Members Practice Witchcraft," was typical:

> Two Elmira women left the Women's Encampment for a Future of Peace and Justice in Romulus Sunday, claiming protestors there called themselves witches and are "intolerant."
>
> Lucinda Talbot, 31, said she and Sharon Chapman, 32, were criticized when the two objected to women stamping on an American flag.
>
> Talbot said they were disturbed with activities in the camp, including what she described as singing in a circle and howling. Many women wore necklaces with double axe blade pendants that the women said was a symbol of worship, she said.
>
> "They told us it was witchcraft," Talbot said.
>
> She said the women had woven colored yarn "as a way of increasing their power."
>
> But camp member Diana Mueller of Burlington, Vt., said the weaving is an expression of unity among different viewpoints in the camp.
>
> Another camp member, who identified herself as Shad, said the pendants are an ancient symbol of matriarchal history. She said some of the camp members practice what they call witchcraft, but she added, "There's a big difference between Satanism and white witchcraft."
>
> Ann Jochems, of Brooktondale, said Talbot and Chapman did not get along with "committed" camp members. With no official directors at the camp, "It's hard not to have strong leaders emerge," she said.
>
> The two women spent about a week in the camp, and by last weekend were unable to converse with the other camp members, Jochems said.
>
> Talbot, a Quaker, said the women "worship a goddess" and are "very much opposed to God."
>
> "They are tolerant of their own beliefs, and if you don't believe what they do, they put you down for it," she said.
>
> Talbot said that at a consensus meeting, the women agreed not to desecrate the American flag. But later, she said, she found some women stamping on a flag.
>
> She said she objected to the flag "desecration" because "Some Sisters that are feminists and pacifists do believe in this country."
>
> Talbot said she plans to form a group in Elmira "to pray for the camp."

The stories Talbot and Chapman told about what they found frightening, perverse, and threatening about the encampment spread rapidly the first week after the encampment opened. Because the Elmira women had, at least temporarily, been encampment insiders, their accounts seemed to provide a unique view of previously hidden aspects of the encampment activities.

Chapman and Talbot felt their problems with encampment women had begun even before they got to Romulus. When a group of women who were walking from North Carolina to the encampment for the opening ceremonies passed through Elmira, Talbot and Chapman had joined the marchers. The other women had set a pace that the two from Elmira couldn't match, had refused to talk to Chapman and Talbot, and had offered them unappealing food to eat. Talbot and Chapman were soon hot, tired, sore, and discouraged. They decided to abandon the marchers and drove to the encampment, but when they arrived they were told that they could not drive their car to the back camping area but had to carry all their equipment and possessions by hand. Soon, physical trials and discomfort gave way to a sense of alienation as Chapman and Talbot became aware that feminist spirituality, witchcraft, vegetarianism, and lesbianism were practiced at the encampment and that many participants harbored what the two from Elmira considered to be anti-American sentiments. Chapman and Talbot freely associated these practices, assuming that they were related because they all occurred in the same place:

Talbot: Unless I saw somebody kissing somebody or they happened to mention that they were a lesbian witch, I didn't call them a lesbian witch unless they told me so.

Question: You're making a connection between the term *lesbian* and witch; if a person was one, were they the other?

Talbot: Usually.

Question: Yea?

Talbot: I don't think there were any heterosexual witches.

Chapman: No, I don't think so.

Talbot: I mean I saw one witch who wasn't vegetarian, or if she was she was maybe trying to wean herself off meat, I don't know, cause she was eating vegetable beef soup. And she blushed when I mentioned it to her; so she probably was trying to wean herself off meat.

In connecting lesbianism and witchcraft to food, the two women were employing a common code for talking about what appeared to be somewhat shocking and unfamiliar subjects. They could use food sharing, food preferences, and the symbolic use of mealtimes as a shorthand to convey some of the dramatic differences they perceived between their own habits and those of the encampment. Food provides a particularly telling device for voicing differences because it is a conventionalized way to express concerns about larger social issues. According to anthropologist Mary Douglas, "If food is treated as a code, the messages it encodes will be found in the pattern of social relations being expressed. The message is about different degrees of hierarchy, inclusion and exclusion, boundaries and transactions across boundaries. Like sex, the taking of food has a social component, as well as a biological one. Food categories therefore encode social events" (1975:249). Through food codes we feel we can see and judge various political, social and cultural tastes and inclinations. What people eat is thought to be a good sign of who they are. As Sidney Mintz explains, human beings believe that "food preferences are close to the center of their self-definition: people who eat strikingly different foods, or similar foods in different ways are thought to be strikingly different, sometimes even less human" (1985:3). Chapman and Talbot took the food habits of the encampment as an indication of who the encampment women "really" were and what relationship could be developed with them.

The two attributed the distaste they felt for the encampment's food choices to a fundamental disagreement over food preferences. The encampment favored vegetarianism, but Chapman and Talbot considered themselves omnivores. Talbot explained: "They called people who weren't vegetarians carnivores. I tried to explain to them that it was omnivore for the simple reason that human beings do eat vegetables too." Talbot and Chapman thus identified the normal human being as omnivorous and perceived vegetarianism as somewhat abnormal. They complained about the blandness and unfamiliarity of vegetarian meals and worried about the potential nutritional dangers of avoiding meat:

Chapman: The meals were very bad, really. We're talking serious nutrition now.

Talbot: Well, you've got to remember too that they were cooking over an open fire.

Chapman: Yeah, they had some potato salad, at least they alleged it was potato salad, but it tasted like they dumped vinegar on it. And they had stuff with a lot of curry in it, and that tasted kind of weird too. And you know, before we even went up there we asked and we were assured that there would be provisions made for people who liked to eat meat. And after we got there we were told that "we don't like to slaughter animals for food; therefore you can't have meat because it offends some of us."

Talbot: I was told the smell of cooking meat offends them. And it wouldn't hurt people to eat a vegetarian diet. And it doesn't hurt people to eat a vegetarian diet provided that they follow the balanced food group type of thing.

Chapman: And that wasn't available there, I know enough about nutrition to know that it wasn't.

The dangers of being required against one's will to eat such foods are multiple. When the food is unfamiliar and alien ("At least they alleged it was potato salad"); incorrectly made ("It tasted like they dumped vinegar in it"); strangely seasoned ("They had stuff with a lot of curry in it and that tasted kind of weird too"); and just not satisfying ("Neither dish was filling"), all the basic expectations about food are being upset. Eating is supposed to be a familiar, pleasant, sensual event shared with family, friends, and honored guests who have crossed the "threshold of intimacy" that separates meal sharers from strangers (Douglas 1975:257). Meals are *not* supposed to be conflict-generating events that challenge one's basic assumptions. Confronted with these unusual and coercive meals, Chapman and Talbot were not only unwilling consumers but also confused about how to interpret the behavior. Were the encampment women breaking all the rules of etiquette, good taste, and decorum by not accommodating their "guests'" tastes, or were the "guests" the ones who were being ungrateful and rude? Talbot and Chapman got so frustrated with the behavior of the encampment women, says Chapman, that they jokingly debated "which one of the lesbian witches would taste best barbequed on a bonfire."

Moreover, these aspects of taste and choice had implications beyond mealtimes. Dietary practices are often taken as powerful indicators of both individual and social health. For example, Americans tend to promote the idea that dietary habits affect the mental stability as well as the physical well-being and even the moral rectitude of the individual (B. Turner 1984:77). Many American diet programs and books promise multifaceted benefits, claiming that followers will live longer, feel happier, have better mental capabilities, and have a better outlook on life. One patient who followed the Pritikin diet, for instance, reported:

> I've never felt this good in my life, but I don't know why. I felt well when I went to the [Pritikin] Center, but I feel more alive, more alert now. Maybe it's just the weight loss.
>
> It's a kind of joie de vivre. I hope you won't laugh when I tell you that I feel like laughing and singing a lot. I never felt this way before—except when I had some very good news. There's a correlation, I feel, between a feeling of well-being and mental and emotional stability. (Pritikin and McGrady 1979:99)

Dietary management of the body is considered necessary not just for individual health but also for group stability. As Bryan Turner notes, "Diet is a cultural practice regulating quantities and types of food for designated categories of person" (1984:170). It is useful and necessary, therefore, for identifying and maintaining social categories. Serving or eating the right food "conveys the message that proprieties are being observed" (Murcott 1983:2), that the world is in its proper order. The choice of the correct food, designated by the judgment of "good taste," is "simultaneously a question of aesthetics and ethics. Eating what is 'good for you' is always more than a matter of mere nutritional value" (Atkinson 1983:17). It is also a matter of knowing what defines you as a proper member of your chosen community.

These relations between dietary habits and the social system are played out in a variety of ways in everyday life. For example, different foods have differential values to the variously situated members of a society. In the American tradition red (bloody) meat has until recently been designated as the most valued food, followed by "bloodless" poultry and fish, eggs and cheese, and, at the bottom, fruit, vegetables and grains. Some believe that it is the redness or the bloodiness of meat that gives it preeminence. Julia Twigg claims that blood has historically been significant because it is "associated with ideas of the living force, carrying aspects of energy and violence, of the arousal and stimulation of the passions and of the distillation of the particular essence of the animal and thus of animality itself" (1983:22–23).

We can see the connections among food categories, the hierarchy of social relations, and the categorization of persons when we look at who is supposed to eat red meat in the United States. Despite concerns about fat and cholesterol, red meat meals are considered necessary particularly for males because of the perceived fit between the animal qualities Twigg lists and proper masculinity. A failure to ingest enough red meat could potentially leave the question of a man's masculinity in doubt. In a television commercial for the beef industry, the rugged and very "masculine" actor James Garner promoted the superiority of beef over other types of food using the slogan, "Beef. Real food for real people." Beef eaters are still perceived, despite some changes in American dietary habits, as tall, muscular, well-fed animals, and those who consume little beef are seen as effeminate and weak, questionable "real men." More recent beef industry ads have replaced the aging and less than healthy Garner with muscular athletes and younger celebrities. A billboard in North Dakota promotes beef with the slogan "Because the West wasn't won on salad."

A discussion of food preferences, then, talks not only about what and how to eat but also about the moral and cultural implications of these choices. Food preferences are a very visible way to confirm membership in a category and to judge the category of the person in question. Because food is such a strong indicator, food-related metaphors are often useful for talking about the relations between things inside and outside a category. Just as the digestibility of food can indicate category membership, so the "digestibility" of ideas can indicate whether they are acceptable or not within a category. Problematic ideas can be "food for thought," but more likely they are "difficult to swallow" or they can "turn one's stomach" and "not sit well" in the (digestive) system.

If food is "one of the means by which a society creates itself and acts out its aims" as Margaret Visser claims (1986:12), the encampment food habits were revealing to Lucinda Talbot and Sharon Chapman an unexpectedly un-American and antisocial world. Vegetarianism, they came to believe, was a symbol and a product of antisocial political aims, not a natural choice based on apolitical bodily needs or urges. Talbot and Chapman believed their own diet was designed to fulfill natural needs and appetites, those nutritional requirements of the body that must be met for continued existence. Their several references to the outside authority "Nutrition" suggest that proper dietary guidelines have been scientifically and objectively defined. Appealing to this authority by expressing the dangers of the encampment eating habits in nutritional terms ("It doesn't hurt people to eat a vegetarian diet provided that they follow the balanced food group type of thing") lent legitimacy to their judgment that the (eating) behaviors of the encampment women were unacceptable.

These two women believed that others at the encampment were using food to fulfill an appetite based on political desire rather than bodily, natural needs. The Encampment women were unwilling to stay within the bounds of their natural appetites, were indulging in unnatural choices that perhaps shouldn't be made. These choices involve a redefinition of what is proper and natural for women's bodies, and what control women should or should not have over their bodily functions. These are central issues of feminist activism. The female body has often been the site of disputed discourses, political controversy, and power struggles. Thus the control that women seek over their bodies is manifested in challenges to established notions about women's sexuality, motherhood, lesbianism, abortion, rape, birth control, battering, and the public and private roles of women. But the issue of control over women's bodies has divided feminists as often as it has united them, for there is no standard feminist stance on any of these controversial matters. Nevertheless, because women are seen as written or determined through their bodies in a way that men are not, feminists do not ignore the political and discursive implications of taking the power to define the female body.

Chapman and Talbot did not express a feeling of being out of control of their own bodies except when the encampment tried to force a vegetarian diet on them. Both saw their own food habits as proper for themselves, as logical and freely chosen, and as superior to those of the encampment. They were surprised and offended when others seemed unwilling to share the superior food they had brought with them. The encampment cooks shunned the canned chow mein they donated, for example, and it never appeared during mealtime. "To the best of my knowledge," said Chapman, "it's still there." This experience made them more wary about sharing their food. Although they wanted the encampment women to know that vegetarianism was unacceptable, they were not willing to give up their own secure provisions and abandon dietary control just to make this point.

The refusal to share their food provided Chapman and Talbot with some autonomy but not complete peace of mind. They still felt compelled to conform to the vegetarian standard in public. They claimed they had been misled about the encampment's endorsement of vegetarianism to the exclusion of all other eating habits, and in fact, none of the orientation material handed out in 1983, including the *Resource Handbook*, mentions a vegetarian meal policy. The handbook has no section on food, and the supplementary orientation handout did not mention the use of meat. Nor did the "respected policies," the loose "rules" that had previously been agreed on, mention vegetarianism.

Although Talbot and Chapman were correct in saying that the encampment did not specifically ban meat, only an outsider, someone not previously active in feminism, would have been unacquainted with the association between a vegetarian eating style and feminist activism. One vegetarian-feminist who was later to be active at the peace encampment wrote in a 1982 article that vegetarianism was a political act akin to feminism and nonviolence (Salamone 1982). Like feminist nonviolence, vegetarianism was seen as necessary for the change back to a "natural" order of social and ecological peace and harmony.

Feminism has been strongly attracted to vegetarianism because both "isms" propose a basic reordering of the world: vegetarianism challenges the hierarchy of food values and the resulting relationship with animals and "nature," and feminism challenges the hierarchy of "male" values and its attendant social relations. In this interpretation, Twigg says, "meat, both through the cruelty involved in its production and daily acquiescence to this involved in eating it, is here seen to stand for egotism, selfishness and coldness of heart that denies the natural empathy between human beings and beasts. Vegetarianism from the late nineteenth century and before has been linked with a growing ideology of intuition that has revolted against what it see as the coldness of rationality and the fragmented nature of modern consciousness" (1983:27–28). These same ideas were also at work at the encampment. Like many habits that are so familiar to a group as to seem scarcely worthy of comment, vegetarianism was taken for granted in this feminist community. It was a basic assumption about encampment participants; therefore, the choice of whether or not to abide by this unwritten code was one way to judge how well a person fit into the encampment community.

Chapman felt that she was generous in her efforts to tolerate the peace encampment women despite her differences from them. She could understand and accept vegetarianism, however unpleasant, as an acceptable alternative, but for her lesbianism and witchcraft were religious "abominations" that were completely unacceptable. She explained, "Now I was putting up with a lot just being there, and not saying to them, this is biblically wrong, because things like this can bring the whole land under judgment from God."

Talbot's approach was a bit different. She tended to be more analytical in her descriptions and discussions, always attempting to get the facts "straight," to choose her words carefully and precisely, and to comment only on those things she herself actually observed. For her, the normal, acceptable world was not based on or explained by religious convictions as it was for Chapman. Talbot expressed her dissatisfaction with the encampment in practical rather than religious or personal terms and according to criteria she considered easily specifiable and logical. For her, the problem with the women of the encampment was that their beliefs and actions were not genuine or convincing; rather, they seemed hastily formed, carelessly practiced, and not supported by scientific research.

Talbot seemed somewhat interested in the witchcraft and spiritualism of some of the encampment women but hated to see them dissolve into silliness. She described a witch she had met at the encampment: "She said she used to be a Quaker and then she read a book that told about how women are oppressed by all Christian churches, and then she stopped being a Quaker and started being a witch. Yeah, I remember Katy; she said she flew around the Encampment but actually she drove a car. Really!" Talbot has a portrait of herself on the wall of her apartment in Elmira. In this portrait, which was drawn by a friend, she has flaming red hair, a symbolically painted face, and a bright yellow, pointed aura. In discussing the portrait, Talbot revealed that she is not at all opposed to alternative forms of spirituality. It is just that these alternatives need to be approached carefully so that the experience can be "genuine." She did not reject witchcraft and spirituality as much as take a different approach toward them:

> If I were to get interested in witchcraft, I would seek out someone who had a coven, and I would be a learner before I was a teacher. It seems to me that their witchcraft was, is, as shallow as their politics. . . . Now if they had been been English, if they had gone through the apprenticeship to be an English witch or if they had gone through the apprenticeship to be American . . . shamans . . . but the fact is they didn't seem to have the training. . . . You don't form a coven by finding thirteen like-minded people and taking off their clothes and dancing.

Talbot treated lesbianism with similar scientific detachment. Rather than express surprise or disgust at lesbianism as Chapman did, Talbot attempted to comprehend it by quoting "scientific" sources:

> Right after this [the Encampment] happened there was an article in the *Psychology Today*, and it stated that there was a theory that the majority of lesbians had been sexually abused. Well, I don't know, 33 percent of the whole female population has been sexually abused so, and the proportions [of lesbians in the general population] are not like that. And then there was this other article that said that, the DES children who

were treated in the embryo with male hormones were 25 percent lesbian, which is a good portion... so, [sigh] you do wonder.

Lesbianism for Talbot wasn't an abomination so much as just incomprehensible, especially when women told her that they were lesbians because it was the politically correct thing to do. Being a lesbian by choice didn't make sense to her. What she had read seemed to indicate that there were biological reasons for the development of lesbians. Choosing to be a lesbian seemed to be just another example of disingenuousness. In her view physical causes left no room for conscious choice. Like vegetarianism, political lesbianism seemed unnatural to Talbot because it defied natural bodily needs and desires.

Talbot's and Chapman's difficulties with lesbianism (that it was immoral or a false issue or both) are prevalent in feminism, as in the larger culture. Defining homosexuality as a sexual "preference" (as some factions of both the heterosexual and the homosexual communities do) reinforces the idea that a decidedly conscious choice is involved, but lesbianism as a possible choice presents several problems for the heterosexual community in general and for nonlesbian feminists in particular. The association of feminism with lesbianism has always been a touchy subject in feminist political circles. Some lesbian feminists, most notably Adrienne Rich, have designated heterosexuality as, in Ann Ferguson's words, "the key mechanism underlying and perpetuating male dominance" (Ferguson 1981:159). Heterosexual women are accused of being implicated in this system of dominance, and a lesbian consciousness or lifestyle has often been promoted as the only correct political position. Heterosexual women in turn have blamed lesbians for the failure of feminist principles to be more widely accepted. Many feminists consider the identification of feminism with lesbianism undesirable; they prefer to focus attention away from sexuality and other controversial issues. Lindsy Van Gelder comments in a *Rolling Stone Magazine* article on lesbians, including some encampment women, "The mainstream women's movement ... is sometimes similarly queasy about word getting out to the New Right that, yes, feminism can turn you into a lesbian" (1982:14).

Van Gelder notes that political lesbianism is also an issue within the lesbian community itself. Just as it challenges the notion of what is natural in the heterosexual world, political lesbianism challenges the "natural" basis of lesbian identity, and in either community such a challenge is often unwelcome. Van Gelder explains: "The gay movement ... has a vested interest in pushing the theory (advanced by a number of respected sex researchers) that sexual preference is set in bronze by the time a person is three years old or so" (ibid). Political lesbianism is to some extent considered a lesser form of lesbianism in both the heterosexual and the lesbian community. Van Gelder notes that some "old time dykes," women who acknowledged being lesbians before it was the politically correct thing to do, are suspicious of women who are attracted to lesbianism for its rhetorical power. One lesbian told Van Gelder that such women seemed less committed to gay sexuality, seemed to "go back to pricks" after the attraction of lesbianism had worn off. Whether or not these characterizations are widely held in lesbian circles, there does appear to be a fair amount of discussion and disagreement about "choosing lesbianism" as a political statement. As one contributor to a lesbian newsletter explains in a letter titled "Choosing Lesbianism," "I often hear lesbians talk about their sexual 'preference' and how they have chosen to love women. Maybe I'm weird but I really can't imagine sitting down and choosing to love someone. I seriously chose to love men for thirty years but, try as I might, I could never love one. . . . If I could, I would choose to be a lesbian. As it is—I am one" (*Lesbian Connections*, 1985:10).

That Talbot and Chapman were able to come to the encampment and participate in its activities shows that the encampment did indeed attract a wide range of women. But although the encampment was open to all women, not all women felt equally welcome or at home there. Like any community, no matter how feminist its politics, the encampment had criteria for judging the "fitness" of the women who wanted to participate. Without this judgment, there would be no way to define who was inside the group and who was out.

At the encampment, this judgment of fitness was not always overt. Often it was a much subtler determination of who was "politically correct" and who was not. The criteria for political correctness in this combined feminist–lesbian–peace-activist community cannot be definitively specified because they shifted with the ever-changing membership of the encampment. But at the beginning, at the time that Chapman and Talbot were there, a woman's ability and willingness to accept and not to criticize the "lesbian-vegetarian-witches," as these two women called them, was a good basic way to judge if a woman shared the political views of most encampment women. Out of the need to construct a shared community identity, the women developed a complex folk categorization that was used to classify participants for community membership.

The lesbian-vegetarian-feminist-spiritualist was taken as the prototype (see Lakoff 1987:87), or best example, of the politically correct woman, but other women were not completely or automatically excluded from acceptance. Rather, all women were potential community members. If some did not fit the prototype perfectly, many "excuses" could be employed to allow them entry to the category despite their lapses. These excuses explained why these women could not or would not want to be politically correct at the moment. Thus, a woman who had been battered or who was black or poor or who was an older, nonpolitical lesbian had a reason, derived from her position in the patriarchal society, for not meeting the prototype, and she was excused. As two peace encampment women joked, feminists make so many different kinds of excuses to avoid excluding any women from their community that they end up with such categories as "Jewish, middle-aged feminist with two kids" in order to account for all these deviations.

The encampment afforded the opportunity for women whose politics were not usually considered correct (nonlesbians, nonvegetarians, women who approved of violent actions or didn't like feminist process and consensus) to measure their loyalty to and appreciation of these criteria for shared community. Even if a women were not a prototypical lesbian-vegetarian-witch herself, she could gain some acceptance if she avoided criticism of the prototype. The fitness of a woman visiting the encampment would be judged according to this protocol, and the effects of actively rejecting the encampment system can be seen in the experience of Talbot and Chapman.

These two women created a dilemma for the encampment. By its own express policy of openness to diverse women, the encampment had to attempt to accommodate Talbot and Chapman's differences. But at the same time, the two Elmira women caused a furor that threatened the encampment's internal coherence. The threat was not just that they disagreed with what was going on at the encampment; many women disagreed with or could not meet the criteria for political correctness, and some even objected to the unspoken but obvious hierarchy the criteria created. No others, however, challenged these issues as vehemently, publicly, and persistently as did Chapman and Talbot.

The peace encampment decided to deal with the two in several ways. One was to see the women's challenge not as a deliberate critique but as an unfortunate incident beyond Talbot and Chapman's personal control, caused by their particular circumstances in the patriarchal society. Encampment members speculated variously that their complaints and their resulting divisive actions might be based on such diverse elements as their physical condition, their religions, their materialistic attitude, their social class, and their unfamiliarity with feminism. Several of the encampment organizers tried to describe why Chapman and Talbot became a problem:

Shad: They were women who had been involved in peace issues but they had never really been involved in an alternative culture.

Jody: I don't know what class they were, maybe working class.

Shad: I would say they were probably working class.

Jody: And they were very unusual. Were they Quaker women?

Michelle: No, they were Jehovah Witness.

Jody: Oh dear.

Shad: Was it Jehovah's Witnesses?

Michelle: I think they were Jehovah Witness.

Shad: I never knew that.

Some of the encampment women based their explanation of Chapman and Talbot's behavior on nutrition, in much the same way as Chapman and Talbot had judged the encampment. They believed that the Elmira women's diet was inappropriate for the situation and left them emotionally and physically unfit. One herbal healer said they were not drinking enough water and were overweight. Another woman said they had problems because they ate too much sugar. The encampment thus had to create an image of these two women that could explain why and how they could behave in this way in the context of a supposedly unified female space.

To admit that the women had legitimate complaints that should have been dealt with more carefully would be to admit that the encampment was not as cohesive as it needed to appear. The public representation of the encampment had to be that of an internally consistent and cooperative community, a model of peaceful existence unlike the outside world. If this image were destroyed, the entire basis of the encampment as a viable alternative to the patriarchy could be called into question.

The encampment women made a concerted effort to counter Talbot and

Chapman's accounts and to maintain an image of internal tranquillity. In attempting to explain to the newspapers the encampment's view of what had happened with the two Elmira women, one encampment woman said, "I don't think there was nearly as much antagonism toward the women as they perceived" (*Finger Lakes Times*, July 11, 1983). Others said that they had simply mistaken feminist spiritualism for witchcraft or were claiming to see things no one else had witnessed.

It became necessary for the encampment to put all of its processual mechanisms into full gear in order to deal with the two women. At Talbot and Chapman's request, meetings were called to rediscuss the flag issue, and the two women attempted to make themselves heard at evening circles. They complained about the anarchists who destroyed flags, and other women countered that Chapman and Talbot had been disruptive because they carried around little American flags for several days. They also wore rosaries around their necks to counter the powers of the witches and tried to get the encampment women to see that the way they were living was offensive to the surrounding communities. Like the early Encampment organizers, they feared that some "good old boys" from the area would come to the peace camp and "bash their heads" unless they stopped the lesbianism, witchcraft, goddess worship, and flag stomping.

These two women could not accept this world of lesbian-vegetarian-witches. The peace camp women seemed to be asking them to change just about everything that had always seemed right and natural and comfortable. When they finally had more encampment food and encampment ideas than they could stand, they took drastic action. They began by cutting all the yarn webs at the encampment with scissors and threatening to throw paint on a large web painted on the side of the barn. When the encampment women tried to stop them, Chapman and Talbot claimed they were legitimately using the encampment's own protest techniques to express their dissatisfaction with the system:

Chapman: Well we asked them part of their theory about violence, and they were saying that violence against property is not violence, defending the fact that they went and did damage and stuff to the Depot.

Talbot: So we violated some property.

Chapman: So we went over and cut the webs, and they said you can't do that, that's violence. And we said violence against property is not violence; you told us so yourself.

By cutting the web of the encampment rather than staying within its protective bounds, the two Elmira women were challenging and rejecting some of the basic premises of the encampment. The web was supposed to represent unity despite diversity, the interconnectedness of all issues (including the rights to be "lesbian-vegetarian-witches" and to practice alternative sexual, religious, and eating behaviors), and the power women can have by joining together. The breaking of the web, both the symbolic web and the communal web of the encampment, had the power to destroy the encampment's representation of itself. Perhaps even more significantly, in vocalizing their problems with the peace encampment, the two women raised the question of the differences within the encampment, which until that time had not often been publicly acknowledged. One of the encampment organizers recalled Sharon and Lucinda's departure with humor but also chagrin: "They packed, they had their boyfriend come, and they loaded up their stuff and they went away. And we go, 'Who were those two masked women?' [laughter] as the encampment is in shambles."

On July 7, 1983, three days before she left the encampment, Sharon Chapman wrote the following poem and posted it on a bulletin board at the peace camp:

> I don't need to be told
> That I am different from you.
> I can see it for myself.
> It's okay with me.
> You have the right to be you
> as much as I have to be me.
> Differences are special
> because you see the beauty
> I might miss
> and I can show you
> The wonders I see.
> But when you use the differences
> to shut me out
> to push me away
> Then you are wrong
> you deprive yourself and me.
> If we add our differences together
> we increase.
> If you refuse to know me
> we decrease.

And that's not right.
We both lose.
And who wants to be a loser?

In 1985 Chapman wrote the following note to explain this poem:

I don't know if I feel this way now. I think when I wrote this poem I was trying to make them see that they *have* to accept people as they are, that different opinions make life better. But they were real heavy into the "I'm right and that's it" idea, and they had no more idea of being tolerant than they had of making love with men. I think it would have taken a nuclear bomb to open their minds to thinking again—they were that narrow-minded and intolerant. Phooey on them!

And I've definitely changed about one thing: I don't see why I should be tolerant of someone who won't be tolerant of me. I'll pray for them—that's my duty as a Christian. But associate with that kind again? No way.

12

Ease on down the Road

If the residents of Waterloo continue such actions to curb the nuclear disarmament movement, it would only serve them right if the Russians' missiles were aimed directly at the village of Waterloo.

—Phone call to Rochester *Democrat and Chronicle*, August 7, 1983

Textuality pervades every aspect of an anthropological project. Of course anthropologists must consider the textual material created by our subjects, but we must also become aware of the textuality of our own writings and pronouncements. Anthropology has turned its eye on itself, and as we come to see "culture as composed of seriously contested codes and representations" available in textual form (Clifford 1986:2), we also begin to see our own textual productions as problematic and less than transparent.

In our efforts to represent another culture at the same time as we are questioning the possibility of representation at all, we find ourselves in a paradox. One reaction to this paradox has been for anthropologists to take a critical interest in the form and rhetoric of anthropological writing. Anthropology, like many other disciplines, has begun to be reflexive and self-critical as it analyzes not only social and cultural systems but also itself as a discipline and a creator of textual representations.

But why is it important for anthropologists to be aware of their own productions *as* texts? When we turn the same critical eye on our own texts that we turn on the texts of others, we are just as obliged to account for the way we create representations. And just as representation is an issue of power and authority in our subjects' texts, so it is in our own. James

Clifford explains: "The focus on text making and rhetoric serves to highlight the constructed, artificial nature of cultural accounts. It undermines overly transparent modes of authority, and it draws attention to the historical predicament of ethnography, the fact that it is always caught up in the invention, not the representation, of cultures" (1986:2). The word "invention" signifies not that ethnography is false but that like every text it is subject to discourses that constrain what it includes or excludes. Since discourse affects the way cultural phenomena are selected, recorded, and analyzed, the anthropologist who is aware and critical of ethnographic writing can highlight the dominant discourses that constrain her writing. In response she can develop resistant, questioning ethnographies that emphasize the constructed, patchwork nature of representations.

What would this resistance to transparent representation look or sound like? One way of resisting the authority of the ethnographic text is to use variations in textual styles to highlight the impossibility of ever directly reflecting a culture in a text. We can never get away from representation but we can continually fight the notion that there is a direct line between the thing represented and its textual description. Since this description in traditional anthropology has tended to be in the form of "scientific" prose, resistance could be attempted through styles that do not claim to be objective and realistic. Another approach is to use information from previously overlooked or underutilized sources. Paul Stoller and Cheryl Olkes have used multiple sources effectively in their memoirs of life among the Songhay of Nigeria (1987), as has Steven Feld in his book *Sound and Sentiment* (1982), and I want to try the same thing here.

In the next two chapters, I present the events leading up to and surrounding the incident that occurred at a bridge in Waterloo through two alternative textual forms—a fictionalized narrative account and a dramatic reenactment. Neither reports firsthand anthropological fieldwork (from which most of anthropology draws its authority). Rather, each is a collage constructed from multiple sources including interviews with participants, audio- and videotapes, gossip, police records, circulating rumors, hearsay, newspaper accounts, photographs, maps, drawings, letters, and other information provided both by participants and by those who never got close to the events. They are designed, as is much postmodern ethnography, to evoke rather than represent important actions and people. As Stephen Tyler defines it, "a post-modern ethnography is a cooperatively evolved text consisting of fragments of discourse intended to evoke in the minds of both the reader and writer an emergent fantasy of a possible world of commonsense reality" (1986:126).

This commonsense world is in conflict with the "impossible worlds of science and politics," as Tyler calls them (122), and it is the tension between them that is the desired effect. The purpose of placing these truly ethno-graphic texts in the heart of a basically familiar text of reportage and analysis is to break away from the everyday speech of anthropological discourse and so to create a moment of awareness, to admit other possible voices, styles, common senses, and interpretive strategies. It is the same approach taken by the encampment women as they tried to rewrite nuclear discourse with their protests. It is also the strategy of the people of Waterloo, for at the bridge the unthinkable almost became real, and common sense was rewritten to include violent actions, virulent name-calling, abuse of authority, bizarre non sequiturs, and abandonment of one's community.

The purpose of this experiment in voices and styles is not to evoke a sense of "being there" but to disrupt the sense of being grounded in the comforting scientific text of traditional ethnography, to deny the objectivity of the representation. Rather than provide guiding orientations to the culture under study, this textual strategy provides productive disorientation, or what Edward Said (1978a) might call a deorientalizing, a refusal to treat the subject like a ventriloquist's dummy, like one whose voice is created by others. (Vincent Crapanzano's *Tuhami: Portrait of a Moroccan* [1980] was one attempt to address this issue.) This disorientation forbids a search for the "truth" of the events and encourages uncertainty about who was right or wrong and who was effective, powerless, oppressed, fetishistic, or simply boring. It is in some ways a duplication of the fieldwork experience as much as the ethnographic event.

Perhaps the most distinct mode of this type of ethnographic experiment is the collage, the piecing together of seemingly unrelated and incompatible voices, events, observations and interpretations into a text that is both abstract and concrete, realistic and irrealistic. Collage, because it challenges the logic of the real and valorizes the imaginative, is able to overthrow "the barriers erected by reason, education, habit, and experience" (Matthews 1986:143). Collage, which puts together disparate and seemingly random elements, can be used to reorder and recode "reality" in such a way that we see the constructedness of that reality.

Anthropology has yet to see widespread use of the postmodern strategy of textual collage. Multiple voices are occasionally introduced, and a few works take an antiauthorial stance (see Paul Rabinow's *Reflections on Fieldwork in Morocco* [1977] or Dan Rose's *Black American Street Life* [1987]). Anthropologists still seem to be uncomfortable with the possibilities of pastiche, parody, collage, and irony in their "scientific" writings. The confusion of author and authority, reality and imagination, constructedness and reflection which I employ in the following two textual constructions will, I hope, suggest the value as well as the pitfalls of such antirealist ethnographic experiments.

Let us begin with the letter that informed the sheriff's department of the march that sparked the Waterloo bridge incident (see figure 4 for the poster advertising the march):

July 17, 1983
Sheriff
Seneca County Sheriff's Dept.
44 West Williams Street
Waterloo, NY 13165

Dear Sheriff:

I am writing to let you know of plans for a walk we are taking on Saturday, July 30th from Seneca Falls to the Women's Peace Encampment in Romulus at the Seneca Army Depot. Corinne Guntzel, of Seneca Falls, may have spoken to you about it, but I'm writing to confirm our plans and give specific information.

On Saturday, July 30th, at 9am we are meeting at Van Cleef Lake Park. We'll begin our walk around 10am and walk on Cayuga Street to West Fall Street (rt 414) and then take route 5 (20) to Waterloo. We'll then take route 96 to the Peace Camp. We will be all women. It is difficult to estimate how many of us there'll be. I would say anywhere from 50–100. We are making the walk to honor upper NY state women from our past who have worked for freedom and equality. We will walk peacefully and non-violently, and do not want to cause any disruptions of traffic, etc. We will have our own peacekeepers (women who ensure everyone's safety).

If you wish any further information please feel free to call me in NYC. I can be reached in the evenings at (212) xxx-xxxx and during the day at (212) xxx-xxxx.

On Saturday morning, if you wish to speak with any of us on the walk you might ask for Donna, Amy, or Quinn.

I'm sure that there will be mutual cooperation between us.

Thank You,

Karen
for the NYC Women's Pentagon Action

Figure 4. Poster advertising the march through Waterloo

Marching from Seneca Falls to Waterloo. Photo by Pam Quiggle

The following is a fictionalized collage narrative constructed about the events leading up to the confrontation at the bridge.

A BARROOM, AT LEAST A WEEK BEFORE

Inside the old Franklin Hotel, several of the regulars were pursuing that summer's favorite topic of conversation—the 'lesbian pinko protesters' at that peace camp down in Romulus. The bartender, one of the Augustine brothers who owned the Franklin, passed out the beers as the men talked. Some of them were war veterans, but unlike many of the town's vets, they didn't hang out at the local VFW bar all that much. Maybe it was because they had been in Vietnam, and other vets weren't always comfortable with them; maybe it was even because some of their fathers hung out at the VFW. The hard-core World War II people, the old-timers, didn't always give them credit for having been in combat. Despite the fact that the Vietnam War had been on TV every night and no one could have missed it, and despite the fact that many of the men had visible scars of their rough times there, the old-timers didn't seem to think they had done any real fighting. Anyway, the Franklin gave them a place to get together, talk and drink with other like-minded guys.

Tonight everyone seemed to share the desire to let those peace camp women know what they felt about this protesting, and so they hashed out some ideas over a couple of beers. "This protesting, I mean, in my opinion, never stopped anything, but it always got a lot of people hurt," said Buddy. "Why do you want to go out and protest and get your head beat in by a cop with a billy club? It doesn't make any sense. They always started out peaceful but a lot of them never ended up that way. Kent State all the way down; always people hurting people. They shouldn't be doing this here. I don't want to hear any more of this stuff."

But Buddy did go on, his brain and mouth lubricated by the bartender's prompt service. "I got drafted in '69. I had to do what I had to do. And I got to watch TV about three or four times when I was in Nam and they showed the towns protesting."

"Instead of protesting against us, they should have been with us. That's the way I see it," someone down the other end of the bar interrupted.

"I mean," Buddy continued, "the protests against was always louder than the people that were on our side more or less. The whole idea of a communist country taking over a country that doesn't want to be communist is what it's all about and that's what Vietnam was all about. If you ever spent some time with the Vietnamese people, they're nice people."

Ben, the man sitting next to him, took up the story as Buddy's mind slid back to his beer. "You have your good and your bad, white and black, I don't care what race you have, if you've ever been through any of the villages and seen the way they look, they don't want to be in a communist group. First off, all's they do is spend all day in rice paddies."

"Yeah, but what's theirs is theirs, they had their own economy. Going communist they wouldn't," someone interrupted.

"As far as I'm concerned, the United States run out on them," said Bob, two seats down from Buddy at the long straight bar, "and it makes me mad because I believe what I was fighting for, and that's against communism. But when I got back, HAH! You know what it feels like to be spit on?"

A few heads seemed to nod in agreement but no one bothered to answer.

Bob continued, "It didn't happen to everybody, but when I came back to California, those people waiting right there on the tarmack, right where the plane landed, with banners, you know—'Go home!'—you know, spit on, yelled at, you know?"

"People are screwed up," said Bill, the man on the other side of Buddy. "These people that talked about us bad, you know, baby killers, war mongers, dope heads, you know. People are screwed up. It doesn't help any when you get in the paper, 'Viet Vet Kills Family.'"

Buddy nodded and added, "People today blow people away. Every time they find out it was a Vietnam vet, they got to put it in big headlines. Not, 'Korean vet' or not 'World War II vet' goes off the deep end."

Bob started remembering his own return from Vietnam and said, "By the time you got home, you dug yourself into a hole. That's all. You went to work and you drank and you spent twenty-seven hundred dollars over a bar in three and a half minutes. Lost a wife and a kid. Come home with thirty-five hundred, put seven hundred down on a car, and spent the rest over a bar, and then run out of money and they say, well, it's time to go to work."

"What work?" Bill asked.

"I could smell the jungle today," Bob said suddenly in a chilling voice. "When it rains, the jungle is not here, the smell of the jungle is not here, but in my mind I can smell the jungle with my nose. No one else can smell it, but we can smell it. It started raining after two last night and that's when I woke up and I ain't been to bed since. Can't sleep, close the windows, still hear it, still smell it. That stuff doesn't ever go away."

"My uncle was in Korea," said Buddy, "and he still gets that feeling too. They did a lot of street fighting, like in cities, and whenever he walks into a blank doorway, he stops. It's automatic. He stops and then he looks, and then he goes in. It's never left him, you know? How do you write about something in your mind. How do you say, well, it's stuck in his brain. That don't sound right. There's other ways to word it but I ain't never come up with a real good one."

Someone turned the conversation back to more recent events: "Okay, so what are we going to do about these bitches when they come through town on Saturday?"

All the men had heard through the grapevine or had read in the paper that some of the protesting women were going to gather in Seneca Falls, the town next door, on Saturday morning and were going to walk down Routes 5 and 20, past the Polar Freeze Restaurant that marked the boundary between the two rival towns, past the tiny Memorial Day Museum, and up to the four corners that indicated the heart of Waterloo. And then they were going to turn onto Washington Street, go over the bridge that spanned the old, muddy barge canal, and go right past the Franklin Hotel. It was a hell of a long walk, twelve or fifteen miles before the women reached the Seneca Army Depot gate on Route 96 in the southern part of the county. And the march was going right past their own Franklin Hotel, a family restaurant and bar just southwest of the bridge in Waterloo. The Franklin was a special place. Years later, when it burned down, someone would paraphrase the words of sixties antiwar activist and musician Joni Mitchell: "Yup, they tore down paradise and put up a parking lot."

The men in the bar that evening discussed this planned march over the next several drinks and decided that something had to be done about the "peace" parade. "You have to do what you have to do," was the reason Bob gave. So a couple of them, including Buddy, some of the other veterans who didn't like this protesting, and, it is said, the Augustine brothers who owned the Franklin, decided to let the "ladies" know what they thought of this nonsense.

Some of them had already seen the women "in action" and didn't like them one bit. "I don't know if you know some of the things going on there," one man explained to the others. "When a woman pulls a pad out from her private parts, all covered with blood, and hangs it on the fence of the depot, what has that got to do with nuclear armament?" "I'll give you another example," said Bill. "I was at a picnic at Sampson Park and these two women were with drawings on their breasts, like they were drawings of hands on their naked breasts like you would see in *Playboy* or something. The troopers had to come and take them away. They were, phew, embracing on the beach, two females doing this on the beach in front of impressionable children. If you want to do it out there at that camp, it's okay with me, but don't push it down my nose, because I don't like it."

And of course everyone knew they wouldn't fly the American flag.

The men decided they would stop the march, just for a short time (or so they would later assure the chief of police, Doyle Marquardt), just to make their point. They would do this by blocking the bridge with a banner held by the vets and, hell, by anyone who wanted to join in. So one night a few of them got together to make the banner, a long, long fabric sign that had to stretch all the way across the bridge (the width of a generous two-way road) and that had to say what they felt. They argued about what the sign should say but finally agreed and painted it in time for Saturday's counterdemonstration. The spray-painted banner, which stretched at least twenty feet, read: "MANY MEN AND WOMEN HAVE EARNED THE RIGHT FOR ANYONE TO PROTEST IN AMERICA. RESPECT THEM, OUR FLAG, AND OUR COUNTRY." They were ready for Saturday.

SATURDAY, JULY 30, EARLY MORNING, OUTSIDE WATERLOO

Some of the residents of Seneca County who knew him said that Jay Cooper liked to go hunting on Saturday mornings. On this last, hot Saturday in the month of July, Jay picked up his faded workshirt and shoved a handkerchief, a pack of Pall Mall cigarettes, and a box of .22-

caliber shells into his jeans pockets. He lifted his rifle onto his shoulder, shifted its position until it was comfortable enough so he could barely feel it but not so comfortable that he didn't know it was there, and left his home in Fayette, just south of the town of Waterloo, on foot. Ever since the motorcycle accident that left him, as people would say, "just a little bit looney," he tended to walk a lot, walk and wander into town and out, into the woods and along the railroad tracks. One day someone found him lying right down on the tracks, asleep.

Jay headed out onto Route 96, which connected Fayette to Waterloo. This way into town led past the Franklin Hotel, over the barge canal bridge on Washington Street and through the intersection known as the four corners. It was still early and everything was hazy and almost empty and quiet, a good day for hunting squirrel, or maybe some rabbit.

At the four corners you could go right and head toward Seneca Falls, three miles or so away; or you could go left onto Routes 5 and 20 and head past the sheriff's department and the Waterloo High School with its monument to Memorial Day. Straight ahead, past Elisha Street where the VFW hall was, were the laundromat, the American Legion, and farther on, the county fairgrounds. No one knows how Jay Cooper left town that day. They only know how he came back.

SATURDAY MORNING, AT THE FRANKLIN HOTEL AND THE BRIDGE

After the fact, a lot of people took the credit for organizing the blockade at the bridge in Waterloo. The men from the Franklin Hotel proudly discussed the grapevine network and the community spirit that they were able to draw on to produce the crowd that numbered about four hundred. Others, however, disputed their organizational skills and commitment to the cause. Missy Barker, a young resident of Waterloo, had her own opinion about how it really got organized.

Missy got a call from a lady friend, who asked her to come over and help with the blockade. "I heard that the guys at the Franklin Hotel are getting up a sign to spread across the bridge and they want to stop the women," she explained. "Can you help get people to join in?" "Of course," said Missy cheerfully as if she had just agreed to provide a cake for the church bake sale. Missy made a few phone calls of her own, and then she and her friend made some signs and drove over to the Franklin Hotel well before the encampment women were even in sight. As cars went by, Missy would wave them to slow down. "Haul it over if you're a proud American," she would say, repeating the slogan on her sign and explaining that the peace camp women were on their way through Waterloo and that the townspeople were going to stop them right there at the bridge. Missy and her friend were alone on the street with their signs but they could see the men going into the Franklin Hotel and could hear the laughter and clinking of cool beer mugs over the hot, heavy air.

Missy recognized one of the cars that drove by. It belonged to Jerry McKenna, a decorated Vietnam veteran who, she heard, had helped organize the blockade. But what was he doing driving back and forth over the bridge? Why didn't he stop and help them get more people interested? "He acts like we're some kind of crazy fruits standing out here," Missy said angrily to her friend.

"Are the guys at the Franklin really giving away free booze?" Missy heard someone in the growing crowd ask. Her work was paying off, and after about an hour (it was now near eleven o'clock) the bridge was filled with people getting more and more excited and—some of them—more and more drunk. Someone from the VFW or American Legion hall a few blocks away brought some little American flags and passed them out to the eager crowd. Some people held them, some waved them, some just put them under their arms or in their back pockets as they waited for the "parade" to start.

The sidewalks were filled with joking, milling people when someone shouted about 11:30 that they saw the women coming. The crowd burst onto the street, forming a human barricade across the bridge. Missy and her friend and some of her neighbors joined hands to form a strong barrier, but by now the men had come out from the Franklin and formed a line in front of them, the line hold the big, long banner. "I guess they just want to protect us," Missy shrugged; "what if those women have something they try to hit us with?"

The marchers came in sight as they turned the corner and headed toward the bridge. Angry people lined the road on both sides, and as the women passed through their ranks they shouted, "Go home lezzies," "Assholes," and "Get out Jews," and held up signs that said "Pinko Dykes Go Home" and "God Is on Our Side." The crowd surged closer to the marchers, about seventy-five or one hundred of them, after the police car escorting them moved by.

Two police officers nervously got out of their car and came up to the line of men blocking the bridge with the sign and asked, "You guys aren't going to do anything? You guys aren't going to do anything, are you?" Missy stretched over the linked bare arms of two of the men in front of her and said, "No, we're not going to do anything, but they're not coming across this bridge." "Well you can't stop them from coming across the bridge," returned the cop. "Well they can swim under water and jump over it, cause they're not coming across it," said Missy firmly as she stepped back and let the men continue the argument, her eyes drifting to the muddy water chugging through the dirty barge canal twenty feet below.

As Missy looked down to the other end of the bridge she saw that her sister and her ten-year-old niece, Michelle, had finally arrived. When Michelle and her mother had driven by the bridge that morning on the way to the grocery store, Missy had recruited them to phone other people to come down and join the protest. "I'm keeping Michelle back from the front of this crowd," Missy's sister shouted. Missy thought it was a good idea, for the crowd was getting angrier. "Well," she joked to Michelle, "at least I got you to your first 'peace riot!'"

TWO BLOCKS AWAY, WATERLOO

The Seneca Community Players had completed their second performance of *The Wiz* the night before, and it had seemed to go even better than opening night. The dancing, costumes, and special effects sparkled as Dorothy, played by Tom and Melley Kleman's daughter Mazie, went brightly on her way with her dog Toto, destroying the Wicked Witch of the East, and combating the Wicked Witch of the West as she headed to the Emerald City to see the Wiz, the only one who could get her back home again.

It had been terribly hot at the Friday evening performance at Mynderse Academy in Seneca Falls, and Mazie had invited some cast and crew members to her parents' house in Waterloo for a swim on Saturday around lunchtime, so they could cool off before the next performance. Since it was so hot and humid, the Klemans were already sitting by their pool when one of Mazie's guests arrived. He came hurrying in and said, "You should see the excitement, *real* excitement, downtown. It's got something to do with the peace camp women. I've got to go back to see what's happening. I just stopped because I told you I would be here at one."

Melley and Mazie put their clothes on over their bathing suits while Tom, who was the president of one of the local banks, got dressed quickly and grabbed the bank keys. "I should go down and see what's going on," he said. If there was trouble downtown, he hoped it wasn't near the bank. They all got into their car and drove the few blocks to the four corners, parking amid a jumble of other cars.

They passed many people going both toward and away from the bridges over the canal, including Jay Cooper, wearing a camouflage jacket and carrying a rifle on his shoulder. Melley saw a lady, an older woman she knew from church, and asked her what was happening. "They're going to get those whores," the woman screamed as she quickly disappeared into the crowd, leaving behind a stunned Melley.

As they came in sight of the bridge Melley and Mazie saw rows of policemen in riot gear, a huge crowd shouting and waving little American flags, and a small group of women sitting on the bridge. Straight ahead they saw a line of men holding a long hand-painted sign that stretched all the way across the bridge. To the right they saw a huge sign strung between two buildings near the Franklin Hotel which read, "NUKE EM TILL THEY GLOW THEN SHOOT THEM IN THE DARK."

13

The Bridge: A Drama

Cast of Characters

DEPUTY ARCANGELI: chief deputy, Seneca County Sheriff's Department
SHERIFF'S DEPUTIES
POLICE CHIEF: Doyle Marquardt, of the Waterloo police
WATERLOO POLICEMEN AND FIREMEN
SHERIFF: Ken Greer, elected sheriff of Seneca County
KIM: an encampment mediator, native of Geneva, New York, six feet, six
   inches tall
REPORTER: male reporter for local radio station, carrying tape recorder
MELLEY KLEMAN: fifty-six-year-old Waterloo resident
MAZIE KLEMAN: her daughter
TOM KLEMAN: Melley's husband, local bank president
YOUNG MAN: friend of the Klemans'
LONNY: Vietnam veteran, thirty-five to forty years old
WOMAN WITH LONNY: his wife
MATRONS: employees of sheriff's department
ARRESTED WOMEN FROM PEACE CAMP
MEN, WOMEN, AND CHILDREN IN CROWD
WOMEN PROTESTERS FROM PEACE ENCAMPMENT
PEACEFUL MAN: encampment sympathizer
JAY COOPER: man with rifle

Scene 1

A crowd has gathered on the bridge over the barge canal in the town of
Waterloo, New York. It is midday, sunny and hot. Crowd rumblings rise
and fall. Occasionally group chants and individuals shouting can be
discerned. The crowd has been on the bridge over an hour, blocking a
march by a group of women antinuclear protesters.

The crowd consists of about three hundred to four hundred people of both sexes and all ages including many teenagers; people are dressed in summer clothes: tank tops, T-shirts, shorts. Some women are in hair curlers; many men are bare chested. At least half the crowd is holding or waving small American flags; some people are holding large American flags; one person waves a large black and white POW/MIA flag. A group of men thirty-five to forty-five years old are holding a banner across the bridge that reads: "Many men and women have earned the right for anyone to protest in America. Respect them, our flag, and our country." Others hold hand-lettered cardboard signs that say, "You Can't Overrule God," "Go Home," "We're Proud to Be Americans," "Dyke Farm That Way," "If You Love America, Protect It," and "Pinko Lesbians, Go Home!"

Sitting in a circle in front of the crowd is a group of about thirty women of different ages. Most are wearing white bibs with the names of historically important women written on them; they talk to each other and to other women standing around them. Some are crying, some look frightened, some seem passive. Occasionally they sing protest or peace songs. When they attempt patriotic songs the crowd takes over and drowns them out.

The crowd is chanting, "Go home! Go home!" and people are jabbing their flags into the air above the seated women. Several sheriff's department cars pull up in the background.

MAN 1 *(screaming):* Come on lesbians, lick communism, not each other! *(Laughter by several people around him).*

WOMAN 1: Right!

MAN 2: That was a good one.

WOMAN 2: Arrest them.

YOUNG WOMAN 1 *(screaming):* Hey you bunch of commies.

CROWD *(several times):* Get out of here. Go home.

YOUNG WOMAN 1 *(screaming):* Hey you fucking commies.

CROWD *(repeatedly):* A-mer-i-ca! A-mer-i-ca!

MAN 3: Go back to Russia!

Sheriff's deputy Dale Arcangeli gets out of a car and walks up to the police chief, who is standing calmly at the edge of the crowd talking to some men.

DEPUTY ARCANGELI *(to police chief):* Hey, Doyle, What's going on?

POLICE CHIEF *(to man 4 in crowd as Deputy Arcangeli listens):* So you're going to stop them here on the bridge just for a little while?

Encampment women in circle on Waterloo bridge. Photo by Pam Quiggle

Protesters, sheriff's deputies, and residents face off at bridge in Waterloo.
Photo by Pam Quiggle

MAN 4: We're going to hold them for a little while and then let them go.

POLICE CHIEF: Nobody's going to get physical, right?

MAN 5: Nobody's going to get physical, nothing.

Woman protester 1 approaches crowd and tries to talk to them. Her words cannot be heard over the chant "Go home!"

MAN 1 *(addressing woman protester 1 but turning away at an angle):* Get out of here; we don't want to hear it. Listen, we're decent people, not lowlife like you.

WOMAN PROTESTER 1 *(sarcastically):* Thank you for allowing me my freedom to....

MAN 2: Up yours. Get out of here. We're decent people; we don't have trash. We got enough trash in this town.

CROWD: Go home!

Buddhist drum begins beating in background.

MAN 6: Now's the time to move in, stomp the piss out of them, and throw them in the canal.

WOMAN 3: You all need psychiatrists.

Other women protesters are mingling with the crowd, having both calm and angry exchanges with them.

WOMAN PROTESTER 2 *(To man 10 in crowd):* . . . so we want nuclear weapons stopped.

MAN 10: You can't just get rid of the weapons. With the situation the way it is we'd all be dead. You have to face reality.

WOMAN PROTESTER 2: The reality is that we have to change things now.

MAN 2: Bullshit! You people want ERA, you join the fucking army, you go to Vietnam.

CROWD: U-S-A! U-S-A!

MAN 2 *(to woman protester 2, disgusted):* Oh, go home.

CROWD: Go home! Go home!

WOMAN PROTESTER 3 *(to people in crowd):* If you'd like to talk to us, we'd like to listen to you.

MAN 10: Ma'am, that's not going to accomplish anything at this point.

WOMAN PROTESTER 3: Okay, but....

MAN 10: It's not going to accomplish anything at this point.

MAN 4: Communists! Go protest in Russia. That's where you belong.

WOMAN PROTESTER 4 *(To man 1 and woman 5):* The situation we're in now, it's like a bathtub filled with gasoline with two people standing in it

Encampment women and residents on the bridge in Waterloo. Photo by
Pam Quiggle

and one has 780 matches and one has 762. It doesn't matter how many
matches you have, the first match will do it.

WOMAN 5 *(laughing):* Well if there are two men standing in a bathtub, I
hope the American is the first to light the match!

MAN 1: Get out of here. We don't listen to commie lesbians.

Crowd tries to poke protesters with the ends of their flag poles.

POLICEMAN 1: Hey, come on. Keep it up straight, keep it up in the air,
Bobby.

*A man named Lonny is in the front line of the crowd. Somewhat intoxi-
cated, red in the face, and agitated, Lonny continuously screams and
gestures at the women.*

POLICEMAN 2: Come on, Lonny, don't get hot.

WOMAN WITH LONNY *(trying to restrain Lonny):* Lonny, please.

LONNY: No! I goddamn fought for my country and it's fucking time we
won right.

MAN IN CROWD: Wave that flag! Wave that flag!

LONNY *(shouting to policeman 1):* Officer, there's not no permit for this
parade, right? There's no permit for this parade.

MAN 11: We don't want you here.

WOMAN 6: Com-mies! Com-mies!

REPORTER *(holding microphone up to Lonny):* What are you doing here?

LONNY *(his voice cracks):* What am I doing here? I'm a goddam Vietnam veteran, that's what I'm doing here.

REPORTER: Have you got a permit to block the bridge?

LONNY: Nobody's got a permit.

REPORTER: Then why don't you get out of the road?

MAN 12 *(to reporter):* Why don't you shove that mike up your ass, pal.

MAN 13 *(To reporter):* What are you, queer like them?

Policeman 2 comes up and takes Lonny's arm.

LONNY: Get your fucking hands off me please officer.

WOMAN WITH LONNY: Lonny, will you get out of here!

POLICEMAN 2: I'm going to arrest you if you don't....

Woman with Lonny tries to get him away from reporter and policeman 2.

WOMAN WITH LONNY *(to man 10):* Will you get him out of here? *(to Lonny)* Lonny.... Lonny!... Lonny please!... Lon-ny!!

CROWD: U-S-A! U-S-A!

LONNY *(to reporter):* Give me that mike! I'll tell you what I got. I got three goddamn brass stars. I got injured twice defending my country, and defending you and this officer. *(Reporter gives a mock bow.)* Oh yeah, okay, a nice bow. You know what we get from the VA? Nothing! They say we're all nuts!

WOMAN WITH LONNY: Lonny, let's get out of here. Lonny, come on *(pleading).*

LONNY: I got home from Vietnam, I got shit *(voice cracks).*

WOMAN WITH LONNY: Lonny, come on.

POLICEMAN 3: That's enough, Lonny.

LONNY *(Turning suddenly to reporter):* I got your face pal *(groaning)* oh, yeah.

WOMAN WITH LONNY: Lonny, goddamn it.

LONNY *(turning back toward protesters, screaming):* No goddam permit.

MAN 11: We did our thing, man. Hey, we did our thing.

LONNY: I did my thing. You people sent me out to do it better. I'll tell you, the vet will survive. They will survive.

WOMAN 6 *(to policemen):* Why do we get arrested? Arrest them!

WOMAN WITH LONNY *(growling):* Lonny, you're going to get arrested, just stop.

LONNY: No, goddamn, arrest nobody. It's not even a civil disturbance.

WOMAN WITH LONNY *(growling):* God almighty!

MAN 12: I'll tell you I'm a disabled vet, and I protected my country to look at this shit?

POLICEMAN 1 *(to Lonny):* You have proved your point, come on.

LONNY: We have proved no point.

(Another part of crowd)

MAN 13: Hey, go home and smoke that crap.

MAN 14: Go home and get the hell out of here.

MAN 13: Hey, we live here, we don't worry about it.

CROWD: Love it or leave it. Love it or leave it.

MAN 15: You fucking don't belong here.

WOMAN 7: You're a sick specimen of woman with your tits hanging out.

MAN 16: Communists! Bunch of communists! We fought for you when you were growing up and now you're turning against us.

WOMAN 5: Hey, my brother was killed when they bombed Pearl Harbor!

MAN 14: You're just a bunch of fucking communists that supported the goddamn people that put us in Nam.

WOMAN PROTESTER 4: We love our country too.

WOMAN 7 *(to woman protester 4):* You can't change things by doing this. You think you're gonna change it? Giving my daughter literature on lesbianism, that's going to change it?

MAN 18: Why do you get your goddamned nose involved? Cause you can't do a goddamn thing. Leave! Go back to where you're from. We don't want to hear your bullshit. Go on! Go on! Save your breath, honey!

MAN 15 *(to woman shaking rattle):* Don't put no fucking hex on me, you bitch.

(Another part of crowd)

MAN 18: Go protest in Russia—that's where you belong.

MAN 19: If you were doing this in Russia, they'd lock you up, send you to Siberia.

WOMAN 9: You can't do these kinds of things in Russia. They don't let you climb fences and stuff. So why are you doing it here?

Women protesters sitting on ground start singing "God Bless America."

CROWD: Go home, commies! *(repeatedly).*

CROWD: Go home, lezzies! Nuke the lezzie Jews!

VOICE ON POLICE RADIO: Dispatcher says they have a full scale riot at the bridge.

(Another part of crowd)

WATERLOO POLICEMAN 1: Sheriff just told me he wants them all to march up back to the village square and have people from the encampment come out and pick them up and truck them down. He doesn't want them walking through Waterloo anymore.

DEPUTY 1: Yeah, but those guys won't let them through, and I'm not sure what will happen if more encampment women show up.

The sheriff is talking to a group of the women protesters.

SHERIFF *(impatient):* Lady, you are asking for trouble here.

WOMAN PROTESTER 1 *(to sheriff):* We're not doing anything.

WOMAN PROTESTER 5: They're the ones who are asking for trouble. We're not....

WOMAN PROTESTER 6: They're the ones who are blocking the road.

WOMAN PROTESTER 4: We're just walking.

SHERIFF: Do as I tell you. You are the people that came into this town.

WOMAN PROTESTER 3: That's true.

SHERIFF: You are the outsiders. Now get it up and come on. Come down here and gather in the parking lot.

(Women complain all together that they have a right to cross the bridge.)

SHERIFF: I can't listen to four yacking ladies in my ears at the same time.

WOMAN PROTESTER 5: I don't know why you are not considering that they are inciting a riot.

SHERIFF: Move it out ladies.

WOMAN PROTESTER 1: Why?

SHERIFF: You are invaders in this village.

WOMAN PROTESTER 1: We're not invaders; we belong to the same country.

SHERIFF: You know, I've got total uncooperation from you people. Now you were advised when you went to that encampment that they didn't want problems with the sheriff's department. And now they are sitting here irritating the situation to no end.

WOMAN PROTESTER 2: We have a right to walk on a public highway

SHERIFF: I, god*damn it*, I know you do. I'm asking you to move it.

WOMAN PROTESTER 4: That's your job to have us keep the law.

SHERIFF: It's my job and I'm going to have to arrest every one of you if you stay here.

WOMAN PROTESTER 6 *(calmly and sarcastically)*: I guess you might have to.

SHERIFF: Well I just might do that *(sarcastically)*.

WOMAN PROTESTER 6: You might have to.

SHERIFF: What are you, the spokesman for this group?

WOMAN PROTESTER 6: No, I'm speaking for myself.

Sheriff's department paddy wagon pulls up. A deputy gets out of the front seat and opens the back door. One man in riot gear quickly jumps out. The deputy angrily tells him to get back in so they can all jump out together. Sheriff's deputies in riot gear (helmets, face shields, body padding) carrying batons, then jump out of the paddy wagon. The crowd cheers when they see them. When the deputies head toward crowd and place themselves between the crowd and the seated women, the crowd hoots and jeers. Firemen with walkie-talkies and WFD (Waterloo Fire Department) baseball caps begin to infiltrate the crowd.

MAN 7 *(nodding toward the line of sheriff's deputies)*: Where the hell do they think they're going.

WOMAN 3: They look like Martians coming in for a landing.

MAN 8: This is ridiculous. Just get those stupid women out of here.

TEENAGERS IN CROWD: Get out of here, you jerks, you assholes.

MAN 9: Take the long way.

CROWD: Go home! *(ten times)*

The sheriff walks away disgusted from the women and starts giving directions to deputies in riot gear.

SHERIFF: Start loading them up. We're going to start loading them in the patrol car and arrest them *(crowd cheers)*. Have these officers swing over the ambulance and we're going to start loading them up, and I'll see to it that every damn one of them goes a month before they're arraigned. *(Turns back to the group of women he was talking with.)* You go to jail if you don't move it.

PEACEFUL MAN *(comes up to sheriff and interrupts)*: The reason they are sitting there, sir, is because they're not being let through.

SHERIFF: I've got a riot on my hands and I don't need your advice. *(Turns to a deputy; points at peaceful man.)* Get this guy's full name and address. If he causes any more problems, I want to have him arrested.

Sheriff gets on hollow-sounding bullhorn; the crowd is suddenly silent.

SHERIFF: Attention, ladies! You were advised when you entered the anti-nuke encampment that they did not want problems with the local taxpayers and the county sheriff's department (*one boo*). You are not keeping that promise. If you remain here... (*silence*) inciting a riot... (*another silence, interrupted as crowd begins to cheer*). I am asking you.... If you do not follow the patrol car and disperse, I will be forced to arrest (*cheers*). You will not be issued a mild letter (*louder cheers*). Attention! This is Ken Greer, sheriff. I am ordering you to follow that patrol car back to the parking lot at the sheriff's department. If you follow the patrol car to the parking lot, you will be allowed to continue your march later. This message is for those women from the antinuke encampment. I am asking you for your cooperation.

Kim is talking to some of the men who blocked the bridge. Many of them come up only to her chest.

CHILD *(taunting Kim):* Hey, bigfoot!

MAN 20 *(to Kim):* Go out of here and don't bother us. We'll all make sure; we'll help these deputies and make sure nobody gets hurt. As long as they go down this road and get out of town we won't bother them. They'll be free and we'll even protect them to get out. Nobody will touch them or bother them. No one.

KIM: All right, well, what we have said, what we have agreed is that if we start going that way, you will stay here and we're going to go that way.

MAN 4: The crowd will hold back, we promise.

MAN 20: We'll hold the crowd here. Just don't come back this way.

KIM: Okay, I wanted to let you know that I talked to....

WOMAN PROTESTER 5: What about our cars here?

MAN 22: You're going to have to figure out a way to get them, like we said.

WOMAN PROTESTER 6: Well we don't got helicopters.

MAN 23: When you got arrested at the depot they dropped you off at the other end—you had to get back to your cars too. Worry about that—that's your problem—we didn't call you here. You came. You should have thought about that before you came here. This ain't Romulus. We care about our town.

KIM: My name's Kim.

MAN 20: Okay, just get them out. We want them out.

Kim Blacklock of the encampment talks to Sheriff Ken Greer in Waterloo.
Photo by Pam Quigle

MAN 21: Tell them we want them going.

MAN 22: That's all we want.

SHERIFF *(to crowd, on bullhorn):* Please cooperate. I'm asking the individuals or group who is on the other side to disperse, to go back to your business establishment or your home.

Tear gas is released by someone in the crowd.

PEOPLE IN CROWD: Tear gas? Tear gas? Are they bringing out tear gas? Did somebody just leak some tear gas?

REPORTER; Someone's leaking tear gas. Shit, I didn't think they had tear gas in Waterloo!

SHERIFF *(on bullhorn):* I'm asking the local citizens to disperse and return to your homes. Please. This is a volatile situation and I am asking for your cooperation. Those local citizens that are gathered here—any expenses resulting from this demonstration or from a riot situation will be passed down to the local taxpayers.

REPORTER *(To sheriff's Deputy):* Hey, Dale, you guys using tear gas? What's that smell?

DEPUTY ARCANGELI: No, somebody threw it; it's somebody here.

SHERIFF: ...the cost will be attributed to you if you refuse to disperse. In addition, *you* will also take the chance of being arrested for inciting a riot. All children are also to leave. All citizens are requested to leave. Immediately. *(Gives bullhorn to encampment woman.)*

WOMAN FROM THE ENCAMPMENT *(on bullhorn):* In the spirit of free activity, in the spirit of searching for alternatives, in the spirit of teaching the community here that we love them and they are part of us and we are part of them, I urge you that we accept an alternative route, that we continue our march, that in about five minutes we turn around, we take our walk as we did before, that we follow the red car over there. The police has promised us, Sheriff Greer has promised us he will back us up. We search for alternatives to peace. Let's search for an alternative right now, in the spirit of reconciliation.

(Light applause, some boos from males; the women seated refuse to go.)

SHERIFF *(to same peaceful man who interrupted him before and is standing nearby):* I don't know who you are, fellow, but I'm not backing down, and I just gave you an order a few minutes ago for the citizens to disperse. Now *move it!* folks. Move out. Go back to your homes. What are you waiting for? You are disobeying a police order. You are, by remaining, inciting a riot situation. *(Crowd starts chanting "Go home" again.)*Ladies from the encampment, I am asking you also to disperse. I am asking you to immediately move out.

The sheriff gives orders for the women on the ground to be put into waiting ambulances and paddy wagon. The crowd, which was beginning to disperse, comes rushing back as the deputies grab the women by their ankles and wrists and carry them away. Most of the women go limp. The crowd cheers and jeers, calling out to the deputies by name, telling them they are doing a great job. Jay Cooper, wearing a fatigue jacket and carrying a rifle on his shoulder comes walking toward the women on the ground. Several sheriff's deputies and firemen see him and wrestle him to the ground. He is taken away.

Melley Kleman and her daughter Mazie come to the front of the crowd and find themselves next to the group of seated women. About twenty-five women have already been dragged away. About nine or ten are still sitting in the circle. As one woman is removed, another encampment woman sits

Woman being arrested in Waterloo. Photo by Pam Quiggle

down to take her place. Melley and Mazie watch; then Melley goes over to her husband Tom, who is talking to a newspaper reporter.

MELLEY *(to Tom):* What are they doing?

TOM: Well, the women tried to walk through and, uh, the townspeople formed a barrier and wouldn't let them through.

MELLEY: But what are they doing? Who are they arresting?

TOM: They're arresting them, the women.

MELLEY: Well, why are they arresting the women? Why aren't they arresting the people who won't let them walk through?

TOM: I, uh....

Tom is interrupted by someone who starts talking to him. Melley walks away. She returns to Mazie, who is still standing near the seated women. They watch as the police come over to the group and roughly drag two women to the truck. The police are red faced and angry. Next they return and pick up an elderly woman who is dressed in a neat wraparound skirt and a T-shirt. They grab her by the wrists and ankles and roughly lift her so that her skirt goes flying over her head as they carry her away. Melley watches in disbelief. After the next woman is carried away Melley sits down and takes her place in the circle. Mazie is obviously amazed. A sheriff's deputy comes over and starts to grab her wrists, but Melley stands up and faces him instead.

DEPUTY 2 *(surprised when he recognizes her):* What are you doing here?

MELLEY: What are *you* doing here?

Deputy 2 looks away, walks her over to the police van, puts her in.

MAN IN CROWD *(standing near Tom Kleman):* That's awful funny, the wife of the bank president being put in the police truck like that. *(Calling out to Tom)* Hey, Tom, they just took your wife away!

YOUNG MAN *(Runs up to Tom):* Mr. Kleman, Mr. Kleman, they just put Mrs. Kleman in the paddy wagon!

TOM: Come on, this is no time for fooling around, this is serious.

YOUNG MAN *(sincerely, with wide eyes):* I'm not kidding!

Scene 2

Inside the police van. A sheriff's deputy armed with rifle, pistols, and extra ammunition gets in and closes the door, standing next to it. Inside, the truck is dark and steamy.

ARRESTED WOMAN 1: I wonder where they're going to take us. How long are we going to be in here?

MELLEY: You're only going to go two blocks

ARRESTED WOMAN 1: You know that? You mean you're from around here?

MELLEY: Yeah.

Melley starts to stand up.

DEPUTY 3: Get back on that floor.

MELLEY: I only want to look out the window. My husband doesn't know I got arrested. I want to see if I can see him.

DEPUTY 3 *(angry):* Sit down!

Truck starts to move away. Women are silent and frightened until they arrive at the sheriff's department. The door opens and the arrested women are led into an outdoor recreation yard. One side is fenced and three sides are concrete walls. A broken basketball hoop hangs from one wall; two broken picnic tables stand in one corner. Little patches of grass pop up from the otherwise bare dirt. About forty arrested women are already in the yard as this last group of about fourteen arrested women comes in.

ARRESTED WOMAN 1 *(just getting out of the van):* We're the last ones.

SEVERAL ARRESTED WOMEN: We need to form a circle. Let's form a circle.

Arrested women begin to gather in a circle. Several women stay outside the circle's edge. Melley and another woman sit on the picnic tables. Several others stand in the shade, crying. The arrested women begin to talk in turn, introducing themselves and expressing thoughts and ideas.

ARRESTED WOMAN 3: My name is Kerry, and, uh, I'll speak first. First, are there any doctors or lawyers here? *(The arrested women look at each other but no one answers.)* No? *(One arrested woman puts her hand up tentatively.)* Are you?

ARRESTED WOMAN 4: I'm just a legal assistant.

ARRESTED WOMAN 3: Okay, then, our first job is to get some lawyers in here.

ARRESTED WOMAN 5: I've got to go to the bathroom.

ARRESTED WOMAN 3: Yeah, we've got to set up some sort of facilities here.

SEVERAL ARRESTED WOMEN: Yeah, we need it, we'd better soon *(giggles).*

ARRESTED WOMAN 6: We need some water too.

Arrested women within the circle continue discussing the situation. Deputy 3 comes in while they are talking.

SEVERAL ARRESTED WOMEN: We need a bathroom. Yeah, and some water. Can you hurry up please.

Deputy 3 goes out and reenters with a matron a few minutes later.

MATRON: Okay, whoever wants to use the bathroom, I can only take you out one at a time. *(Arrested women groan.)* Line up!

A few arrested women get in line. The rest wait in the circle. The matron walks out with one woman. Other arrested women continue talking in the circle.

ARRESTED WOMAN 7: I usually don't give my name when I'm arrested. I go by Jane Doe and I'm going to do that this time too.

ARRESTED WOMAN 8: Look, they're going to come out and threaten us if we don't use our right names. They're going to threaten us with very long jail terms, but don't be afraid of that. They can't do that; that's just a threat. Don't let them scare you.

MELLEY: What's wrong with giving your name? I'm going to give my name because I want, you know, to get out of here.

ARRESTED WOMAN 1: She's the lady that's local!

ARRESTED WOMAN 9: Can you tell us where we are?

MELLEY: This is the sheriff's jail in Waterloo. This is the county seat of Seneca County so this is the county's jail. We're just a few blocks from the bridge; they didn't take us far. I live here in Waterloo, and I don't know what happened. It just looks like everybody was nuts, you know. I just can't believe this happened. But I can't believe anything else bad will happen to us, I hope. But I don't understand why we can't give our names, why you don't want to give your names.

ARRESTED WOMAN 9: I was just, some of us were just arrested for protesting nuclear subs in Groton, Connecticut, and if they find out I was arrested before, they'd treat me worse now.

ARRESTED WOMAN 10: Yeah, if they find out that you are a repeater they get more harsh. Some of us have already gone over the fence at the depot. I'm going as Jane Doe too. *(Other women nod in agreement.)*

Deputy 3 comes in. He angrily reads an announcement that the women are going to be arrested and that they must give their true names or face three to five years in jail.

ARRESTED WOMAN 3: We're getting hungry. Can we get some food, some sandwiches or anything?

DEPUTY 3 *(red and angry):* Who the hell do you think you are. You don't deserve nothing and we don't have to feed you until dinnertime. You disrupted this town, this jail, completely. We'll do what we can but we can't handle a bunch of people like you. We'll be coming back soon to process you, so line up.

Deputy 3 leaves. Arrested women continue to talk in circle. Deputy 3 returns with deputy 4.

DEPUTY 3: Okay, who's first? *(Melley raises her hand, but he doesn't see it; he angrily grabs an old woman in front of him and shoves her toward deputy 4.)* You're first. Get going.

MELLEY: I'll volunteer.

DEPUTY 3: Okay, you're second. Come with me *(grabs her arm and leads her out).*

Deputy 3 leads Melley to a room in the jail, where she sees another woman sitting on a chair, sobbing. Deputy 5 tries to measure her height but fumbles with the measuring device. Melley is taken over to have her picture taken. A sign with her name and number is put around her neck. She is told to hold it in front of her chest. Deputy 6 complains she is too short, and he can't see sign. She puts it higher, but it is tilted. Finally, the picture is taken. Melley is then directed to a seat across the table from matron 2. The other woman is seated at a similar table next to her, sobbing. Two deputies are standing behind matron 2, who is nervous.

MATRON 2: What's your name.

MELLEY: Mrs. Melley Kleman.

MATRON 2: Date of birth?

MELLEY: November 6, 1927.

MATRON 2: What's your address? *(She writes the answer.)*

MELLEY: Waterloo.

MATRON 2: What race are you?

DEPUTY 7 *(leans over to her):* We're putting them all down as Caucasian. It doesn't matter what they say.

MATRON 2: What color are your eyes?

MELLEY: Blue.

MATRON 2: What color is your hair?

MELLEY: Gray.

DEPUTY 7 *(interrupts before she can write it down):* Gray is not a legal color.

Matron and Melley look at each other. No one speaks for a few seconds.

MELLEY: Well, you know, I used to be blond.

MATRON 2 *(looking up at deputy):* Well, what do you want me to write?

DEPUTY 5 *(leaning over and looking at Melley's hair):* I still see some blond there. Put blond-gray down. Yeah, put blond-gray.

Matron 1 writes on form. Next to Melley, the other woman is sobbing and refuses to answer any questions.

DEPUTY 8 *(screaming at other woman):* You're going to sit here till you tell us your name, lady. Don't think you're gonna pull this stuff on us. I don't care what you do when you're arrested at the depot—we aren't gonna take that sort of stuff. You can pull that off in the city, but you can't pull it off here. We're going to fill out this form if it takes five days. What is your name? When were you born? What is the color of your hair.

The woman continues to sob.

DEPUTY 3 *(to Melley):* You're done. Take her back to the bullpen.

Melley stands up, but doesn't know which way to go. Matron 4 comes up behind her, pushes Melley's back.

MATRON 4: Walk along, you.

Melley and Matron 4 walk back to the area where the arrested women are gathered. They all rush over to greet Melley since she is the first to return. She explains what happened. Arrested women come over one by one to thank her.

ARRESTED WOMAN 10: Thank you for doing this with us. It means a lot since you're from around here.

ARRESTED WOMAN 11: Yeah, really, you're really brave.

MELLEY: I don't think of what I did as brave.

ARRESTED WOMAN 12: It's so wonderful. Thanks.

Deputy 3 brings in a woman lawyer, who addresses the group.

LAWYER: I'm a lawyer from the encampment. Things are a little crazy and confusing outside. The townspeople have gathered outside the jail, and a lot of the women from the encampment are there too. The cops have separated the townspeople from us, but it is still very threatening. I don't think there will be another confrontation, but I don't know. The women are setting up a vigil to wait for you. We're working to get you out. First thing, don't let them frighten you. You don't have to give your name if you don't want. They can't force you. This whole thing is going to be really slow because the police are not prepared for this. Also, they know they are in the wrong and don't know what to do.

Deputy 3, who is standing there listening, grabs the lawyer's arm and starts to pull her back out the door.

DEPUTY 3: That's long enough. You've had all the time you can have with them.

He pulls the lawyer out the door. Deputy 4 comes back in with sobbing other woman. Arrested women gather around her as she cries. Deputy 4 stays near the door.

ARRESTED WOMEN: What happened? What did they do to you?

OTHER WOMAN *(sobbing):* Just give me a minute.

The other woman walks over to the fence, puts her hands on it, and bangs her head lightly against it as she cries. Deputy 4 comes running over, grabs her arm, and spins her around.

DEPUTY 4: Look, lady, I don't know what kind of pigpen you come from, but we keep a clean, neat jail here, and you ain't going to rub hair grease all over our fence. You keep you hands off that fence. We ain't going to repaint it after you.

Several arrested women come over to the other woman, put their arms around her, and lead her away as she tells them about her interrogation. Several other arrested women come up to Melley.

ARRESTED WOMAN 13: We don't know if we will ever see you again, but can I thank you now?

MELLEY: Oh, you'll see me again.

ARRESTED WOMAN 14: Oh, I don't think so. Thanks. You'll be going soon.

DEPUTY 3 *(shouting):* Melley Kleman? *(Melley raises her hand.)* Come with me.

Melley walks out with deputy 3. Arrested women say goodbye.

14

Good Americans

Our nation is not embroiled primarily in a battle of the sexes, but a battle of philosophies . . . between those who hold the pro-family biblical values up-on which this nation was founded, and those who embrace the humanist/feminist philosophy.

—USA Committee

For weeks afterward, Waterloo bridge was *the* topic of private com-munications and public discourse in Seneca County. The blockade of the bridge and the arrest of the encampment women came to be seen as the central event of the summer of 1983. But the potential for violence so vividly demonstrated at Waterloo never fully developed that summer. Several other events after Waterloo threatened to erupt into major inci-dents, and a few did result in small-scale physical confrontations between the encampment women and local people. But all the fears that the encampment would be bombed or burned to the ground, that women would be shot, beaten, or driven out of town by angry mobs did not materialize.

When Melley Kleman walked out of the sheriff's jail, she saw large crowds of local residents and encampment women shouting at each other and waving flags and signs from opposite sides of the street in front of the sheriff's department. Much later that night, the fifty-two arrested women were transferred to a makeshift jail in a school at Interlaken in the southern part of the county, far from Waterloo. For five days afterward, small groups of encampment women who held vigils at the school were shoved, punched, jabbed with flags, and verbally harassed by counter-demonstrators. Several of the women were eventually arrested, but no counterdemonstrators were.

About a hundred people threatened to attack five peace camp women during a late-night demonstration at the depot gate if the police did not arrest the women for crossing over the yellow line that marked the boundary between legal and illegal entry. When the police refused, the crowd surged around the women, punching and kicking them. Most reports of the incident say that the sheriff's deputies watched the attacks but did nothing to intervene. On August 1, between fifteen hundred and three thousand women took part in the central demonstration of the summer, a march to the depot. About two hundred to five hundred local residents watched but did not interfere as 240 women climbed the depot fence and were arrested. Several days later, the women who had been arrested in Waterloo (minus two who had escaped) were cleared of all charges and released during a raucous trial at the Waterloo fairgrounds. In terms of reference events that the community could share and discuss, the rest of the summer was anticlimatic. None of the other incidents took on the symbolic import of the Waterloo bridge blockade.

The name Waterloo is most closely associated with Napoleon Bonaparte's defeat in 1815, and to "meet one's Waterloo" is to suffer a final, decisive defeat. Several days after the incident at Waterloo bridge, T-shirts with the slogan "I survived the women who met their Waterloo" were being sold in town and were available from a clerk at the sheriff's department. Yet this battle of Waterloo did not really provide a clear-cut victory for either side. The encampment, for example, saw some positive signs in the incident, suggesting that it was the point at which many of the local people turned in their favor. Many local people visited the encampment in the following days to apologize and make donations. The encampment participants took the visits as evidence that the residents were taking a stand in their favor.

It is probably better, however, to see the incident as a drama with an ambiguous and problematic conclusion. All the narrative developments of the summer led up to Waterloo bridge. Here the criteria defining who was a proper member of the local community and who was an unwelcome outsider should have been decided. Also on the agenda was determining proper membership criteria for the larger American community. At issue that hot summer's day on a bridge in upstate New York was nothing less that who could count as a real American.

To make this judgment, the local residents needed a way to measure their actions and beliefs against those of the encampment women. They needed an American prototype, an ideal reference point for their judgments. Much cultural knowledge is arranged in terms of such prototypes, and we judge quality and legitimacy in terms of ideal cases (Lakoff 1987: 87).

For many of the Seneca County residents, particularly those involved in the bridge blockade, the prototype of the Good American, the example against which to measure all other potential Americans, was the male war veteran. This choice of the veteran as the American prototype was not just a retroactive valuing of the actual men, particularly the veterans, who instigated the bridge blockade. Rather, Waterloo saw itself as America writ small and, in some ways, writ better than the rest of America. Besides being the "home of the concept of the Pullman Car and the forerunner of modern embalming," according to a local newspaper (*Reveille*, August 3, 1983), Waterloo is the birthplace of Memorial Day. It was the first town to consistently celebrate the holiday designed to remind all Americans that it was the veteran who defined America.

The historical marker in front of the high school identifies Waterloo as the center of the discourse on American identity. On this marker, the town's creation of the observance is described as complete, comprehensive, and genuinely original, an old-fashioned community effort of the sort that still characterizes Waterloo. The marker reads in part:

> On May 5, 1866, the residents of Waterloo held the first complete, community-wide observance of Memorial Day. They dedicated the entire day to honoring the Civil War dead in a solemn and patriotic manner. Throughout the village, flags, draped in mourning, flew at half mast. Ladies prepared wreaths and bouquets for each veteran's grave. Businesses closed, and veterans, civic organizations and townspeople marched to the strains of martial music to the village cemeteries. There, with reverent prayer and patriotic ceremonies, the tradition of Memorial Day was born.

Waterloo prided itself on being the true source of this commemorative day (despite challenges from other communities that also claim the honor) and on celebrating the "real" day, not the convenient three-day weekend version set up by the federal government. In 1984, the year after the encampment, Waterloo decided to return to a traditional May 30 celebration. In 1991, the town held a major celebration of the 125th anniversary of Memorial Day.

War provided the veteran with the most direct and time-honored access to the category Good American by having him risk his life to defend the very definition of the nation and its people. War, Elaine Scarry tells us, has a very particular function: it provides an arena in which the "national self-definitions of the disputing countries that have collided" can be played out, where each side can attempt to force the other to "retract, alter or relinquish its own form of self-belief" (1985:114). The designation of winner and loser in war refers as much to this alteration of "national consciousness, political belief, and self-definition" (ibid.) as it does to the loss of life, territory, and property. The United States has usually been the "winner" in war, retaining its self-definition and forcing its opponents to alter theirs.

With Vietnam, the United States had to face the other side of the war experience; it had to question its identity, its sense of itself as a nation and a united people. The veteran of a successful war comes back to a country whose self-definition has been renewed and affirmed, but the veteran of a war like Vietnam loses this status as defender of the national identity and the easy entrée into the category Good American which goes along with "defending the country." If military experience is supposed to give a young man immediate status as a Good American, the Vietnam War did just the opposite: it blamed the Vietnam veteran for the loss of national purpose and identity. Instead of creating veterans who were automatically considered Good Americans, it made veterans who were thought to exhibit the most antisocial and "un-American" characteristics.

The Waterloo bridge incident, in taking the veteran as the prototype, produced an interesting twist, one of the effects of Vietnam as a different kind of war. As Vietnam veteran and Waterloo resident Jerry McKenna explained, "My own true feeling of the bridge was this was like the Vietnam veteran get-even time. You know, now we're gonna strike back at the radicals that struck at us." The Vietnam veterans believed that the protesters of the 1960s had robbed them of a proper war experience and thus an easy entrée into the category Good American and all the benefits that go with it. As stand-ins for the earlier protesters the present-day demonstrators might provide the Vietnam veterans the chance symbolically to right the wrongs of ten to fifteen years earlier. After the start of the war with Iraq in 1991, news coverage of antiwar protesters emphasized that during this war, unlike Vietnam, Americans came out to show their support for the troops. Again the anti-war protesters stood in for those of the 1960s. Efforts by the military and the press to stress that the Persian Gulf War was not going to be like Vietnam were at least partially directed at the postwar status of the soldiers.

The early 1980s saw the first signs that the Vietnam experience was being revised. The Vietnam Memorial in Washington, D.C., was dedicated in 1982; Vietnam veterans began joining the American Legion and VFW in larger numbers; and plays, books, comic books, and Hollywood movies began using Vietnam more frequently as a topic, reevaluating and rewriting the Vietnam story. The Waterloo incident occurred two years before Sylvester Stallone's blockbuster movie *Rambo: First Blood, Part II*, but it had a similar theme. As John Rambo asks when he is sent back on a rescue mission to Vietnam, "Do we get to win this time?" Throughout the early 1980s the Vietnam veteran was slowly being brought into the prototypical category of Good American, and the proper narratives about veterans were being restored.

How does the veteran define the Good American better than other possible candidates? First, the veteran has physical proof of his membership in the category, having given his body "in the service" of his country. The veteran is the literal embodiment of the category because he has offered his body for use by America to maintain "herself." Whether or not the veteran has been in actual battle and despite any fear, loathing, or anger he may have experienced in the service, he has proven himself willing and able to put his life "on the line" for his country. This relinquishing of the control of his body is unusual for the American male (except perhaps in team contact sports) and is adequately justified only if bolstered by a mystique of transcendental necessity: he has to make this sacrifice for the good of the country (or the team).

Veterans whose bodies bear the record of wounds from combat possess a visible reminder of the sacrifices they made, and their bodies display the intertwined history of their own and their country's involvement in combat. Wartime experiences intricately tie the body to the state, so that the body stands for the state on the field of battle (Scarry 1985:112) and subsequently, when the soldier is transformed into a veteran. Several veterans of Seneca County urged their fellow citizens to remember that this physical sacrifice was a significant measure of being a "good American." In one letter to the editor, two veterans wrote: "The women seem to have forgotten how many of their countrymen perished in burning planes, sinking ships, flaming tanks, murderous beach assaults" (Syracuse *Post-Standard*, July 26, 1983).

That the women of the peace encampment ignored or denigrated this kind of sacrifice and chose instead to criticize the military seemed especially insulting, considering that women as a group were implicated in the motives for waging wars. Apparently, the idea that "women's removal from the ultimate sacrifice constrains their direct critiques of the wars" (Higonnet et al. 1987:14–15) was operating in Seneca County. For women to be ungrateful to the men who fought on their behalf and to criticize these men for defending their families and their country seemed ludicrous to many veterans.

Military service gave knowledge to the combat veteran that women could never have, and this knowledge, veterans believed, made them the best judges of proper American behavior and the proper authors of narratives about American life. The narratives of what it means to be a Good American had to harmonize with what they had learned in the service. Veterans are thought to develop the personal qualities associated with an ideal American in the military service if they did not already possess them. Loyalty, integrity, a respect for authority and tradition—all are traits that veterans value and believe Good Americans must exhibit. One Seneca County veteran made such a connection between his war experience and being a good, loyal American by telling the following story about his entry into the service and its relation to his immigrant father's ideal of a Good American:

> Now my father emigrated to this country when he was eleven years old, and the First World War broke out, and he volunteered, [but] he couldn't read or write English. . . . He could not go overseas of course because he could not read or write, but this man had such a love for this country. Now when I went in, and I was leaving, he took me by my hand to the door, and he said, "I want you to know that this is my country. I went away and I served it, and now you are going to serve it. There are two ways through that door," he says; "you can go out of it and you can come back, but you can only come back if you serve and you love it. If you don't and you discredit this country in any way, or me, because this is my country, I do not want you to come in this house again."

Was this use of the veteran as the American prototype peculiar to Seneca County or was it a more widely shared means of making judgments about people in the United States? Another place to see veterans serving as prototypes is in a public incident larger than any that occurred in Seneca County. The congressional hearings on the Iran-Contra scandal held in the summer of 1987 provided a splendid opportunity to see the Good American category and its prototype, the veteran, in action. In these hearings, which focused on the the sale of arms to Iran and the use of proceeds from these sales to supply money to the Contras in Nicaragua, many of the participants invoked their status as veterans and as good veteran Americans to justify their actions or establish their credibility. Many witnesses described who they were by providing details of their military service. Lieutenant Colonel Oliver North, for example, described his naval academy training and his service in the Marine Corps in his introductory statement. North also described National Security Council director (retired) Admiral John Poindexter as a distinguished naval officer, and he called CIA director William Casey "a renowned lawyer, a war veteran of heroic proportions," even though both men had long been civilians.

When the loyalty and patriotism of the congressional committee was called into question because it was criticizing the Reagan administration, committee cochair Warren Rudman, in order to prove to the listening and watching audience that there were indeed Good Americans on the committee, referred to the military records of the committee members to prove their status: "Represented on this panel are sixteen members who served in the service, eight who served in combat, a number with great distinction—with medals for valor and heroism from Guadalcanal to the Lingayen Gulf."

In the Iran-Contra hearings, the veteran's literal embodiment of the category Good American was utilized most effectively in relation to two of the participants, Oliver North and the committee chairman Senator Daniel Inouye of Hawaii. North, although he had not been on active duty with the marines since his 1981 assignment to the National Security Council, nevertheless appeared in his marine uniform and medals, presenting a striking military appearance that the press repeatedly remarked upon. One editorial cartoon showed North's empty but erect uniform sitting next to his lawyer at the witness table. The caption read, "Colonel North couldn't make it to the hearings today, but he sent along his uniform for questioning."

On the last day of North's testimony, the vice-chairman of the committee, Senator Warren Rudman, announced that the committee had been receiving calls and messages that contained "ugly racial slurs" against Chairman Inouye (who is of Japanese descent and thus suspected by many who use World War II as a reference point) because of his treatment of Oliver North. Rudman bolstered Inouye's reputation as a good American with the most concrete of evidence: he reminded the audience that Inouye had sacrificed an arm for his country and had surely proven his loyalty whatever his ethnic heritage. These incidents from Iran/Contra suggested that the veteran could claim status as a Good American with little fear of contradiction.

In the controversy that developed when George Bush selected Senator Dan Quayle as his running mate in the 1988 presidential elections, the criterion was used against the candidate. The Democrats criticized Quayle for using family influence to avoid military service during the Vietnam era, and they questioned his integrity and his status as a Good American. By contrast, the Democratic candidates both emphasized their own active military service to bolster their own claims to be Good Americans. The Republicans countered by questioning the Democratic candidate's stance on the Pledge of Allegiance and the American flag.

The category Good American, as our commonsense notions and folk categorizations seem to indicate, involves not legal criteria of citizenship but judgments about behavior, beliefs, and attitudes. These judgments are made not by comparing persons to a list of traits but by comparing persons to other kinds of persons, particularly to the prototype, the veteran. Although it was clear to Seneca County residents that the encampment women were not prototypical veteran Americans, they were nevertheless expected to admire and emulate the prototype.

Although some Seneca County residents could not accept anything about the protests or the protesters, many separated content from style and said that *what* the women were trying to do—the nuclear protest—was basically acceptable but *how* they were doing it was completely out of line. Seneca residents expressed the opinion that the protesting had to be done in a particular way for it to be legitimate, acceptable, and believable, that there was a right way and a wrong way to protest, and these women were just not playing by the rules. Many residents agreed that, "nobody wants a nuclear war." One woman said she told the protesters, "I'm for it, and I admire you, but not the way you're doing it." A Waterloo woman said in a newspaper interview, "I think it has had an effect on the people in this area by making people more aware of the issues, not only here but in other areas and countries. Even though it may be a good idea, they are going about it the wrong way" (Syracuse *Post-Standard*, July 21, 1983).

The residents suggested a hierarchy of protest strategies, from the most proper step—working within the system by electing officials and lobbying Congress—and progressing to public demonstrations only as a last, unpleasant resort if it seemed that the system was clearly not going to bring about the desired results. In any case, they believed, the purpose of a protest was to right some wrong, not to dismantle the entire system within which that tiny wrong existed.

A secretary in one of the county offices explained how proper protesting should begin—not with the weird rituals of the encampment but with systematic political action: "If they want to prove something, then start getting some funding for the people they want in the elected positions. Instead of paying for this peace encampment with civil disobedience and their activity, get those women to contribute to a candidate they want to run for office, put him in office, and make him fight for them. That's how the system works." One man asked in the Rochester *Democrat and Chronicle* (August 3, 1983): "Why don't they go and elect someone who will listen to them? Why don't they go home and around election time vote for Jane Fonda? She opposes nuclear power and arms." A past commander of the Waterloo VFW post used the VFW as an example of how protesting should be done. Local VFW posts, he maintained, do not get involved in politics. Unlike these peace camp women, the VFW doesn't march in the streets when it wants its voice heard. Instead, it maintains permanent lobbyists in Washington. That's where the women should go if they want to be heard. If the local VFW (which has more than five hundred members) doesn't like something that is happening, it tells the regional headquarters in Albany, which relays the information to the national headquarters in Kansas City, and the lobbyists go right to the source of power, to the president if necessary. When the lobbyists go in, they know they are representing two million members. The women, this veteran thought, were going about it the wrong way: the people at the depot did not make the decisions; the source of power was not locally based but entrenched in the nation's capital.

Many local people believed that the system provided the means for bringing about changes without the total disruption of everyday life Seneca County was experiencing. That these methods for challenging the system required money, influence, or group memberships that were not accessible to all people did not seem to be criteria for judging the effectiveness or fairness of these routes of protest. Some of the local residents seemed to think that the encampment women had not given the system already in place a chance. If the women had already tried established routes of protest and were still frustrated, it might be all right to demonstrate publicly, but the demonstrations had to be conducted properly.

Some of the local veterans were able to suggest ways that a public demonstration could be carried out without threatening the whole American system. One vet suggested, "I would have had a representative from the organization [the encampment] approach this organization [the VFW] and the American Legion, maybe your Marine Corps League, saying that they wanted to protest the nuclear whatever they have that we don't know about out there." Another vet thought it would be logical to contact the military organizations first: "they asked us to go to war for them, didn't they? Why didn't they ask us to go to peace for them too?"

The next proper step in the public display of dissatisfaction with American nuclear policy would be to have a "parade or something" organized by all the groups and led by the color guard from the military organizations. It would have been okay, one vet explained, "if it were orderly and it was... no, not discrete, we didn't want it discrete... if it was brought out in the open with a big parade, like you have on the Fourth of July or Memorial Day."

From the point of view of some of the local people a parade would have been a much more effective form of demonstration than something like the Waterloo bridge incident. With a parade, the women could have walked from Seneca Falls and through Waterloo without incident because they would have had a military escort. As it was, many of the local people saw the women as deliberately "attacking Waterloo," not just marching through it. If all the people had walked together in one color-guard-led parade, one vet explained, then "Ivan Roosky [could] read [about] this and say, 'Well, look at the big parade they're having to show they don't want a nuclear war. Okay, they don't want it any more than we want it; we don't want it any more than they want it.' And if it had been presented in the right way, then they [the Russians] would have seen it." What we didn't want the Russians to see, this man and several others insisted, was that Americans were weak or fighting among themselves or disagreeing. That would give them the wrong impression and would make us vulnerable.

If a parade were not to the peace camp's liking, there were other possibilities. One veteran explained, "I wouldn't go into your county and do the things they done. I may go into your county and protest something I don't like, but I'd do it in the way the Constitution says you have the right to do it," which, he said, is with "pickets" who are orderly. "You protest the way the law allows you to protest," said another veteran with experience in Vietnam. He continued, "There's rules and regulations for protest. . . . You don't protest by hanging dirty signs and you don't run around bare naked."

Vietnam veteran Jerry McKenna described a proper protest he had seen at the depot one day:

My wife and I took a ride one night; we went all the way around Seneca Army Depot. . . . There was some cars from out of town, and these people [were commemorating] the atom bomb they dropped on Hiroshima; very nice well-dressed people get out of their cars, they took their signs out of their trunk, they walked over, got on the grass, sit down in their lawn chairs, put their signs up next to them, and they protested the bombing of Hiroshima. . . . They voiced their opinion, and more power to them. They didn't come in my back yard; they didn't come into the town where I live.

McKenna compared these pleasant middle-aged Asian protesters with an experience one of his friends had with two encampment women:

> Two women stopped in front of these peoples' house. One of them hikes her skirt up, squats down, and pees in the middle of the street, right in front of these kids. The kids go running back in the house, "Ma, you should see what just happened!" [She says], "I don't believe something like that!" The woman walks up—sure enough. She says, "Hey, there's the wet spot right in the middle of the road!"
>
> [The other protesters] were older people. . . . Some of their ancestors might have been Japanese, Koreans, or whatever it was. To me, that was more the right way to do something. You get the same publicity, and they did, they got the same publicity. Photographers went out there. Here's a guy that I'll never forget, he had on a pair of light, real light yellow pants and a darker yellow shirt, very well dressed. Nice shined boots. The woman, very nice dress on, another woman very nice pair of slacks, blouse. . . . The car, I think it might have been about a two-year-old automobile. But they came in, they did their thing, they caused no one any problems.
>
> If you want to go out there and protest and you walk up and down the road and you carry a sign that says, "I protest Reagan and the Cruise missiles," I have no problem with that. *But*, if you go out and you walk up and down that road, and you have two other women with you, and all of a sudden about twelve o'clock when it's time for dinner, I call the kids and they come around the corner and you're making out with one of the women that are with you, then we have a problem. . . . You got a tambourine out there, and I'm trying to sit in here and listen to my TV, and it's nine o'clock at night, and you're running up and down the road with candles in your hand beating on a tambourine, you and me got problems.

Some of the women from the encampment did make proper protests. Several of the local residents and government officials remembered fondly and favorably a group of protesters from Minnesota. These women especially delighted them because they were so "normal," so unlike the rest of the encampment women, and because they fit the notion of what a proper protester should be, do, and say. Robert Zemanek, the director of public information at the army depot, said he liked the two busloads of women from Minnesota because they looked like his grandmother. They were terribly polite, he explained, and said, "Yes, sir," and "No, sir," and "Can I have a bar letter now?" after they had committed civil disobedience and gone over the depot fence. They were interested in having the bar letters (notices from the depot warning against repeated trespassings), he said, because they wanted to show their grandchildren that they got arrested in Seneca. Zemanek did not take the letters as a sign of the women's commitment to serious political action; he thought of them as "souvenirs" of their adventures. The women were "cute," Zemanek explained, and the military personnel certainly preferred them to the other women protesters. A local woman who owned the diner across from the depot main gate remarked of the Minnesota women: "They're more respectable. They're just so much different than the other women. They don't come around in short skirts and Army boots." A cook at the same restaurant agreed: "They're sweet, little old ladies" (Syracuse *Post-Standard*, July 22, 1983).

Other antinuclear protesters who were mentioned as fitting the local idea of the proper protester were the members of the religious groups, especially the nuns, who regularly demonstrated at the depot. One local counterdemonstrator explained, "We've had demonstrations down there from some of the religious groups. Churches in Ithaca and Rochester have come down to protest, and pretty much they held prayer vigils. They were very calm about the whole ordeal." The nuns and religious protesters would also quietly hand out flyers to the workers and would clean up after themselves when they left.

Like the women from Minnesota and the Asian protesters Jerry McKenna saw, these protesters met the local expectations of what protesters should be, do, and say. The grandmothers from the farm country of Minnesota, the middle-aged, middle-class Asians, and the religious women of upstate New York had protested by the rules—that is, they had been quiet, nonaggressive, unobtrusive, discreet, and not at all youthfully exuberant or disrespectful. Moreover, they were stereotypically asexual; they had neither flaunted their sexuality nor made an issue of it in public discourse. It was in many ways the aura of open and active sexuality associated with a strong and aggressive feminist identity that made the encampment women so objectionable to the residents of Seneca County.

The idea that the content of the protests could and should be separated from their style was important for the local residents to propose. Defining content as what is being said and style as how it is said (Goodman 1978:23), the local people implied that the women should not mix feminist politics with antinuclear protests. Whereas the encampment women saw it as absolutely necessary to put the American nuclear weapons policy into the context of the larger web of social, political, sexual, and economic relations, the Seneca County people saw this strategy as unnecessarily complicated and confusing, and they were alarmed that it seemed to implicate "your average American" in the whole mess. They were particularly concerned by the attempt to relate feminism to nuclear opposition. A letter to the editor published in July soon after the encampment opened ran under the headline "Don't Let Feminist Cause Overshadow Nuclear Weapons Fight." The writer explained:

> Unfortunately, and most disturbing however, is that such a peaceful oriented and educational cause for nuclear disarmament has become caught up in a quagmire of gender-rooted issues. It seems that the nuclear disarmament dispute has become misconstrued by the organizers of this encampment in such a way as to divert its central focus and attention from the dangers of nuclear arms proliferation to one involving solely feminist causes.
>   While the feminist cause is obviously a valid and worthwhile endeavor, it should not be allowed to overshadow the present cause which it attempts to rectify. There is no place for partiality when dealing with such a meritorious goal. (*Democrat and Chronicle* July 10, 1983)

Many local people shared this man's fear that feminist issues were taking attention away from nuclear issues. This may seem a curious stance for a community that had till this time exhibited little concern about these same nuclear issues, but perhaps by July the antinuclear protests came to be seen overall as less threatening than the feminist concerns being expressed and acted out. The feminist approach connected all women's issues in a web of interrelations that implicated every aspect and every member of society in patriarchal nuclear practices. Nuclear weapons and the policies that established and supported them were not separate from the content of everyday life, according to this view. Several local people expressed the notion that it was the "big chiefs" in Washington and Russia and not the "little Indians" locally who were responsible for the national nuclear policy, but a feminist critique of the depot placed some of the blame on local supporters.

Style, when it is too noticeable (as the peace camp's was said to be), is often thought of as a barrier that detracts from the pure or accurate reception of a text, story, event, or work of art. But there can be no such thing as a styleless, neutral text that delivers content without tone or attitude or manner. Those who deny style often promote the idea that people who consciously choose a style to deliver their content are being insincere or are needlessly intruding upon their message. Concentrating on content and dismissing style was a way to allow the local people to control the discourse about the protests. By taking the content of the protests out of their performative context, out of the realm of social action and exchange, people could abstract issues so that they can be judged on their "inherent" merit, apart from their role in a larger system of political, economic, sexual, and social conditions. Unfortunately for the Seneca County residents, the women's style of protest brought up exactly the hidden aspect of nuclear arms policies and patriarchal culture that the local residents needed to repress. In a sense, the women's style of protest acted as the uncontrollable unconscious of society, revealing things the society wanted left unsaid and unseen.

Some differences in style are due to differences in content, according to Nelson Goodman (1978:25). This seems particularly true for feminist-style protests, which have resistance as their content and resistance as their manner. Feminist protests done in a "normal style" are not as much of a challenge because they are acted out in the exact marginal space assigned to them by the central figures in the society they are supposed to be challenging. In the alternative approach that the encampment women seemed to be taking, the nuclear discourse was applied not only to atomic bombs, deterrent strategies, weapons systems, and the potential apocalypse but to the very foundation of the Western world, what Jonathan Culler calls "patriarchal authority, unity of meaning and certainty of origin" (1982:61). This system, which Culler and others call phallogocentric (phallocentric in that the male/phallus is set up as the universal standard; logocentric because it relies on the notion of unity of identity in the self and the possibility of perfectly matching sign and signified), takes the atomic/nuclear as the metaphor for the organization of all social and political life, history, and thought. Nuclear weapons are just one manifestation of a larger, underlying, and in many ways objectionable system that feminists feel must be opposed.

Any discourse that opposes this phallogocentric discourse can be called antinuclear. The anti-nuclear challenges not just nuclear weapons but also the nuclear discourse that structures social life and thought, and so it is a particularly appropriate metaphor. Feminism and the antinuclear have always had an affinity for each other because each recognizes the nuclear discourse informing Western social and political life. Feminist and anti-nuclear activism can also be seen as models of and for other social forms and thoughts that oppose the phallogocentric order, including any of the voices in a complex, plural society that refuse to be assimilated, appropriated, or neutralized.

The feminist and the antinuclear offer a set of desires different from those of the patriarchal and the nuclear. They suggest an elimination of binary oppositions, expose the fictionality of coherence, and favor an emphasis on the play of differences. This desire for difference rather than acquiescence in the nuclear elimination of difference, Josette Féral notes, "opens up the system to the prospect of the plurality of possibilities whose recognition, up to the present time, has been forbidden" (1980:92). This is the great promise or, depending on one's position, the great threat of the feminist, nonnuclear future.

15

The Difference Within

If it wasn't for women, us men would still be walking around in skin suits carrying clubs.
—Ronald Reagan, August 3, 1983

The discrepancy between what the local communities thought the women of the encampment should be and what the women actually seemed to be caused a mighty uneasiness among the residents of Seneca County. They expressed this uneasiness in one very revealing way—through a critique of the use of the word *women* to refer to the encampment participants. When they used the word, they often qualified it, said it sarcastically, or put it in quotation marks. In whatever way they could they tried to indicate that the encampment misfits did not properly occupy the category called Women. Not only, then, did the protesters fail to achieve the category Good Americans, but they were also being eliminated from the most basic form of identity, as Women.

A secretary in the office of one of the local officials noticed the phenomenon. "It's funny," she said, "because people always put those quotes around women." She said, "THE WOMEN," in an exaggerated, deep tone that both emphasized and mocked the word. Her boss, a member of the Seneca County Board of Supervisors, also demonstrated. People would ask, he said, "How are [pause] THE WOMEN [pause] doing?"

One local man, describing to a group of fellow veterans his dislike of the encampment's protest style, could hardly bring himself to use the word: "The kind of protest that these—." He paused, then said in a quieter aside, "Now, I'm using the word *women*." He spoke as if he the label were being forced on him. Another man in the same group shared this reluctance to use the label for these protesters. He was giving an example of what he disliked about the protests. "I was at a picnic at Sampson, at the state park, and there were two of these [pause] 'WOMEN.' "Is that what you call them," another man asked. "Yes," he replied in a resigned voice.

In calls and letters to the local newspapers, residents also qualified the word or put it in quotation marks. They often justified their judgment about category membership by listing the proper qualities that Women have and that the peace camp "women" lacked. One caller to the Rochester *Democrat and Chronicle* said, "I would like [to] comment about the so-called women who are protesting at the Seneca Army Depot. I think they should be thoroughly ashamed of themselves. They are not the typical American woman. What they should be doing is out working, making a decent living, taking care of their children, helping the unfortunate, doing volunteer work (July 17, 1983). Another woman wrote: "And despite grandiose and presumptuous claims to represent 'women,' the group in Romulus is like any group anywhere that has the time, money, and inclination to get together: it represents only its own members" (*Finger Lakes Times*, July 7, 1983).

Some of the women who wrote letters or called used themselves as examples of what Women should be:

> I am a woman with a career (nursing), a husband (of 36 years), three grown children (two boys and one girl) all married, and five grandchildren. For all of our 36 years of marriage I have worked side by side with my husband, raised my three children (who to this day enjoy our company as much as their peers) and do not feel left out of anything.
>
> It certainly seems to me that those "women" could find something better to do with their lives and those of their children, who some saw fit to bring with them, besides belittling the men of our country who are there to protect us and our security system, rather than acting like "fools." (*Finger Lakes Times*, July 21, 1983)

One local woman paid for a full-page advertisement in the *Pennysaver* (August 9, 1983) in order to have her say:

> A WOMEN'S PEACE (?) CAMP in Seneca County
> The last time I read the meaning of the word "Peace" in the dictionary, it said something about tranquility and calmness. The "women" in Romulus are grouped together in a "Peace" camp, but the feeling these

"women" are spreading throughout our county is certainly NOT one of tranquility and calmness...

The ideas these "women" came to Seneca County with were perfectly justified, but the way they are carrying out their protest is certainly not—and the attitude they are creating about themselves within the people of Seneca County is equally justified. Did they expect the tax-payers to just sit by and let them get away with all they are doing without some kind of retaliation?

We all love our country and the flag that stands for her. Granted, where have we all been keeping our American flags until we wanted to show these "women" how we felt about their putdown of our flag? A lot of us don't put our flag out even on holidays—we don't even see many vendors selling them at parades anymore. But when someone puts down our country and her flag, we want to show them just how important they are to a real American. Let's not put our flags away in the cellar or closets anymore—keep them flying and keep the feeling these "women" have brought out alive and strong. I think they deserved the reaction they got in Waterloo on July 30th, and since that colorful Saturday. Our tax money, which we all work hard to pay for, is being spent on extra law enforcement and other necessities to keep these "Peace" demonstra-tors in line. Yet they continue to knowingly trespass on government property, they display activities that are making many people uncom-fortable—enough to even think about moving away from the "Peace" camp area. If one of us were to enter the depot unlawfully, or even to take showers in a public carwash, would we be arrested for indecent exposure or trespassing, given a letter and released? Certainly not.

County residents have lived and worked at the Depot for over 40 years—at least we hold jobs and have earned the protection of our law officers! IF there were any "weapons" stored at the depot, the govern-ment certainly did not ship them in just to give the "women" something to protest over—and IF they are there, the government will leave them there whether the "women" like it or not—but we will continue to live with and work at the depot.

These "women" have brought out many feelings of anger that were put to rest years ago—is that why they came here? If they wanted a "Peace" protest, they should have just remained on their little farm and left the people of Seneca County—and the law enforcement and tax money—out of it! This angry summer will not be over soon enough for some of us, and unfortunately the memory of all this will remain long after. Why can't these "women" who have already made the point that they wanted to make go back to their jobless lives wherever they live and let Seneca County return to being the quiet, peaceful place it used to be. Maybe they don't mind having their children subjected to nudity and intentional lawbreaking, but we don't want our children to be brought up with that in their everyday lives!

A Disgusted and Tired of "Women's Peace Camp"
Taxpayer of Seneca County
Who Holds A Job and A Husband
(paid advertisement)

Some of the letters sent directly to the encampment also put the word *women* in quotation marks; several were addressed "Ladies?" or "Ladies (I use that term very loosely)." One Waterloo woman said that those at the peace encampment shouldn't even be called women, never mind ladies. They were a disgrace to womanhood, she said, and she was ashamed she was the same gender. The local people called the encampment participants many different things (including kooks, dykes, Gypsies, goofballs, crap-asses, dirty scuzzy wrinkled hippies, communist pigs, disgusting comical hypocrites, a bunch of nuts, sluts and witches, weirdos, perverts, dirtbags, peaceniks, bitches, stupid hairy beasts, and the devil's children), but they steadfastly refused to acknowledge them as Women (without the quotation marks).

To many local people, the encampment participants' problematic status as Women seemed directly related to their feminism and style of protest. They collectively characterized this "feminist approach" as disruptive of everyday life, defiant toward authority, and focused on the public display and discussion of sexuality. They disapproved of the physical appearance of the protesters, their noisiness, their way of drawing attention to themselves, and their apparent lack of adult responsibilities. Each of these characteristics seemed a distinct challenge to the patriarchal system and the phallogocentric tradition that supported it.

Appearance was an especially sharp sign for the local people that these feminists were not Women as they knew Women to be. Appearance or image holds a special place in the patriarchal order because it is the initial way to make the all-important gender identification; this gender designation sets the tone for any subsequent encounter between social beings (Henley 1977:91). The body bears the burden of identity, and the body's appearance carries the specific conventions of a gender identity. The members of an interpretive community share a conventional, expected image of Women. Even though the image may not be exactly the same for every member of the community, "the degree of uniformity is remarkable," according to George Lakoff, and it is useful for judging a person's fit into the category that the image represents (1987:447).

Appearance is also important because it is thought to be an outward sign of the internal state of the human being, an easily read, accurate representation of the character of its bearer. The body's appearance has an aura of inevitability and naturalness about it, a concreteness that belies any effort to conceal what it is forced to display. The personality of a person is thought to shine through any attempt to disguise it through costume and cosmetics.

The "women" who did not look like Women in Seneca County presented an immediate challenge to the standard gender categories. Few peace camp attendees appeared in stereotypically feminine dress or in makeup and elaborate hairdos. Because "clothing powerfully defines sex roles," as Sandra Gilbert notes, women whose clothing was seen as unfeminine were perceived as falsely appearing and dressing as men (1982:195). This judgment was readily passed on the women at the encampment who had short haircuts and wore more "masculine" clothes—work boots, shorts or pants, and T-shirts and workshirts. These "women" who appeared more masculine caused discomfort because cross-dressing, says Annette Kuhn, threatens to "denaturalize the phenomena held in our culture to be most evidently and pre-eminently natural: sexual difference" (1985:54). A female who hides or denies her inner femaleness by cloaking it in masculine garb can be seen as perverting both culture and nature.

The thousands of women who came to Seneca County certainly must have presented a wide range of appearances and demeanors to their new neighbors. The local residents, however, tended to see them all as the same, as a type of woman whose body was uncontrollably displayed and exercised. Despite their differences in hairstyles, clothing, complexions, personal grooming, and body size, despite the fact that the women actually wore everything from prim suits to shorts and T-shirts, despite bathing habits that ranged from obsessive to lackadaisical, and despite armpits and legs that ranged from hirsute to hairless, all the women were thought to fit the model of the braless, smelly, inappropriately dressed, and unshaven female that was often called a "dirty, disgusting pig."

Many people attested to the filthiness of the "women." One woman reported that she had told some of the encampment "women," "I've never judged a woman by the way you dress, the length of your hair, or the color of your skin, but I do wish you ladies could get more showers" (*Democrat and Chronicle*, August 8, 1983). The acting police chief of Seneca Falls described the encampment "women" as "the dirtiest, smelliest people" he had ever seen. One local environmental conservation officer commented that one "woman" had had a nice face but she was really hairy and hadn't "taken a bath or washed her hair in two years." As they would say on the TV program *Hill Street Blues*, he said, she was a "real dirtbag." "I don't know who she was trying to impress," he continued, "but she didn't impress me."

"They're not very clean," one woman watching them demonstrate at the depot said. "I wouldn't go out in my yard the way they come dressed here tonight, most of them." Another woman, like many of her neighbors, postulated a connection between the "women's" appearance and their political stance: "It would be one thing if they came here looking halfway decent and demonstrated something decent, but when they come here dressed the way they are, with no bras on and filthy dirty, I mean, how can you look at them as a woman; I mean, what are they making of themselves?" "It makes all women look bad," she concluded.

The "women's" purported filth was also associated with the potential for disease and for pollution or infection of the local residents who had contact with them. Only a few people mentioned the possibility of AIDS at the encampment in 1983, but some thought that venereal disease and dysentery must be rampant there. One man claimed that people called the encampment "herpes village." A sheriff's deputy reported that local fears that the "women" would leave germs and bugs in their makeshift jail at the Interlaken School resulted in a reassuring fumigation of the school at the county's expense, despite the fact that no contamination was found there. Several complaints to the sheriff's department claimed that the "women" had dirtied showers at Sampson State Park with their filth, and one complainant in a letter to the editor claimed the "women" were picking lice off each other in the bathroom:

> My family was shocked to find that with total disregard for the law and regulations of the area, they proceeded to use the bathroom facilities which they left in such a filth that a pig would have been insulted.
>
> This alone would not have caused me to write this letter. It was the fact that my wife overheard and saw two of the women asking and checking each other to see if, after washing, all of the lice were gone.
>
> In my opinion, these people cannot be for peace and justice when they knowingly break the law and contaminate local facilities. (*Finger Lakes Times*, August 17, 1983)

Anthropologist Mary Douglas (1966) has suggested that many peoples make this association between filth and human beings that they consider "other" to themselves. According to Douglas, dirt is a metaphor for social disorder, for things out of place; it is also a moral judgment that is designed to cast an aura of inferiority and impropriety on all that is "dirty" and different. To call the encampment women dirty was not only a judgment about their appearance; it was also an evaluation of their moral fiber, for dirty things are judged to be outside the proper order of things. If we analyze those things that are clean in a society and those things considered dirty, we have some sense of how people order their symbolic and social world; the residents of Seneca County clearly saw the encampment women as dirty and out of place.

Some people found it particularly disturbing that some of the encampment women didn't wear bras. Their refusal to wear bras contributed to their image as women whose bodies were out of control. One local woman commented that not wearing a bra was just like going around undressed. She didn't always like to wear a bra, but a woman has to do it, she explained. One local man described a woman whose breasts "hung down to her knees like some African" because she had gone for years without her "over-the-shoulder-boulder-holders." Some locals thought the "women" were deliberately using their bodies to disturb people. All the men in their fifties and sixties "had heart attacks," said the owner of a Waterloo antiques store, when the "women" were walking around without bras.

Another feature of the "women's" failure to achieve status as real Women was the disruptiveness of their behavior. Some of the local people saw the "women" as guests who were rude to their hosts and abused local hospitality; others found the "women" guilty of more than just transgressions of etiquette. The "women" were described as "vociferous and damned pushy," both noisy and annoying, like a barking dog nipping at your heels, explained Waterloo police chief Doyle Marquardt. What particularly perturbed many locals was that the "women" were actively seeking attention for themselves and their causes. Instead of remaining silent and invisible as Women traditionally would, the "women" flaunted their behavior and forced the world to take note of them.

"I think the women are getting exactly what they want by getting front-page coverage," said one caller to the *Democrat and Chronicle* (August 4, 1983), as if attention seeking in itself were a fault. Many locals believed the real goal of the encampment was an "egotistical" desire for attention, a sort of selfish, narcissistic drive that Women shouldn't have. "They're here to get attention. They're not here to worry about the nuclear war," one man said. Mary Jacobus explains that the "narcissistic" woman who acts self-sufficient and self-defined seems threatening because of "her indifference to man's desire" (1986:105). This "monster woman," Toril Moi elaborates, this woman "who refuses to be selfless," who "has a story to tell," is rejecting "the submissive role that the patriarchy has reserved for her" (1985:58).

Some local people grudgingly admitted an admiration for the encampment "women's" ability to work the media, but their success at gaining visibility was a threat that had to be neutralized. One way to neutralize this challenge of female narcissism was to claim that the "women" were dependent for their very existence not on the strength of their beliefs but on attention from the news media. The solution to this problem of female narcissism, many thought, was to cut off media coverage of the encampment activities and so force the "women" to abandon their cause. Media coverage was seen as a sort of fuel for a narcissistic machine; take away the fuel, many claimed, and the encampment would fall apart. As one man explained, "If the television and the newspaper didn't play it up, they'd be dead." Another wrote: "If it weren't for the notoriety they got from the news media, the women probably would have gone home (where they belong) by now or would have stayed there in the first place" (*Democrat and Chronicle*, August 6, 1983).

The "active, belligerent feminism" also disturbed some of the local feminists, who saw it as a threat to the personal and political gains that they had achieved over the years. They worried that the encampment tactics might come to be associated in the local mind with all "women's libbers," even those who were interested in women's rights and equality, not in changing all aspects of society, even those that seemed beneficial to women. The local feminists favored women's rights and equal pay, but they liked to work quietly and behind the scenes. Drawing attention to feminist activities by using the encampment tactics (especially the emphasis on homosexuality, some of the women said) was not the way to get things done. The local women were afraid they would be identified with the hysterical image that the encampment women were allowing to develop.

The image of hysterical females implies that the encampment feminists were victims of their emotions. Yet while the notion of hysteria serves this conservative function of reinforcing the idea that women's behavior is determined by their biological urges, it also introduces a disturbance that cannot be so easily dismissed; the hysteric is an example of woman's "aberrant otherness," according to Charles Bernheimer 1985:4). Hélène Cixous and Catherine Clément explain the ambiguities: "The feminine role, the role of sorceress, of hysteric, is ambiguous, antiestablishment and conservative at the same time. Antiestablishment because the symptoms—the attacks—revolt and shake up the public, the group, the men, the others to whom they are exhibited. . . . The hysteric unties familiar bonds, introduces disorder into the well-regulated unfolding of everyday life, gives rise to magic in ostensible reason" (1985:4).

The designation of feminism as hysteria is a common way to attempt to neutralize the feminist refusal to cooperate with the patriarchy, but "hysterical" behavior has also been a successful political weapon for feminists who seek to express rather than repudiate feelings of anger and resentment against male-dominated institutions (Hunter 1985:113). The local people acknowledged that this hysterical behavior interrupted everyday life in Seneca County. They resented the encampment, one woman explained, because it "disturbed daily routine." People couldn't work in their offices or even sit down for a quiet evening at home without being bothered by the protesters. One letter to the *Finger Lakes Times* complained, "They seem to feel that it is their right to march through our streets, deface our areas with their slogans and disrupt our daily lives. What about our rights, the residents of this area?" (July 20, 1983).

The right to be left alone, not to be forced to consider issues that are best repressed, is an idealized American notion of the dual aspect of freedom—freedom *from* as well as freedom *to*. Local New York state assemblyman Mike Nozzolio told his constituents that summer that the right to protest does not extend to "disturbing the peace and mind of the community." "The issue here," he wrote, "is not to challenge the women's right to protest but to take command of the situation in order to ensure that they are not infringing on the rights of others" (*Trumansburg Free Press*, August 8, 1983).

When the "women's" activities disrupted the routine of everyday life, they were attacking the facade of coherence and order that every community claims to maintain through routine. The notion of a repetitive, consistent routine fits into a scheme that sees the world as a coherent, predictable place where disruptions are easily identified and swiftly dispatched. Everyday routines are comforting because they are thought to be unchanging, cyclic, enduring, stable behaviors that have served and will continue to serve the community's interests and needs. Repetition without change presents the illusion that the world can be mastered and understood and that differences and disturbances can be kept at a distance. Thus any disruption of community routine and of the narratives that define that community is more than a minor inconvenience: it is a threat to all that holds a community together.

Sudden and uncontrolled change may be exciting, but it is not necessarily seen as a good thing for the community as a whole. One man who lived on a farm just a few doors down from the army depot's main gate told a story about a local lottery winner to illustrate this point: "A local woman, who was not very well off financially, won a million dollars in the lottery. She used some of her winnings to buy a new mobile home. She moved into the new trailer with her boyfriend and two kids. One day soon after she had moved into the trailer, she got killed in a car accident. Maybe if she hadn't won the lottery she wouldn't have been driving on that road near her new trailer and she would be alive today."

The introduction of new people into a community was not enough in itself to break daily routine, and several local people cited the case of the Amish and Mennonites to prove this point. Wisner Kinne, a descendant of one of the Revolutionary War soldiers who settled in the area on government-supplied land, explained that these two groups, although culturally and religiously distinct from other Seneca County residents, had been easily accepted a few years ago. The reason, according to Kinne, was that "they tend to withdraw; they don't go out. Now the peaceniks went out and made fools of themselves." The Amish and Mennonites were non-threatening because they seemed to remind the locals of their own Puritan roots, Kinne said. These people were "essentially like us, and the peaceniks are not like us." One difference Kinne emphasized was the very traditional role of the Amish and Mennonite women, a "terribly exploited role," mind you, but reassuring nonetheless, just as the "use of horses is very reassuring" and indicates that somewhere traditional values are being sustained.

The encampment "women" were not worthy of the label Women because they appeared to have none of the personal and social responsibilities that real Women usually have. Since they were at this camp, they were obviously not home taking care of their husbands and children or working at a job. "If these women had anything to do," said one man, "they wouldn't be here messing around doing what they're doing. . . . If they had a job or something to do they wouldn't be messing around in this goddamn thing, that's for sure, would they?"

Many local people defined the "women" as drifters who "run from place to place trying to 'find a cause'" (*Finger Lakes Times*, August 9, 1983). Drifters, says Elizabeth Meese, are frightening because they "embody everyone's human potential to cut loose from and be cast out of society; they are the difference within" (1986:62). They are a reminder of the precarious nature of society, of the flux or drift within the supposed stability. Drifters can make a community feel uncomfortable because they represent that border between social order and chaos by seeming not to be anchored in any social milieu. The local people often articulated the significance of the encampment in terms of both the appeal and the fear of being cut loose in this way. Many expressed envy of the "women" because of their seeming freedom from social constraints and rules. Apparently without jobs, houses, children, material possessions, overdue bills, and in-laws, the encampment "women," like the lone cowboys of the American frontier, appeared to be enacting the desire to be free of the burdensome social world.

Some resented the "women" because they "got away with things" for which the local people knew they themselves would be punished. The depot, for example, seemed to have changed the regular rules—those that applied to the local people—and to be applying a different standard to the encampment protesters. "When it's not under protest," said one man, "anybody goes over the wall, you're arrested immediately, but when it's under protest, there's a whole new set of rules set down, and that's not right; it is not right. This is government property now and it's government property when anybody goes over [the fence]." Another person added, "If we wanted to do that, we wouldn't be dragged away." "You would be shot!" the first man concluded, and many of his neighbors agreed. They believed they would face serious violent reaction from depot guards for doing what the "women" were doing.

People were not just concerned that someone else was getting a better deal than they were, however. They also found it disturbing that the protesters were actively engaged in civil disobedience. Civil disobedience (referred to as CD) can encompass many different actions beyond the "normal institutionalized political methods," including boycotts, marches, fasting, refusal to pay taxes, sit-ins, obstructing traffic, vigils, and destroying property (Faison and Irwin 1980:28). All instances of civil disobedience share the goal of challenging established governmental or institutional policies. At the encampment, the term CD was used to refer to nonviolent direct action such as climbing the depot fence, crossing the yellow boundary line of the depot, or blocking traffic—all actions that would presumably result in arrest. The encampment women believed that civil disobedience confronts the authority's right "to command and enforce obedience" (*Resource Handbook* 1983:43) particularly to policies that are considered morally abhorrent.

CD seemed to present a particular dilemma to the local people for two reasons. First, it involved a direct challenge to the authority of the govern-

Protesters climb depot fence. Photo by Pam Quiggle

ment, a challenge of which many disapproved. "We are a society governed by laws," noted Seneca County district attorney Stuart Miller (*Democrat and Chronicle*, August 6, 1983). "To me," Emerson Moran wrote, "civil disobedience is a defiance of the law. To organize civil disobedience is conspiracy to violate the law. Violation of the law as a political act is, in fact, revolt against authority" (*Finger Lakes Times*, July 29, 1983). The breaking of law leads to a disruption of its natural companion, order. "Open protests in our streets," wrote one nineteen-year-old man, "are dangerous to our democracy" *(Democrat and Chronicle,* August 10, 1983); he was implicitly equating law and order with silent acceptance and trust of the authorities who define and interpret the law. Many local people commented that it was none of their business what went on at the depot, that the government had it under control.

Women are considered particularly susceptible to breaking the law in patriarchal societies because in some ways to be a woman is to be natu-rally disobedient to patriarchal law, which requires adherence to male standards from which women are by definition excluded. Women's "lack of loyalty" to civilization (see Meese 1986:12) allows them to challenge the established authorities almost simply by existing as speaking subjects. Women who actively resist, who commit civil disobedience, are doing the unthinkable: they are daring not only to speak but to speak against the very system that claims to define them. Of course this "patriarchal system" is not as stable, as internally consistent, or as all-powerful as the encampment women and other feminists often seem to claim in their political rhetoric, but their protest strategies demanded that they construct a monumental patriarchal enemy for this encounter.

Another decidedly unacceptable feature of the encampment "women" which kept them from being considered proper Women was their active and public sexuality. The local people were less upset that the "women's" behavior in sexual matters did not match community standards than that they made their behavior public. "Hey, you wanna be gay, be gay. I could care less. Just don't bring it on my doorstep," said counterdemonstrator Jerry McKenna. Lucinda Talbot, one of the Elmira women who left the encampment said: "I'm a heterosexual but the shades are drawn when I make love. It's just the way that you do it. We might hold hands; I would hold hands with a man or a woman, [but] only the very young French kiss in public with male and female partners, and anything more than that is simply extremely vulgar. If you're talking about a big city where, you know, people crawl into the bushes . . . but I'm sure none of the locals were French kissing their wives on the front lawn."

The most worrisome aspect of such public displays of sexuality, many thought, was their possible effect on "impressionable children." Many people said they themselves were not disturbed by these displays, but they did not want their children exposed to these ideas and behaviors. One teenage boy watching a protest at the depot gate complained that his ten-year-old brother could see the women with their arms around each other and rubbing each other's bodies. A woman somewhat favorable to the encampment complained nevertheless that she had "two daughters of a very impressionable age. I couldn't imagine taking them to an environment where they see other women loving each other, and blatantly showing it." Another man said his "impressionable" eight-year-old should not be "exposed to this garbage." "In front of impressionable children is out of the question" said one man. "What you do in your private life is your business."

For feminists, this idea that women should not be actively sexual and that sexuality should not be a part of public discourse has been a major point of contention. As Meese explains, "Male control of women's bodies has always been the cornerstone of patriarchy. Women often play out their resistance to this authority in sexual terms. . . . control or the illusion of control over one's sexual expression is analogous to control over one's existence" (1986:117). One aspect of this control over sexuality is the power to make it visible in a form that challenges patriarchal notions of female sexuality. Publicly and actively acknowledging lesbianism and other forms of female sexuality (including the refusal to have sex with men) is one way the encampment forced this visibility.

Public sexuality is problematic not simply because we have puritanical notions that the proper place for sex is in private, behind closed doors, but also because visibility exposes sexuality to discussion, critique, and contradiction. It questions the normalcy of a sexuality that is private and not spoken about in public. It questions the notion that sexuality is apolitical. It questions why this "normal" sexuality should be silently passed on to "impressionable children." This refusal of the encampment women to comply with a structure that promotes the internalization of sexual mores through the private, nuclear family threatens the entire patriarchal system, which depends on the collaboration of women within the nuclear family to keep children in line by teaching them traditional values and roles.

Discussing sexuality publicly brings it into conjunction with the social and political world and forces it to be considered in reference to things with which it does not seem to be "naturally" associated (nuclear weapons, for example). Sexuality brought into the public eye this way becomes a field of discourse that does not just refer to genital activities but encompasses the very nature of existence in the patriarchal society, which uses sexual difference as the basis for judgments and decisions. Shoshana Felman, discussing Freud's flexible and far-reaching theory of sexuality, indicates that it is not to be taken only in its literal, popular sense as referring primarily to the sexual act (Felman 1985:156). Rather, sexuality is a problematized field of rhetoric, a field that has as its essence ambiguity and contradiction. Sexuality in this Freudian sense makes simplicity and certainty impossible because it arises in human being out of conflicting forces.

Thus the "sex" that the local people didn't want their "impressionable children" to see in public is that set of contradictory meanings and ambiguities that the encampment participants, as "women" challenging patriarchal modes of existence, are making visible. These ideas are feared as powerful and contagious, and children are seen as very susceptible to their rhetorical power. The fear that a single exposure to these ideas and actions will turn a child away from normal, patriarchal sexuality suggests that the margins occupied by women present a constant and well known threat to patriarchal standards.

Women, Toril Moi explains, represent that line between men and chaos, between center, the margins, and that wilderness beyond the margins (1985:167). If women don't hold the line and stay in the margins, the system can collapse as men lose control of the definitions of the center and the beyond. The public discussion of sexuality about which the local people complained blurred the important patriarchal boundaries between the public center, held by men, and the private margins, inhabited by women, sex, animals, children, and all uncontrollable things. The encampment "women" were acting like a strange border breed that did not know its rightful territory.

The representation of the encampment participants as unfit for the category Women was another way to attempt to control the summer's narratives. Yet even as the local people tried to take control of this discourse on gender identity and its social and political correlates, they were faced with the fact that the encampment women had complicated this category of Women for them. Their supposed certainty about what Women were and what they were not was challenged by the sheer diversity and overwhelming otherness of the summer visitors.

The possibility of ambiguity in a gender category must be repressed in a phallocentric system that utilizes clear-cut distinctions and binary oppositions such as male/female, masculine/feminine, and man/woman. These binary oppositions are the means of providing distinct gender identity categories that must seem immutable, natural, and biologically given; they make each category seem distinct from the other, limit membership to one category or the other: you are either male or female but not both; you are man or woman but not either; your behavior should be masculine or feminine, not ambiguous.

In our patriarchal tradition, the category Women must be defined and defended closely and carefully if personal and sexual identity for both males and females is to be fixed. The male model of identity is the key reference point in our society, the standard by which all is measured. The female is seen as a separate type of identity that is merely a complement to and an inferior example of the male model. Man in this tradition represents totalizing knowledge (Moi 1985:198); woman is "a man with a lack or a difference, nothing in her own right, a modification or a deviation from the 'norm'" (Meese 1986:136). Since this tradition equates the biological designations "male" and "female" with the social categories Man and Woman, a confusion of the category Woman is a threat to the entire conception of the natural and cultural worlds. Woman is supposed to be unambiguously opposite to man, to be a mirror that confirms his own stable identity. This mirror function requires orientation to the male and forbids orientation to other females. It demands a "compulsory heterosexuality," as Adrienne Rich calls it (1984), in which women must "naturally" prefer bonding to and identifying with males. Compulsory heterosexuality has the effect of ensuring that women who ally themselves emotionally, physically, or politically with other women are branded unnatural and made to question their own desires. And compulsory heterosexuality ensures that man has his sexual, social, and psychic other in order to define himself.

Women who refuse a patriarchal identity maintain that the lack is not in themselves but within the patriarchal system. When compulsory heterosexuality is questioned, women are not necessarily left in homosexuality (whether of a gay-male model or a lesbian-separatist model) but rather in a figurative bisexuality, a feminine opening to multiple and diverse affiliations. Bisexuality is an important theoretical concept for feminism. It does not refer only to sexual activities with both males and females: that is only one specific, literal manifestation of this idea. Nor does it refer strictly to the psychoanalytic concept that each person, male or female, has a bisexual predisposition that allows identification with both the same and the opposite sex. Rather, women in this theoretical bisexual mode can be said to experience a double desire and identification that positions them in a contradictory field. Differences aren't negated but respected and enhanced, and repressed differences are made visible. This alternative mode is part of feminism's "wild complexity" (Meese 1986:ix), which opens women up to the consideration of relations beyond binary oppositions and possibilities beyond those defined by heterosexism and the patriarchy. By emphasizing differences other than those promoted by the phallocentric order, feminists using bisexuality tolerate and even promote ambiguity. Bisexuality puts into question the monosexual discourse of the patriarchy, and according to Féral, "To put discourse into question is to reject the existing order" (1980:91).

This theoretical bisexuality, then, challenges the phallocentric order by questioning the gender differences upon which it is based. The voicing of this bisexual nature of woman threatens a patriarchal system in two distinct ways. First, it engenders the fear that women will compete for the male sphere by acting not only like women but also, or instead, like men.

This fear was expressed in Seneca County when women were accused of not being proper Women because of their nonfeminine or masculine appearance, demeanor, ideas, and actions. Women who were not home taking care of husband and family were acting out the male rather than the female role. Women expressing their political opinions on nuclear weapons were clearly, the locals were certain, stepping out of the bounds of their possible area of expertise. Nuclear strategy and decisions were best left to the experts, the scientists and engineers, several declared; common citizens (especially women) could not possibly have enough knowledge to develop informed opinions in this area. Encampment women who were aggressive and noisy were compared unfavorably with the quiet grandmothers and nuns who seemed decidedly more feminine, not at all masculine, and certainly not blatantly sexual. Women who could not be identified as women were seen as faking it, acting with false faces and borrowed clothes and disguised voices; they were dupes, dopes, and lesbian-vegetarian-witches who acted not out of normal feminine needs but out of uncontrolled desires and ideas.

Women's bisexuality, their "overidentification" with other women when released from or reacting to patriarchal suppression, is threatening in another way. It is not just that female bisexuality puts women in competition for the male preserve, but Tania Modleski argues, "far more fundamentally . . . it reminds man of his own bisexuality . . . , a bisexuality that threatens to subvert his 'proper' identity which depends on his ability to distance woman" (1988:6). If male/female lines are not so sharply drawn and if females, contrary to patriarchal belief, can and do orient themselves to women as well as men, then male identity, which is dependent on a strict separation of male and female, is shattered. Proper heterosexuality requires men to keep femininity at a distance and women to keep masculinity out of their own identities but in sight as a reference point. Women who refuse to marry, who are lesbians, who challenge gender categories, who have close women friends—all frighteningly shatter not only the category Woman but also the mirror that man uses for self-identification. As Modleski explains, "If woman, who is posited as she whom man must know and possess in order to guarantee his truth and his identity, does not exist, then in some important sense he does not exist either, but rather is faced with the possibility of his own nothingness" (1988:91).

"Women" become recognized as the "difference within," the reminder that the binary differences promoted by the patriarchy are illusory and the differences between the categories Man and Woman are, in the words of

Barbara Johnson, "based on a repression of differences *within* entities, ways in which an entity differs from itself" (1980:x). For man, Catherine Gallagher notes, "femininity is dangerous because, by 'infecting' him, it might erase the distinctions which buttress his idea of masculinity"; it might bring to light the metaphorical threat of castration, the loss of "one's property, one's social and economic power, one's very self-representations" (1983:55). Feminism has man inhabited by woman in a way that reveals his construction and her powers.

The suppression of this information about the implications of the other within the self is necessary for a patriarchal system to work. Women like those at the encampment force these ideas into a public discourse that normally does not allow them. These specific women forced the local people to see the differences within their own families, their own communities, the whole country. When neighbors disagreed and family members took different sides of the argument, when women loved women and men and the Soviets all at the same time, when community members sided with outsiders, and when prototypes of the ideal American became an embarrassment at the Waterloo bridge, a reassuring homogeneity could no longer be assumed.

The incident at the Waterloo bridge evoked not just a physical impasse but also a discursive one. A discursive impasse is the point in a narrative that reveals an inherent contradiction, "the moment in the text that seems to transgress its own system of values," as Gayatri Spivak puts it (1976: xlix). Such an impasse can be shown to "embarrass" the system of logic that rules the discourse (Eagleton 1983:133), thus calling into question the power and cohesiveness of the system supporting the discourse.

The discourse the Waterloo bridge impasse interrupted was simultaneously local and national. As Clifford Geertz points out, there is a "continuous dialectic tacking between the most local of local details and the most global of global structure in such a way as to bring them into simultaneous view" (1983:69). A challenge that reveals an impasse in a local situation can thus point to a simultaneous weakness in the logic of the larger discourse. And since the people in Seneca County were using the larger dominant discourse on Good Americans and proper Women to justify and explain their actions, the acknowledgment of this impasse was particularly disturbing.

The discussion about this impasse took its most public form in the wealth of letters and calls to local and regional newspapers in August and September. Some letters supported the bridge blockade; others condemned the citizens of Waterloo for acting in an unacceptable and un-

American way; all contributed to a lively discussion that continued for the rest of the summer and revealed the divisions and factions in the local communities. Emerson Moran contributed a letter to the editor, which ran in the *Finger Lakes Times* on August 3, 1983, under the heading "They Did Not Pass":

> My grandfather, who grew up in Waterloo before the Civil War, always called it Skoi-Yase. That was the Indian name for that part of the community on the south side of the Seneca River.
>
> On July 30, big medicine was made on the bridge that carries Route 96 from the north into the old Indian village of Skoi-Yase. The people of Waterloo, deeply concerned by the presence and antics of the feminist peace demonstrators farther to the south rose up en masse to bar foot passage of such route from Seneca Falls to join their sisters in displays of massive civil disobedience to be directed against the Seneca Army depot near the hamlet of Romulus. Like Marshall Foch, leading the French against the Germans before Verdun in World War I, Waterloo promised, "They shall not pass."
>
> And they did not pass.
>
> In the skies of rural America went new smoke signals. Hopefully, the America watchers at the Kremlin are scratching their heads in perplexity. Which is the real America, that one pulling the college sorority pranks in Romulus, or the determined defenders of the bridge leading into Skoi-Yase?
>
> In a recent interview (*Times*, July 25) Yevgeny Velikov, director of the leading nuclear research center in the Soviet Union stated that decision-making in his country takes much time because decisions are collective.
>
> We pray that there is time for the committee to reach its consensus on the true character of America. In my lifetime our attackers have been those who adjudged us to be weak.

Other letters disagreed with this interpretation of the events. A resident of Waterloo wrote to the editor of the *Finger Lakes Times*, which published the letter on August 2, 1983, under the heading "Black Day for America":

> Saturday was a black day for Americans. The "patriots" of Waterloo forgot what our country stands for. The Declaration of Independence states that all citizens have the inalienable right to "life, liberty and the pursuit of happiness." The Bill of Rights guarantees the rights of freedom of speech, petition and assembly.
>
> We may not agree with what the peace camp women are doing or

their lifestyle, dress or whatever. But as Americans we are committed to defend their rights, too.

Voltaire said, "I disapprove of what you say, but I will defend to the death your right to say it." That's what being a real American means.

Hurrah for Mrs. Kleman, a Waterloo resident who joined the women and was arrested because she felt the women had a right to march through the village.

A resident of Geneva contributed a letter, which ran the same day in the same newspaper under the heading "Working for a Change":

Here's one local resident who won't stop a peaceful march by waving the American flag, carrying a loaded shotgun, or chanting "Go home" to women well within their domain.

Those who call the women protestors anti-American irk and embarrass me: irk me because that cry is really one of "you are not like me, therefore you cannot be a part of my country"; embarrass me because as one who was born and raised in Geneva, I cringe as my neighbors put a parochial, insular, uninsightful foot forward and in doing so, plant an unfortunate notion of these counties' sophistication, intelligence and willingness to engage in enlightening and potentially world-changing discourse.

Civil disobedience is and has been a vital part of American heritage: from the Boston Tea Party to Dr. Martin Luther King's freedom marches, Americans have struggled to make government serve the people instead of blindly serving a government.

An encampment such as the one on Route 96, peaceful, intelligent, concerned with issues of global importance while at the same time sensitive to local concerns, should elicit patient attention, thoughtful dialogue and informed dissent, not loaded rifles.

Those, such as the person quoted in a Sunday newspaper saying, "we cannot allow demonstrations against our government. Somebody had to make a stand for what the majority of the people feel," should confront the contradictions in their own muddled thinking. Patriotism means loving one's country while realizing it is not perfect and democracy (which is as American as that statement is myopic) means having the right, indeed the responsibility to actively work for change.

Another resident of Waterloo continued the dialogue by responding to these criticisms. The *Democrat and Chronicle* ran the letter on August 15, 1983, under the heading "They Were Disruptive":

THOSE PEOPLE who feel Waterloo should "be ashamed" or "rethink their actions" should try wearing our shoes. We are a happy, friendly community that gets along well. We have our shops and our plazas just like Anytown, U.S.A.

These women marched down our streets and sang out loud, waved their signs, etc. We didn't bother their homes, why do they have to come to ours?

The main complaint I heard, and I was there, was not of the nuclear arms, but of the disruption of our home. Not the Earth that they call home, but of our Waterloo. I admit that the standoff may have been a little long but after what was seen, I think it was okay.

There was one woman who urinated on the bridge before the crowd, a girl who blew her nose on the American flag and other things like that.

Don't you people from out of Waterloo pass judgement unless you invite them to your home for a "friendly march" first!

People debated the pros and cons of the actions of the authorities, the counterdemonstrators, and the protesters. Some decided that one side or the other was right or wrong, and some decided that even if the bridge blockers were legally wrong, they had made the right moral decision in standing up to the encampment women. After the incident at Waterloo bridge, the local people seemed to feel that they had accumulated more than ample evidence that the differences between themselves and the encampment women were real, dangerous, and insurmountable. Yet the differences within their own communities had also been vividly demonstrated.

For Seneca County, the incident at Waterloo bridge became an unwelcome revelation about the contradictions and conflicts that exist not between Americans and outsiders but more notably among Americans themselves. The borders between insider and outsider, patriot and traitor, man and woman were constantly shifting and being reoriented. The fact that local people could not agree with each other about the interpretations and implications of these events was frightening. All through the first part of the summer the local people, like the encampment women, had attempted to present a coherent and consistent representation of themselves. One important aspect of that representation said that the local community was homogeneous in its political and social outlook and that everyone agreed that the encampment women were unacceptable and unAmerican.

The incident at Waterloo bridge led to a locally produced deconstruction of the bridge blockade. In this deconstruction residents began to question whether the oppositions they were employing (us/them; Americans/communists; locals/outsiders, men/women, etc.) were as clear-cut and important as they had been made to seem. Such a deconstruction, Terry Eagleton explains, "tries to show how such oppositions, in order to hold themselves in place, are sometimes betrayed into inverting or collapsing themselves" (1983:133). Because actions of the bridge blockaders were seen as just as anti-American as those of the peace camp women, the local and national discourses that had seemed useful for explaining, categorizing, and understanding the encampment women threatened to collapse.

16

The Postnuclear

A group called the Nuclear Union to Kill Everything (NUKE) has set up a camp outside the Seneca Army Depot in Romulus.

The group, which has the slogan, "A mushroom in every backyard," promotes nuclear annihilation of the Earth "so that civilization can start over," a spokesman said.

—Spoof of 1983 news events
written by Seneca County journalists

The activities of the encampment women in 1983 helped to point out the differences and weakness within a system that had seemed so stable and correct. But is such a subversion really possible? Certainly the interaction between the residents in and around Seneca County and the Women's Encampment for a Future of Peace and Justice exemplified what can happen when women try to make a difference on public and private issues. But one very effective conservative strategy in response to such threats is to reify the established order. Local residents, both males and females, did so by expressing what might be called a "nostalgia" for a mythical past when men were men and women were women, when these categories were (supposedly) fixed and natural, and when few strayed outside their boundaries. Differences were carefully defined and thoroughly understood. This nostalgia blamed feminism for abusing and discarding the real categories of Men and Women (see Doane and Hodges 1987) and for negating important differences between them. It becomes necessary to ask, then, if the encampment made any difference after all.

When most of the protesters and staff left the peace camp land in September 1983, the local men and women of the Seneca County region remained. They had to make sense of their challenged lives and communities. In these people, therefore, we can look for evidence of change in the narrative they constructed about their lives and their community. If an interpretive community is defined by the narrative strategies it shares and uses, then a change or difference should be expressed or discussed in the narratives created after a transformative event.

For many of the male officials of Seneca County (men whom the encampment would define as the patriarchal center), the encampment brought about not a questioning of their official roles and identities but a reaffirmation of their place in the established order. For many of the men charged with maintaining law and order in Seneca County, the summer of 1983 turned out to be not so much a threat as a welcome testing of their position and abilities. Many took the women's encampment as a professional challenge, the one big event that a man thinks he will have in his career after he gets out of college, explained Brian Dombrowski, the director of the Seneca County Health Department. In a sense, a man's life story is not complete or comprehensible until he has been tested in this way and has proven himself through such a challenge. For many men in Seneca County, the encampment thus became a means by which a man could write this challenging test and its successful passage into his narrative interpretations.

As director of one of the smallest county health departments in the state, Brian Dombrowski had not foreseen much chance that he would encounter such a character-testing event, but the encampment made this desired test possible. Dombrowski's department had the responsibility to license the encampment as a campground under public health laws. As Dombrowski explained, the health department permit was the only one required by state and local laws. When the encampment became "the hottest thing since the Civil War," local people began to criticize his office for approving the permit (even though, as Dombrowski pointed out, the women easily complied with the regulations). Forced to explain and justify his important decision throughout the summer, he achieved a unique sense of accomplishment that the daily routine did not provide. The decision also thrust him into the media limelight when he had to answer for it both locally and nationally. Dombrowski described the excitement in his office while the national media were calling him all day long, keeping him from doing anything else. He got calls from as far away as California (from the *Los Angeles Times*). Sometimes, he said, "I was quoted in the media and I never talked to them!" Dombrowski had never expected this kind of excitement in his job, or to be deferred to as *the* pertinent authority. For him, in retrospect the encampment was not completely unwelcome.

Robert Zemanek, the public affairs officer of the Seneca Army Depot, was the primary liaison between the encampment women and the depot; he usually met daily with the women. He too felt that the summer of 1983 was professionally rewarding, especially in terms of the contact he had with the international media. He had had to work fifty or sixty hours a week that summer, and one day things got so bad that he was stopped three times for interviews while he was on his way to lunch. But since his job was ordinarily limited to putting out the depot newspaper and arranging tours for local civic or school groups. The encampment protests had brought an element of interest and excitement to a job that was usually pretty routine. Zemanek felt he had done a good job that summer and jokingly confided that if he had been the public relations director for the encampment too, the women might not have made so many mistakes with the local community.

Roman Catholic priests Michael Conboy of Seneca Falls and Albert Shamon of Waterloo, perceived the women's peace encampment as a challenge to which they could apply their religious ideals. Father Conboy took the encampment as an opportunity to show the relevance of Catholic church in the modern world. In May 1983 the National Conference of Catholic Bishops had published a pastoral letter on nuclear weapons and war titled *The Challenge of Peace: God's Promise and Our Response*. The pastoral letter recommended bilateral reduction in nuclear arms, a comprehensive test ban treaty, and a halt to the testing, production, and deployment of new nuclear weapons systems. It also addressed the moral issues of war and peace and declared "Keeping the peace in the nuclear age is a moral and political imperative."

Soon after the document was published the encampment opened, and Father Conboy saw the opportunity right in his own community to take the moral stand suggested in the pastoral letter. He explained: "As the summer encampment began to get under way, we thought it would be a good chance for us to lend a voice, to say that we're concerned about this buildup of nuclear warheads. And if the Seneca Depot is a place where they were stored, then we wanted to get out there on the front line . . . so that the church is not in an ivory tower." Father Conboy spoke favorably of the protests in some of his sermons and also provided breakfast for the women the morning they marched from Seneca Falls into Waterloo. Some of his parishioners were supportive of the encampment and his sermons, but many others were outraged. One parishioner, a former military man, told Father Conboy that he didn't want to hear anything about this in church. To emphasize his point, the man would present a check for his Sunday offering and then rip it in half and hand it to the priest. Father Conboy believed people were too concerned with the extraneous issues surrounding the encampment and were missing the larger implications of the bishops' pastoral letter. He thought the encampment offered an opportunity to show how religious teaching relates to the realities of everyday life, and he was disappointed that his parish showed little interest in these connections.

Father Conboy had been taught in his early seminary years by Father Albert Shamon who in 1983 had the parish in the town of Waterloo. Shamon had encouraged Conboy in his studies for the priesthood, and the two had become friends despite significant differences in personal and religious philosophies. Father Shamon saw a completely different kind of challenge and opportunity in the encampment. He used the protests to illustrate his basic belief that evil in society is caused by individual sin, not the shortcomings of governmental structures. In newspaper columns, Sunday sermons, radio shows and interviews, he took the encampment women, with their "satanism," witchcraft, and lesbianism, as examples of a sinful lifestyle. He found it easy to argue that the encampment women (whom he called communist dupes) were a moral and political threat and that the only real solution to the nuclear dilemma was moral renewal. For each of these priests, then, the activities of the summer of 1983 provided a test of fundamental religious and moral beliefs and an arena in which to demonstrate them.

For Dale Arcangeli, the chief deputy of the Seneca County Sheriff's Department, the summer of 1983 was a big test of his skills as a law enforcement officer. It was, he said, the biggest event of his fifteen-year career; he never missed a protest, and he made eleven thousand dollars in overtime on top of it all. Arcangeli organized the logistics for the sheriff's department. As coordinator of operations for the encampment activities, he arranged meetings with local officials, set up barracks at a local (closed) college campus for the extra police, requisitioned a local school to act as a jail, arranged for food for the backup police officers, and conducted aerial photography of the encampment. From May 10 to July 3 he did nothing but plan for the encampment. That summer he worked sixty-four days without a day off, and he ate, drank, and slept the encampment. He saw little of his new wife and his newborn baby, but even so, Arcangeli considered the summer rewarding. He felt no antagonism toward the encampment women and became friendly with many of them. September was depressing, he said, when the encampment ended and life returned to normal.

Arcangeli began the summer as a lieutenant, but after the first women were arrested, he was promoted to chief deputy and received a raise in salary. Arcangeli was one of only three people authorized to initiate arrests and his list of responsibilities and rewards grew throughout the summer. For Arcangeli the incident at the Waterloo bridge was a welcome test of all his hard and careful planning. He was glad to find that everything worked. After the encampment, he proudly gave lectures to other agencies on preparation, especially emphasizing the cooperation among the different local agencies. In the following years Arcangeli's proven record took him even farther in the sheriff's department hierarchy. The county officials now listened to what Dale Arcangeli had to say.

The sheriff of Seneca County in the summer of 1983, Ken Greer, did not fare as well as some of the other men. Greer didn't talk much to his family about what had gone on at the protests, and sometimes when he came home to relax after a day of protests he would sit and paint. One painting he did at this time showed some cavemen on one side and a nuclear bomb exploding on the other side. The theme of it, his wife, Nikki, explained, was something like "the beginning of the end."

Greer was severely criticized for his handling of the Waterloo bridge incident. As an elected official, he had to answer to the public for his actions. Ken Greer didn't run for sheriff in 1984, partly because he didn't want to deal with the encampment again and partly because he knew he was sick. Greer died in 1985. Many local residents felt that it was the women's encampment and the incident at the bridge—not just the cancer—that had killed him.

Emerson and Carolyn Moran had continuing success with their Jesus nut jewelry business. They continued to pray for peace and had small cards printed with a prayer in English and Russian asking for an end to the threat of nuclear war. They arranged to have some of the cards sent to the Soviet Union. Emerson Moran conducted a short-lived bid for the state senate, and he and his wife eventually left Romulus and relocated to Seneca Falls.

To many women, both inside and outside Seneca County, the encampment seemed like a welcome opportunity despite the stresses and difficulties of the summer. It provided a chance not so much to solidify old identities and communities as to try out and confirm new, challenging ones. For women who had never worked with other women before, it was a way to crack the myth of female competition; for women who did not know many lesbians, it was a chance to see and perhaps experiment with an alternative sexuality; for those who thought in terms of isolated issues, it was an introduction to the idea of a web of interconnected problems.

In some ways, however, the experiences of the women from outside Seneca County and those inside the county were necessarily different. Those from outside did not have to deal with the daily repercussions of the encampment's activities, which often made life for local women difficult. For them, the encampment provided a whole range of experiences that could positively affect the interpretation and writing of their lives. One letter to the encampment women exemplifies how strong the perceived effects could be:

I just came back from the CD over the weekend and am still feeling strong. I wanted to write just to let you know about my feelings about the future of the camp. I am 33, married 12 years, 3 kids, have been a feminist for 8 years. I came to the encampment with that background. I came home loving women, alienated from the culture in which I exist, empowered, depressed, struggling. Re-entry into my previous life is impossible so I struggle to find my own culture. It has been painful, lonely and strangely challenging. I have a close group of women friends, many of whom went to camp also this summer. My affinity group. They are my survival, my hope.

I spent two weeks at the camp and found my life changed forever. I also felt you sent me home without enough knowledge to deal with these changes. I thank the Goddess for my affinity group. I don't know how other women are making it. I wish you could share with me ideas how to maintain a new life of strength, happiness and commitment to myself, my sisters and the world I live in.

The future of the camp is very important to me. I learned I was a woman of worth, love and purpose. I want to do what I can to insure peace. Having a place (the camp) that allowed me to be me for the first time in my life, a space for women only, is too important to just let go. When I was at the camp Monday night, I was able to read the minutes of your last meeting to discuss the future of the camp. I felt after reading them that I could trust all of you to come up with the best answer, but I felt the need to say something too. First and foremost, there needs to be a permanent place for women to come to that is their space. If you touched my life and helped me to struggle for my wholeness, how can we deny other women that opportunity. Maybe it doesn't have to be the same place it is now, but I must tell you I have a strong attachment to the land, the house, the buildings. I am trying not to let that cloud my thinking, it's just how I feel.

. . . Please do not take away a place that has that kind of potential, grow, change, I understand, but we've only just begun. To say we can't "repeat" the peace camp experience is not truth. We should learn from the summer, improve on it, offer it to as many women as possible. Prepare us better to go home and do these things. Give us a place to come back to, to rejuvenate ourselves. So many of us are thirsting for our own culture, I can't find it without you, you're all part of it.

I love all of you beautiful, strong women.

Some of the local women had quite different interpretations of the events of the summer. A woman whose husband was an officer at the depot felt that the encampment women completely misunderstood the military. "Probably the most peace loving people in the world are soldiers," she said, because they are the ones who have to go to fight. The military wives ended up resenting the encampment women, she said, because of the reports of the women's nudity in front of their husbands. One thing the encampment women apparently hadn't counted on, as far as she could tell, was that the military families would all pull together and support each other, bringing cookies and soup to soldiers on duty and entertaining those brought in for temporary duty.

Longtime local resident Pam Flanigan got involved with the encampment for very personal reasons, and she worked with it for years. Nevertheless, she expressed some deep reservations about the procedures and attitudes of the participants. Flanigan became involved because she had given birth to her daughter not long before the encampment opened and started having nightmares about a nuclear holocaust. "When I talked to some of my friends who were in some of my childbirth classes," she said, "I found that [such dreams] seemed to be very common, that after people are mothers, after they have babies, they have terrible dreams like that." She and some of her friends decided to develop a local antinuclear group. The encampment's opening was timed perfectly as a focus for this new group. Despite the disapproval of her in-laws, Flanigan and some friends tried to act as liaisons between the encampment and the local community, especially after the Waterloo incident. They arranged a trip for about ninety local people to visit the camp, to "go and see for themselves" what the camp was about. Unfortunately, Flanigan and other local women began to feel exploited by the encampment women, who would often ask them to do favors but never seemed to empower them or invite them into the "inner workings" of the camp.

They also organized three or four meetings or coffee hours in their homes, which were attended by about fifty people each. At the meetings they talked about the depot and about the problems with the encampment and tried to help the local people see why the women were doing what they were doing. Having originated these coffee hours, Flanigan was disappointed to receive a form letter at the end of the summer asking her to open her home to some coffee hours that encampment women would run so they could talk to the local people. Flanigan was dismayed at what she considered insensitivity in sending her this form letter, with a blank space in which her name had been written, without any acknowledgment of her previous work. Because of rapid turnover among "outreach coordinators" at the encampment, women in the local community were not adequately recognized or appreciated for their contributions.

The women who lived in the Seneca County communities were constrained in ways outsiders didn't understand, explained Seneca Falls resident Gwen Henderson, who called herself a corporate or executive wife, a woman whose identity was based on her husband's position in one of the local corporations. Henderson wanted to talk about her experiences with the peace encampment because she felt others needed to understand what life was like for local women. Only then could they see what the encampment meant to these women, even those who were not actively involved. Henderson sat down on the floor of her comfortable kitchen in Seneca Falls, the smoke from her cigarette flowing into the shaft of light that lit the floor in front of her dishwasher. She explained that the life of an executive wife revolved around the husband: "This is my opinion, I can't include all corporate wives but . . . executive wives have roles to play and they play them out one way or the other. . . . One thing is that there's nothing that I could do in this world that would be as important as what he does because he's the big boss, right?" His activities, his concerns, his schedule determined the entire tone of their lives. "The men in our lives are more like company; we are always on our best behavior; we always try to please them." She explained the reasons for accepting this situation:

I have what probably 95 percent of the things that any halfway smart woman in the world would want: I have two beautiful children, a husband who comes home, does not beat me, does not go out drinking and fooling around, doesn't do anything around the house either [laughter]. . . . And I guess, because of my upbringing or whatever, I have never had a terrible desire to prove to the world who or what I am. I mean, I suppose I should. The *feminists* told me I should go out and get a job and fulfill myself and all this stuff.

But if you're completely happy with what you have, she asked, why would you want to do something that would threaten that happy life? Gwen Henderson couldn't explain why, but she saw her visits to the encampment (twice before it opened) as an exploration of new possibilities. Her reception was not, however, all she had hoped for:

> They wanted me to sign my name. I said I'd just as soon not. I really didn't want my name on anything because I wanted to see what was going on. [The first time] I came in with white tennis shorts on, and a pink shirt and Nike sneakers . . . and I went out there and I was not really well received—like, no one spoke to me hardly at all. . . . So I went out another day, and I had my cutoffs and I was going to work; I was going to help build this pavilion. I knew how to use a hammer and a saw. Once again nobody really extended open arms. . . . And so then I went and I started helping and it got hotter than heck and I took my shirt off, but under my shirt I had on my swimming suit. They're looking at me and they're laughing at me because pretty soon another girl she took her shirt off and she had nothing on and it didn't bother me. I don't care; that doesn't bother me. I mean, we were all women together doing something, enjoying, and it was a hot day and this gal had her shirt off. That didn't bother me, but they gave me rude looks because I had my swimming suit on.

Henderson felt that the encampment women had judged her just as her neighbors sometimes did—according to unimportant differences based mostly on surface appearances. As an executive wife she was expected to act and dress within certain constraints, and now here at the encampment the same thing was happening. Henderson did not go back to the encampment for a while, but she did make another effort to have some relationship to it. While walking through a store in Seneca Falls one day after the encampment opened, she overheard a conversation among some encampment women about the negative attitudes of some of the local people. The women had shaved heads and unshaven armpits and legs, but Henderson, perhaps to test her own theory that people need to look beyond appearances, went up to the women and started to talk to them:

> I said, "Oh bullshit! You want to come home and have a beer with me? I'll invite you home, if that's what you want some of us townies to do." And they said, "yeah, we'd like that." They were testing me. . . . So they came home and here's my husband, here's my kids, here's these weird

women. . . . These are kids [22 or 23 years old]; of course they can do what they want: they're not married, they have no ties; they can do what they want, and they're busting my chops for being a townie, not realizing the restraints and controls that simply choosing this lifestyle, being my age, being, quote, who I am, and all this stuff. They couldn't understand that, and I think that's one thing I wanted to show them, that there are some of us who do support their action. We'd love to be acting with them, but not to the same degree or level of sacrifice that they had made because we can't do that because we have other obligations.

Henderson was impressed by the knowledge these women had about nuclear weapons and continued to talk to them through a swim in the family pool (after jokingly asking them if they had VD or if their hair would clog the filter) and through dinner. She invited them to join her family as they headed for the fireworks at the Seneca Falls Convention Days celebration: "So here goes mama, papa, and my two children, and these two. And I have to admit that [clearing throat] I was a little uncomfortable. It really was uncomfortable, and Jim [her husband] says, 'Can you get rid of those guys?'" After the women left, her husband asked:

"What have you gotten into now? Goddammit, Gwen, you get into the craziest situations." I said, "What did I do? I was trying to be nice, to let them know that everybody in town didn't hate them." I said, "I think that's important for them to take back to the encampment that there are some people in the town that don't hate them. They may be different looking, they prefer different lifestyles, they maybe had different politics, but we don't hate, we wouldn't do anything mean to them."

Henderson worried about being seen with the weird encampment women because she still had her husband's reputation to protect. Her husband always got teased because of her activities, and she worried about the backlash. "I think it is fearful for these men to know," she speculated, "that we are close to someone else, our lives are not centered completely around them, and when they're home that's exactly what they want." But she worried about something else more. Whenever Gwen opens the kitchen cupboard that holds her coffee and cups, she sees the 1983 women's peace encampment poster tacked up inside. This reminds her that she had done something productive about this other concern:

I don't really give a damn that people see it because somewhere in my heart I felt like I was counted. Didn't sign my name to anything, but I was counted. . . . What if I died tomorrow or whatever, or a nuclear disaster happens and we're all totally wiped out and we go up to heaven and God says, "Gwen. So, Gwen Mary Henderson, did you not know about the nuclear issue that was taking place on the planet earth?" And I say, "Yes, God, I knew." "Then, Gwen, how come you didn't do anything to stop it?" And somewhere inside of me it's like displeasing your father. I know he doesn't want us fooling around with this kind of shit, and I want to say, "I did something. I didn't do much, but I did something and I really want to do something but I don't know how. And it seems like you have to let someone greater than me fix it. I'll help fix it if I can but someone greater than myself has to fix it.

Conclusion

There is certainly no way to judge how the encampment affected all the women in Seneca County. Gwen Henderson's and Pam Flanigan's stories are probably not typical, but they do show that within the county there were women curious about other types of community life. For local feminists, women more actively involved than women like Gwen Henderson, the events of 1983 did not seem to provide any particular benefits. The post office always mixed up the mail for the Women's Hall of Fame with the mail for the National Women's Historic Park, and now it added the peace camp to the jumble of correspondence. Nor did local feminists welcome the visibility for feminist causes; they tended to do things quietly, behind the scenes, and politely. "Those women are libbers," said one local feminist, comparing herself and her friends to the peace camp women, "and we are for women's rights." One woman declared that the local women's community was "not activist at all" and consisted mostly of separate groups who were not coordinating their efforts very well. "We're not going to accomplish anything by being activist in this area," one woman explained. "If we were in New York City or even Syracuse or Rochester, we might be able to get somewhere through activist measures, but we won't around here. In fact we'd be ostracized just like the encampment was."

Some local feminists certainly were active with the encampment, but many echoed the words of the women who claimed that things were different in Seneca County. Even though it was the birthplace of women's rights, many explained, the women here are no more aware or more active than in other places. Local women were not as "wowed" by Seneca Falls and its history as outsiders were, said one woman. "They take it all for granted and don't really care."

The encampment continued to hold regular regional meetings throughout upstate New York after the first summer, trying to keep the encampment going by sustaining the active participation of many women in decision making. Some of the encampment organizers were also interested in evaluating the effects and processes of the encampment. They wanted to see what the camp had accomplished and what it meant to women after they left. I attended a series of these meetings from 1984 to 1987, and some considered my study a contribution to this overall evaluation.

The evaluations conducted by the encampment itself after the summer of 1983 indicated many triumphs but also several areas of concern, including the relationship between the camp and the local people, the internal structure of the encampment, and the lack of diversity among the women who attended. The women realized that they had provided much valuable information on what was happening at SEAD, but they admitted that they had not anticipated the reactions of the residents to the things they did and represented. Some women felt that the encampment had closed down lines of communication to the local people instead of working hard to keep them open. Some women had worked effectively with local contacts, the press, and their neighbors, but others had seemed not to care about the effects of what they did on Seneca County residents.

The internal structure of the camp presented problems because the ideals of consensus and shared labor and responsibilities were not realized in practice. Whereas women thought it was exciting and valuable to try out these alternative arrangements, it seemed that responsibilities and decision making always came back to a few staff members. Everyday tasks such as emptying garbage and cooking large-scale meals did not seem as politically important as talking and demonstrating about nuclear and patriarchal issues.

The encampment evaluators were also disturbed, according to one written evaluation, because they had to acknowledge that the encampment was "basically white/middleclass/feminist . . . egocentric, classist, racist, etc." Some women thought the participants had been diverse, but others, contradicting each other, saw it as too oriented toward lesbians or straight women; feminists or nonfeminists; younger, radical women or older, more conservative ones; witches or those who feared them. The self-evaluation seemed to suggest that whereas the encampment has been effective for women personally (many attested to their changed lives and new consciousness), it had not offered an alternative social space where differences were celebrated and new structures were successfully enacted. It should be remembered, however, that many feminist groups, including the encampment, tend to disparage or downplay the positive accomplishments of the group if such pressing issues as race, class, and sexual preference still keep women from working harmoniously together.

In November 1984 a series of newspaper articles in the Syracuse *Post-Standard* (November 29–30, 1984) further polarized the women and the local communities, and the different types of women within the encampment. The articles, titled "Witches of Seneca," seemed to demonstrate that the encampment had truly fulfilled the representations the local people had developed about them in 1983. The stories were written by a reporter who, with the knowledge of the encampment women, spent several days at the camp. She wrote of the women that "all of them are lesbians, all are vegetarians, and many practice witchcraft as part of their everyday lives." The article described in detail the practice of witchcraft and feminist spirituality at the encampment and described and showed photographs of a fire-walking ritual.

Letters to the editor from the local people continued the debate on the propriety and sanity of the women and their activities. The encampment women themselves disagreed about the way to evaluate these activities, some appreciating the publicity for their alternative lifestyles, and some disliking the attention taken away from the Encampment's mission as a base for antinuclear protests. In 1985 two naked women who could be seen from the street were arrested for public lewdness. Despite several warnings from the police and long discussions at the encampment about how they were disregarding long-established "respected policies" against public nudity, the women decided that they had the right to go nude anywhere they wanted.

In the next several years, antipatriarchal and antinuclear graffiti on local signs and buildings became more common and one car was apparently vandalized by encampment women. Fewer women came to the encampment to protest, and fewer were arrested at the depot. The public information director of the depot cited the decline in the number of women committing civil disobedience each year as proof that the encampment had played out its game.

In the view of many of the women attending the regional meetings, the encampment was drifting away from its original goals. Passionate and tearful arguments at the meetings often turned to the same question of lifestyles and antisocial behavior that had occupied the local people for so long. Many of the meetings focused on problems with women who refused to abide by "respected policies" governing encampment behavior (issues of particular concern were vandalism, illegal actions, nudity, and the consumption of meat, alcohol, and drugs). Many of the women who had been involved with the encampment from the beginning expressed distress that lots of women had withdrawn their financial and spiritual support because the encampment now seemed open only to lesbians and those interested in "anarchy."

As the encampment changed, much attention began to be focused on the issue of "zapping." The women believed that the army depot was directing microwaves at the peace camp, which, they believed, were making women edgy and nervous and making it hard for them to concentrate and be productive. Some women who spent a winter in the house supposedly being zapped said they had nightmares with common themes: men with guns and knives chasing them through the woods. All literature that went out from the encampment contained the warning that pregnant women and children should not come to the land

In the summer of 1990 after several years in which only a handful of women occupied the land and many women nationwide lost touch with the peace camp, the organizers began a series of discussions about its future. In a message to the women on its mailing list they explained: "On July 4, 1989, Twilight [one of the early encampment participants and organizers] read the peace camp's astrological chart. One of the main themes of her reading was that the next few years will be a time when the encampment will either 'transform or die.'" At the "transform or die" meetings, the encampment came up with several possible scenarios for its future. One plan was for three to five women to reside on the land and maintain it as a safe haven for women who had nowhere else to go. If this plan were chosen, the women would have to open contacts with former supporters of the encampment who had drifted away because of changes in the camp. A second possible scenario was to open only from the spring to the fall and possibly to sell part of the land or the house. The third possibility was to give away the entire peace camp, perhaps to women of color or native American women. Some expressed doubt that consensus on giving up the land could ever be reached, however, because some women were so attached to it.

Meanwhile, the town of Waterloo began making plans for the 125th anniversary of the first Memorial Day, which was celebrated in 1991 with a month of parades, museum displays, speeches, concerts, memorial services, and the issuance of a special commemorative American flag postage stamp. Waterloo, eager to celebrate itself as the home of the Good American, in many ways seemed unchanged.

Nevertheless, there were suggestions in the narratives of participants in these events that the powerful rhetorics bolstering all the communities involved were cracking. The encampment split between those who wanted to be true to the image of 1983 and those who wanted to develop a new encampment that was more friendly to lesbians, women with radical politics, women who desired freedom from all social constraints, and women with physical or emotional problems. The differences just barely discernible in 1983 grew into bitter battles over the definition of an encampment woman and who should have the right to dictate the policies for women living on the land.

In Seneca County the women of the peace encampment had served to remind residents of the "difference within," thus generating fear and hatred in the local community. They were perceived as dangerous, but not simply because local people feared the loss of employment opportunities, as many have claimed. Nor was the only cost the temporary $195,000 debt the women left the county. The local representations of the encampment women as dangerous creatures (witch-women, pig-women, hysterical madwomen) was connected not so much to a possible elimination of depot jobs as to the more frightening possible elimination of the job of Man to serve as a stable category and reference point for the entire system of patriarchal representation and interpretation. The heaviest cost was to the identity and patriarchal structure of the community.

The dangerous woman displays not her lack—lack of manners, proper sexual partners, stable identity or even clothing—but her lack of a lack, her failure to need and act and plot as the phallocentric system insists she should. Instead of needing the patriarchal system, the dangerous, feminist, bisexual woman desires in ways that are forbidden and monstrous. She is the unconscious of the patriarchal system, the one who dredges up those things usually repressed and hidden. As the early encampment organizers perceived, placing her in a women-only peace camp was a powerful gesture. In Seneca County the dangerous women of the encampment undermined the local community's certain discourses on man and woman, on nuclear war and weapons, on community loyalty, on political action and power, on the sexuality of adults and children, and on peace, safety, and security in a nuclear world. The women ruined the summer of 1983 for the people in and around Seneca County, and they also ruined, perhaps only for a moment, perhaps forever, patriarchal modes of representation and the easy, comfortable power structures that keep them in place.

References Cited

Altschuler, Glenn C., and Jan M. Saltzgaber. 1983. *Revivalism, Social Conscience, and Community in the Burned-over District: The Trial of Rhoda Bement*. Ithaca: Cornell University Press.

Anderson, Benedict. 1983. *Imagined Communities: Reflections on the Origin and Spread of Nationalism*. New York: Verso.

Andrew, Dudley. 1984. *Concepts in Film Theory*. Oxford: Oxford University Press.

Atkinson, Paul. 1983. "Eating Virtue." In *The Sociology of Food and Eating: Essays on the Sociological Significance of Food*. Ed. Anne Murcott. Aldershot, England: Gower, pp. 9–17.

Bataille, Georges. 1985. *Visions of Excess: Selected Writings, 1927–1939*. Ed. and trans. Allan Stoekl. Minneapolis: University of Minnesota Press.

Beaver, Harold. 1981. "Homosexual Signs (in memory of Roland Barthes)." *Critical Inquiry* (Autumn): 99–119.

Bercovitch, Sacvan. 1978. *The American Jeremiad*. Madison: University of Wisconsin Press.

Bernard, Jessie. 1981. *The Female World*. New York: Free Press.

Bernheimer, Charles. 1985. Introduction: Part One to *In Dora's Case: Freud—Hysteria—Feminism*. Ed. Charles Bernheimer and Claire Kahane. New York: Columbia University Press, pp. 1–18.

Bluebond-Langner, Myra. 1978. *The Private World of Dying Children*. Princeton: Princeton University Press.

Bolton, Richard. 1988. "Notes on 'Canadian Notes.'" *Afterimage* 15(7): 4–7.

Boorstin, Daniel J. 1985. *The Image: A Guide to Pseudo-Events in America*. New York: Athenum.

Brooks, Peter. 1984. *Reading for the Plot*. New York: Random House.

Broude, Norma, and Mary D. Garrard, eds. 1982. *Feminism and Art History: Questioning the Litany*. New York: Harper and Row.

Bruner, Edward M. 1986a. "Experience and Its Expressions." In *The Anthro-

pology of Experience. Ed. Victor W. Turner and Edward M. Bruner. Chicago: University of Illinois Press, pp. 3–30.

——. 1986b. "Ethnography as Narrative." In *The Anthropology of Experience.* Ed. Victor W. Turner and Edward M. Bruner. Chicago: University of Illinois Press, pp. 139–155.

Bruner, Edward M., and Phyllis Gorfain. 1984. "Dialogue, Narration, and the Paradoxes of Masada." In *Text, Play, and Story: The Construction and Reconstruction of Self and Society.* Ed. Edward M. Bruner. Washington D.C.: American Ethnological Society, pp. 56–79.

Bryant, Anita, and Bob Green. 1978. *At Any Cost.* Old Tappan, N.J.: Fleming H. Revell.

Burgin, Victor. 1986. *The End of Art Theory: Criticism and Postmodernity.* Atlantic Highlands, N.J.: Humanities Press International.

Chilton, Paul. 1985. Introduction to *Language and the Nuclear Arms Debate: Nukespeak Today.* Ed. Paul Chilton. London: Frances Pinter, pp. xiii–xxiii.

Chodorow, Nancy. 1978. *The Reproduction of Mothering: Psychoanalysis and the Sociology of Gender.* Berkeley: University of California Press.

Cixous, Hélène, and Catherine Clément. 1986. *The Newly Born Woman.* Minneapolis: University of Minnesota Press.

Clifford, James. 1986. "Introduction: Partial Truths." In *Writing Culture: The Poetics and Politics of Ethnography.* Ed. James Clifford and George Marcus. Berkeley: University of California Press, pp. 1–26.

Cook, Alice, and Gwyn Kirk. 1983. *Greenham Women Everywhere: Dreams, Ideas, and Actions from the Women's Peace Movement.* Boston: South End Press.

Crapanzano, Vincent. 1980. *Tuhami: Portrait of a Moroccan.* Chicago: University of Chicago Press.

Cross, Whitney R. 1950. *The Burned-over District: The Social and Intellectual History of Enthusiastic Religion in Western New York, 1800–1850.* Ithaca: Cornell University Press.

Culler, Jonathan. 1982. *On Deconstruction: Theory and Criticism after Structuralism.* Ithaca: Cornell University Press.

Daly, Mary. 1978. *Gynecology: The Metaethics of Radical Feminism.* Boston: Beacon Press.

——. 1987. *Webster's First New Intergalactic Wickedary of the English Language.* Boston: Beacon Press.

Davis, Peter. 1982. *Hometown: A Portrait of an American Community.* New York: Simon and Schuster.

De Lauretis, Teresa. 1984. *Alice Doesn't: Feminism, Semiotics, Cinema.* Bloomington: Indiana University Press.

——. 1990. "The Essence of the Triangle; or, Taking the Risk of Essentialism

Seriously: Feminist Theory in Italy, the U.S., and Britain." *Differences* 1(2): 3–37.

Doane, Janice, and Devon Hodges. 1987. *Nostalgia and Sexual Difference: The Resistance to Contemporary Feminism*. New York: Methuen.

Douglas, Mary. 1966. *Purity and Danger: An Analysis of Concepts of Pollution and Taboo*. Boston: Routledge and Kegan Paul.

——. 1975. *Implicit Meanings: Essays in Anthropology*. London: Routledge and Kegan Paul.

Eagleton, Terry. 1983. *Literary Theory: An Introduction*. Minneapolis: University of Minnesota Press.

——. 1986. *William Shakespeare*. New York: Basil Blackwell.

Eisenstein, Hester. 1983. *Contemporary Feminist Thought*. Boston: G. K. Hall.

Faison, Gordon, and Bob Irwin. 1980. "Nonviolence Theory and Strategy for the Anti-nuclear Movement." In *Grass Roots: An Anti-nuke Source Book*. Ed. Fred Wilcox. Trumansburg, N.Y.: Crossing Press.

Feld, Steven. 1982. *Sound and Sentiment: Birds, Weeping, Poetics and Songs in Kaluli Expression*. Philadelphia: University of Pennsylvania Press.

Felman, Shoshana. 1985. *Writing and Madness (Literature/Philosophy/Psychoanalysis)*. Ithaca: Cornell University Press.

Féral, Josette. 1980. "The Powers of Difference." In *The Future of Difference*. Ed. Hester Eisenstein and Alice Jardines. New Brunswick, N.J.: Rutgers University Press, pp. 88–94.

Ferguson, Ann. 1981. "Patriarchy, Sexual Identity, and the Sexual Revolution." In *Feminist Theory: A Critique of Ideology*. Ed. Nannerl O. Keohane, Michelle Z. Rosaldo, and Barbara C. Gelpi. Chicago: University of Chicago Press, pp. 147–161.

Ferguson, Margaret W., Maureen Quilligan, and Nancy J. Vickers, eds. 1986. *Rewriting the Renaissance: The Discourse of Sexual Difference in Early Modern Europe*. Chicago: University of Chicago Press.

Fish, Stanley. 1980. *Is There a Text in This Class? The Authenticity of Interpretive Communities*. Cambridge: Harvard University Press.

Fitchen, Janet M. 1981. *Poverty in Rural America: A Case Study*. Boulder, Colo.: Westview Press.

Foster, Hal. 1983. "Postmodernism: A Preface." In *The Anti-aesthetic: Essays on Postmodern Culture*. Ed. Hal Foster. Port Townsend, Wash.: Bay Press, pp. ix–xvi.

Foucault, Michel. 1979. "What Is an Author?" In *Textual Strategies: Perspectives in Post-structuralist Criticism*. Ed. Josué V. Harari. Ithaca: Cornell University Press, pp. 141–160.

Gallagher, Catherine. 1983. "More about Medusa's Head." *Representations* 4: 55–57.

Garner, Shirley Nelson, Claire Kahane, and Madelon Sprengnether. 1985. Preface to *The (M)other Tongue: Essays in Feminist Psychoanalytic Interpretation*. Ithaca: Cornell University Press, pp. 9–11.

Geertz, Clifford. 1973. *The Interpretation of Cultures*. New York: Basic Books.

———. 1983. *Local Knowledge: Further Essays in Interpretive Anthropology*. New York: Basic Books.

Gies, Frances, and Joseph Gies. 1978. *Women in the Middle Ages*. New York: Barnes and Noble.

Gilbert, Sandra M. 1982. "Costumes of the Mind: Transvestism as Metaphor in Modern Literature." In *Writing and Sexual Difference*. Ed. Elizabeth Abel. Chicago: University of Chicago Press, pp. 193–220.

Gilligan, Carol. 1982. *In a Different Voice: Psychological Theory and Women's Development*. Cambridge: Harvard University Press.

Ginzburg, Carlo. 1982. *The Cheese and the Worms: The Cosmos of a Sixteenth-Century Miller*. New York: Penguin Books.

Gitlin, Todd. 1980. *The Whole World Is Watching: Mass Media in the Making and Unmaking of the New Left*. Berkeley: University of California Press.

Goodman, Nelson. 1978. *Ways of Worldmaking*. Indianapolis: Hackett.

Greenhouse, Carol. 1985. "Anthropology at Home: Whose Home?" *Human Organization* 44(3): 261–264.

Griffith, Elisabeth. 1984. *In Her Own Right: The Life of Elizabeth Cady Stanton*. New York: Oxford University Press.

Grover, Jan Zita. 1987. "AIDS: Keywords." *October* 43: 17–30.

Harari, Josué V. 1979. "Critical Factions/Critical Fictions." In *Textual Strategies: Perspectives in Post-structuralist Criticism*. Ed. Josué V. Harari. Ithaca: Cornell University Press, pp. 17–72.

Haraway, Donna. 1985. "A Manifesto for Cyborgs: Science, Technology, and Socialist Feminism in the 1980s." *Socialist Review* 80: 65–107.

Henley, Nancy. 1977. *Body Politics: Power, Sex, and Nonverbal Communication*. Englewood Cliffs, N.J.: Prentice-Hall.

Hess, Thomas B., and Elizabeth C. Baker. 1973. *Art and Sexual Politics: Why Have There Been No Great Women Artists?* New York: Collier Books.

Higonnet, Margaret, Jane Jenson, Sonya Michel, and Margaret Collins Wietz. 1987. Introduction to *Behind the Lines: Gender and the Two World Wars*. Ed. Higonnet et al. New Haven: Yale University Press, pp. 1–17.

Hobsbawm, Eric. 1983. "Introduction: Inventing Traditions." In *The Invention of Tradition*. Ed. Eric Hobsbawm and Terence Ranger. Cambridge: Cambridge University Press, pp. 1–14.

Hunter, Diane. 1985. "Hysteria, Psychoanalysis, and Feminism: The Case of Anna O." In *The (M)other Tongue: Essays in Feminist Psychoanalytic*

Interpretation. Ed. Shirley Nelson Garner, Claire Kahane, and Madelon Sprengnether. Ithaca: Cornell University Press. pp. 89–115.

Jacobus, Mary. 1986. *Reading Woman: Essays in Feminist Criticism.* New York: Columbia University Press.

Johnson, Barbara. 1980. *The Critical Difference: Essays on the Contemporary Rhetoric of Reading.* Baltimore: Johns Hopkins University Press.

Jung, Carl. 1964. *Man and His Symbols.* Garden City, N.Y.: Doubleday.

Kappeler, Susanne. 1986. *The Pornography of Representation.* Minneapolis: University of Minnesota Press.

Kertzer, David. 1988. *Ritual, Politics, and Power.* New Haven: Yale University Press.

Kuhn, Annette. 1982. *Women's Pictures: Feminism and Cinema.* London: Routledge and Kegan Paul.

———. 1985. *The Power of the Image: Essays on Representation and Sexuality.* Boston: Routledge and Kegan Paul.

Lakoff, George. 1987. *Women, Fire, and Dangerous Things: What Categories Reveal about the Mind.* Chicago: University of Chicago Press.

Lippard, Lucy. 1972. "Flagged Down: The Judson Three and Friends." *Art in America* 60: 48–53.

Manoff, Robert Karl. 1986. "Writing the News (by Telling the 'Story')." In *Reading the News.* Ed. Robert Karl Manoff and Michael Schudson. New York: Pantheon Books, pp. 197–230.

Manoff, Robert Karl, and Michael Schudson. 1986. "Reading the News." In *Reading the News.* Ed. Robert Karl Manoff and Michael Schudson. New York: Pantheon Books, pp. 3–8.

Marcus, George E. 1986. "Contemporary Problems of Ethnography in the Modern World System." In *Writing Culture: The Poetics and Politics of Ethnography.* Ed. James Clifford and George Marcus. Berkeley: University of California Press, pp. 165–193.

Marcus, George E., and Michael J. Fischer. 1986. *Anthropology as Cultural Critique: An Experimental Moment in the Human Sciences.* Chicago: University of Chicago Press.

Marcus, Steven. 1985. "Freud and Dora: Story, History, Case History." In *In Dora's Case: Freud—Hysteria—Feminism.* Ed. Charles Bernheimer and Claire Kahane. New York: Columbia University Press, pp. 56–91.

Martin, Wallace. 1986. *Recent Theories of Narrative.* Ithaca: Cornell University Press.

Marx, Leo. 1964. *The Machine in the Garden: Technology and the Pastoral Idea in America.* Oxford: Oxford University Press.

Matthews, J. H. 1986. *Languages of Surrealism.* Columbia: University of Missouri Press.

Meese, Elizabeth A. 1986. *Crossing the Double-cross: The Practice of Feminist Criticism.* Chapel Hill: University of North Carolina Press.

Meyrowitz, Joshua. 1985. *No Sense of Place: The Impact of Electronic Media on Social Behavior.* New York: Oxford University Press.

Mintz, Sidney W. 1985. *Sweetness and Power: The Place of Sugar in Modern History.* New York: Elisabeth Sifton Books.

Mitchell, Juliet, and Jacqueline Rose. 1982. "Introductions I and II." In *Feminine Sexuality: Jacques Lacan and the Ecole Freudienne.* Ed. Juliet Mitchell and Jacqueline Rose. New York: W. W. Norton.

Modleski, Tania. 1988. *The Women Who Knew Too Much: Hitchcock and Feminist Theory.* New York: Methuen.

Moi, Toril. 1985. *Sexual/Textual Politics: Feminist Literary Theory.* New York: Methuen.

Moore, Sally. 1975. "Epilogue: Uncertainties in Situations, Indeterminacies in Culture." In *Symbol and Politics in Communal Ideology.* Ed. Sally Moore and Barbara Myerhoff. Ithaca: Cornell University Press, pp. 210–240.

Moran, Carolyn, and Emerson Moran. 1979. *Grandma, Grandpa, and the Jesus Nut.* Plainfield, N.J.: Logos International.

Mullett, G.M. 1979. *Spider Woman Stories: Legends of the Hopi Indians.* Tucson: University of Arizona Press.

Murcott, Anne. 1983. Introduction to *The Sociology of Food and Eating: Essays on the Sociological Significance of Food.* Ed. Anne Murcott. Aldershot, England: Gower, pp. 1–5.

Parenti, Michael. 1986. *Inventing Reality: The Politics of the Mass Media.* New York: St. Martin's Press.

Patterson, Maurice L. 1976. *Between the Lakes: The History of South Seneca County 1976.* Interlaken, N.Y.: Publishing Corp.

Philp, Mark. 1986. "Michel Foucault." In *The Return of Grand Theory in the Human Sciences.* Ed. Quentin Skinner. Cambridge: Cambridge University Press, pp. 65–82.

Pritikin, Nathan, and Patrick M. McGrady, Jr. 1979. *The Pritikin Program for Diet and Exercise.* New York: Bantam Books.

Rabinow, Paul. 1977. *Reflections on Fieldwork in Morocco.* Berkeley: University of California Press.

———. 1986. "Representations Are Social Facts: Modernity and Post-modernity in Anthropology." In *Writing Culture: The Poetics and Politics of Ethnography.* Ed. James Clifford and George Marcus. Berkeley: University of California Press, pp. 234–261.

Reiter, Rayna R. 1975. *Toward an Anthropology of Women.* New York: Monthly Review Press.

Resource Handbook. 1983. Romulus, N.Y.: Seneca Women's Encampment for a Future of Peace and Justice.

Rich, Adrienne. 1984. "Compulsory Heterosexuality and Lesbian Existence." In *Feminist Frameworks: Alternative Theoretical Accounts of the Relations between Women and Men.* Ed. Alison Jaggar and Paula S. Rothenberg. 2d ed. New York: McGraw-Hill, pp. 416–420.

Rogin, Michael Paul. 1987. *Ronald Reagan, the Movie, and Other Episodes in Political Demonology.* Berkeley: University of California Press.

Rosaldo, Michelle Zimbalist, and Louise Lamphere. 1974. *Woman, Culture, and Society.* Stanford: Stanford University Press.

Rose, Dan. 1987. *Black American Street Life: South Philadelphia, 1969–1971.* Philadelphia: University of Pennsylvania Press.

Rubin, Gayle. 1984. "The Traffic in Women: Notes on the 'Political Economy' of Sex." In *Feminist Frameworks: Alternative Theoretical Accounts of the Relations between Women and Men.* Ed. Alison M. Jaggar and Paula S. Rothenberg. 2d ed. New York: McGraw-Hill, pp. 155–211.

Russo, Vito. 1981. *The Celluloid Closet: Homosexuality in the Movies.* New York: Harper and Row.

Sahlins, Marshall. 1976. *Culture and Practical Reason.* Chicago: University of Chicago Press.

Said, Edward W. 1978a. *Orientalism.* New York: Vintage Books.

———. 1978b. "The Problem of Textuality: Two Exemplary Positions." *Critical Inquiry* (Summer): 673–714.

Salamone, Constantina. 1982. "The Prevalence of the Natural Law within Women: Women and Animal Rights." In *Reweaving the Web of Life: Feminism and Nonviolence.* Ed. Pam McAllister. Philadelphia: New Society, pp. 364–375.

Scarry, Elaine. 1985. *The Body in Pain: The Making and Unmaking of the World.* New York: Oxford University Press.

Schlesinger, Arthur M., Jr. 1986. *The Cycle of American History.* Boston: Houghton Mifflin.

Shilts, Randy. 1982. *The Mayor of Castro Street: The Life and Times of Harvey Milk.* New York: St. Martin's Press.

———. 1987. *And the Band Played On: Politics, People, and the AIDS Epidemic.* New York: St. Martin's Press.

Shostak, Marjorie. 1981. *Nisa: The Life and Words of a !Kung woman.* Cambridge: Harvard University Press.

Spivak, Gayatri Chakravorty. 1976. Translator's Preface to Jacques Derrida, *Of Grammatology.* Baltimore: Johns Hopkins University Press, pp. ix–xxxvii.

———. 1987. *In Other Worlds: Essays in Cultural Politics.* New York: Methuen.

Starhawk. 1979. *The Spiral Dance: A Rebirth of the Ancient Religion of the Great Goddess.* San Francisco: Harper and Row.

———. 1982. *Dreaming in the Dark: Magic, Sex, and Politics.* Boston: Beacon Press.

Stoller, Paul, and Cheryl Olkes. 1987. *In Sorcery's Shadow: A Memoir of Apprenticeship among the Songhay of Niger.* Chicago: University of Chicago Press.

Suleiman, Susan Rubin. 1986. "Pornography, Transgression, and the Avant-Garde: Bataille's *Story of the Eye.*" In *The Poetics of Gender.* Ed. Nancy K. Miller. New York: Columbia University Press, pp. 117–136.

Turner, Bryan S. 1984, *The Body and Society: Explorations in Social Theory.* New York: Basil Blackwell.

Turner, Victor. 1967. *The Forest of Symbols: Aspects of Ndembu Ritual.* Ithaca: Cornell University Press.

———. 1969. *The Ritual Process: Structure and Anti-structure.* Ithaca: Cornell University Press.

———. 1979. *Process, Performance, and Pilgrimage: A Study in Comparative Symbology.* New Delhi: Concept.

Twigg, Julia. 1983. "Vegetarianism and the Meaning of Meat." In *The Sociology of Food and Eating: Essays on the Sociological Significance of Food.* Ed. Anne Murcott. Aldershot, England: Gower, pp. 18–30.

Tyler, Stephen. 1986. "Postmodern Ethnography—from Document of the Occult to Occult Document." In *Writing Culture: The Poetics and Politics of Ethnography.* Ed. James Clifford and George Marcus. Berkeley: University of California Press, pp. 122–140.

Van Gelder, Lindsy. 1982. "America's Gay Women." *Rolling Stone Magazine,* November 11, 1982, pp. 13–17.

Veyne, Paul. 1984. *Writing History.* Middletown, Conn.: Wesleyan University Press.

Vidich, Arthur, and Joseph Bensman. 1958. *Small Town in Mass Society: Class, Power, and Religion in a Rural Community.* Chicago: University of Chicago Press.

Visser, Margaret. 1986. *Much Depends on Dinner: The Extraordinary History and Mythology, Allure and Obsessions, Perils and Taboos of an Ordinary Meal.* New York: Grove Press.

Watney, Simon. 1987. *Policing Desire: Pornography, AIDS, and the Media.* Minneapolis: University of Minnesota Press.

Watrous, Hilda R. 1982. *The County between the Lakes: A History of Seneca County, New York, 1876–1982.* Waterloo, N.Y.: Seneca County Board of Supervisors.

White, Hayden. 1987. *The Content of the Form: Narrative Discourse and Historical Representation.* Baltimore: Johns Hopkins University Press.

Zicree, Marc Scott. 1982. *"The Twilight Zone" Companion.* New York: Bantam Books.

Zinn, Howard. 1980. *A People's History of the United States.* New York: Harper Colophon Books.

Index

Anthropology of Contemporary Issues
A SERIES EDITED BY
ROGER SANJEK

Library of Congress Cataloging-in-Publication Data

Krasniewicz, Louise, 1952-
  Nuclear summer : the clash of communities at the Seneca women's
peace encampment / Louise Krasniewicz.
    p. cm.—(Anthropology of contemporary issues)
  Includes bibliographical references and index.
  ISBN 0-8014-2635-9 (alk. paper). — ISBN 0-8014-9938-0 (pbk. :
alk. paper)
    1. Antinuclear movement—Social aspects—New York (State)—
Romulus. 2. Women and peace—Social aspects—New York (State)—
Romulus. 3. Seneca Army Depot. I. Title. II. Series.
JX1974.7.K735 1992
327.1'74'09747—dc20   91-55538

DATE DUE

8-15-94			

HIGHSMITH 45-220